MESSAGES FROM ABOVE

Messages from Above

WHAT YOUR LOVED ONES IN HEAVEN WANT YOU TO KNOW

MONICA THE MEDIUM

MESSAGES FROM ABOVE
What Your Loved Ones in Heaven Want You to Know

Published by 444 Publishing
A division of Monica the Medium, Inc.
www.monicathemedium.com
@MonicatheMedium

Monica the Medium® is a registered trademark
belonging to Monica the Medium, Inc.

Cover photograph taken by Danielle McBrayer;
photograph copyright belongs to Monica the Medium, Inc.

ISBN   978-1-5445-0573-2   *Hardcover*
        978-1-5445-0574-9   *Paperback*
        978-1-5445-0572-5   *Ebook*

*To Tyler, for giving the girl who talks to dead people a chance.
For loving me unconditionally and for supporting me every
step of the way. You are my best friend and the love of my life.*

*To my family and friends, for always being there
for me and for accepting me for who I am.*

*To Spirit, for trusting me to be your messenger for so
many people here on Earth, for sharing your wisdom,
and for essentially being the cowriter of this book.*

Contents

Disclaimer

The information in this book is for personal or educational purposes only and is not intended to, nor should it ever, take the place of any medical, legal, financial, traditional psychological, or other professional advice. Monica Ten-Kate (Monica the Medium, Inc.) will not accept responsibility for any decisions made or actions taken by anyone based upon any of the information in this book or any other services or communication. The choices you make and the actions you take are solely your responsibility. The author and the publisher assume no liability.

If you are suffering from depression, you owe it to yourself to seek individual and professional guidance from a licensed doctor and/or grief therapist, as this book cannot substitute the treatment you may require.

In some instances names and personal details in this book have been changed to protect the privacy of the individual or their family.

Introduction

If you're reading this book, it's probably because you've lost someone important to you. If you haven't, I imagine you're simply curious to learn more about life after death and the process of mediumship. Either way, this book is for you.

But if you do fall into that first category of readers, then I want you to know: I can't really think of anything in life that is more difficult than dealing with the loss of someone you love. It's enough to make you feel like the bottom has dropped out of your world. Something as simple as finding the energy to get out of bed in the morning can feel totally overwhelming. It can be hard to know how to move forward.

I know this because, as a medium (or a translator between this world and the Spirit World), I have spent a lot of time talking to people in similar situations to the one you are in right now.

While I can't stop the grieving process or single-handedly heal your pain, what I can do is tell you with 100 percent certainty that, for as alone as you feel right now, your loved ones *are* still with you in Spirit.

Even if you can't hear or see them, they are still around you. They want you to know that they're always by your side.

HOW TO READ THIS BOOK

Since you're reading this book, chances are you have some special interest in the afterlife. Maybe you've recently lost someone close to you, or perhaps you're a medium looking to develop your gift. You might be tempted to glance through the table of contents, find the chapter you're looking for, and flip straight to that page. I understand the impulse, but before you do that, give me a chance to make my case for reading the entire book in order.

This book is laid out in a very particular way. Each chapter lays the foundation for the next, and I will provide pieces of information as you go, so that by the end you can see the whole picture. I give definitions and use analogies that I then rely on for the rest of the book. Without this knowledge, you're going to find it more difficult to make sense of what you're reading. There could also be important messages waiting for you in chapters you might otherwise skip. Often, we find comfort and meaning in the stories and experiences of others, even if their situation might look different than ours on the surface.

There is one exception to this—the first few chapters are about my background and experience coming into my gift and, from there, mediumship career. I included this because, frankly, I don't plan to write another book for a long time. So, I figured it was best to answer all the questions I typically get in one go! For some, especially those who are trying to get into mediumship themselves or who loved watching *Monica the Medium* on TV, this is stuff they want to know. But if you find yourself thinking, "Let's get to the good stuff!" feel free to skim over that and pick up reading about halfway through Chapter Three. (Although, in doing so, just know that you might still miss out on some golden nuggets.)

WHY SPIRIT COMMUNICATES

I believe I've had the gift of being able to communicate with the Other Side (or Heaven, as I like to call it, but really it's all the same) for my entire life, although it took me a while to figure that out. Today, I channel what I call Spirit (the souls of those who have passed on to the Other Side) for people who need to hear from them most.

One of the main reasons Spirit comes through is because they love those of us here in the physical world so much that they want to help us move forward so that we can live the most joyful and fulfilling life possible. They want to send us little hellos from Heaven so that we understand they are still very much alive, even if it's in a way that looks different from how it did before. For as much as you want to connect with your loved ones who have passed, they also want to connect with you. They are aware of your thoughts, grief, pain, and struggle, and they strive to help you through the process.

They want to support you from Heaven. They want to bring you comfort. They want to give you reassurance that they are okay. They want to help you heal and to provide closure. Sometimes, Spirit wants to offer apologies or answers to those burning questions that make you feel as though you can't find peace. And, sometimes, they just want to say, "Hi, I'm here."

On a grander scale, Spirit wants to let all of us know that there *is* an afterlife and that the soul never dies. For many people, this understanding can completely transform their perspective not just on death, but also on life. So many of the struggles we go through as humans are based in fear. We fear our own death and the death of our loved ones, and that colors so many things in our lives, often in ways we are completely unaware of. Receiving evidence that an afterlife exists and that our soul continues on has the power to significantly change one's outlook.

When possible, Spirit will communicate these messages through mediums because they offer a clear channel between the Spirit realm and our own. But, of course, plenty of people are not open to the idea of visiting a medium for any number of reasons, so Spirit also uses opportunities like visitation dreams and signs such as familiar scents, pennies, songs, and flickering lights to try to get your attention and let you know they're right there with you. Just look around and I bet you'll start to notice the many ways that Spirit is in constant conversation with you.

If you've already had an experience of connecting with Spirit, then you know how powerful it can be. If you haven't yet had this experience, I think you will be amazed by what they have to share and want you to know.

Even though this is my life's work, I'm still constantly shocked by the powerful and transformative impact these messages from above can have. I'm amazed by how present Spirit is and how they always manage to get their messages through at just the right moment in time.

There are thousands of examples I could share, but I will start with this one: A few years ago, I was getting a haircut when I felt Spirit coming through to speak with the hairdresser. It turned out to be the hairdresser's mom, who had passed and wanted to communicate with her daughter. This mother brought up the fact that her daughter had been in a state of deep depression and was planning on ending her life later that week. She urged her daughter not to give up. To choose life *for her.* She validated specific details about the difficult situations her daughter had been going through and explained that she understood how, from her daughter's perspective, it felt like there was no light at the end of the tunnel, but that suicide was *not* the answer.

Spirit used every ounce of my energy that morning; it kind of felt like an out-of-body channeling experience for me. Normally, I'm still very much in control of what's happening when I connect to the Other Side, but in this instance I completely lost my sense of self and all of the words coming out of my mouth and the mannerisms I was using were *exactly* how this hairdresser's mother would talk. Her mother communicated that things *would* get better with time and treatment.

That hairdresser has since reached out several times to say thank you and has even told me that hearing from her mother that day was the reason she decided not to follow through with her suicide plan, and to instead seek help.

A few years ago, there was another woman, Michaela, who went through a similar experience after connecting to her son. Michaela won a free reading giveaway that I had hosted; her name was randomly drawn from the nearly ten thousand entries we received. After her son died, Michaela found a sticky note in his handwriting that read, "Have you heard from Monica yet?" She and I both knew that her son had made this reading happen. Michaela contacted me a few weeks after her reading:

> One of the first things you said after accurately describing my adult son's physical appearance and personality, was that you were hearing him call me "Mommy." You smiled and said, "I don't even call my own mom 'Mommy.'" I knew without a doubt you were connecting with my son. He was thirty-six years old, but always called me Mommy. Shortly after the reading, it was like a light switch went off. I no longer spend all my time wondering if I should just leave this world and end my life in order to be with my son. You helped me understand that he wants me to be happy and to live my full life. You have a gift that goes far beyond connecting with Spirit. In many ways, you're saving lives right here on Earth.

Of course, it's not really me at all. It's Spirit. But these stories go to show how important their communication is, if only we can open ourselves up to hear it.

A Note About Grief

Before we really dive into this, I just want to speak to those of you who are currently in the thick of the grieving process. Through my work, I have spent a lot of time with people who are grieving. I can tell you that every single person grieves differently. There is no such thing as a standard or right way to do it. Wherever you're at is exactly where you're supposed to be right now. Please also know that you won't be in that place forever.

Some people move forward with life quickly, and that's okay. It doesn't mean you loved the person any less, and it doesn't even mean that you're not grieving. It's just what your process looks like. Other people grieve by going into a state of solitude. Some people need to talk about their loved one or feel a deep need to be surrounded by others.

You have every right to find your own way through grief, even if your way looks wildly different from that of others. There is no generic advice or timeline that you need to follow. No one has the right answers, no matter how wise they might be or how well versed in grief they are.

Ironically, I often find that because of my work I'm at more of a loss than most people are when it comes to offering words of comfort, solace, and advice to those who have lost a loved one. I usually start off with something along the lines of, "God, you would think I would know exactly what to say, but I really don't." I'll then try my best to provide insights about the afterlife that will hopefully help them heal. But I understand that it's not up to me to take away a person's grief, no matter how much I want to. The truth of the matter is, we all just have to get through it in the way that works best for us.

In this book, I will tell you some of the things Spirit has to offer to assist us in moving through grief, but with the understanding that each one of us has to go through our own very personal process of finding healing and renewed joy.

WHAT IT'S LIKE TO BE ME

People always ask me what my life is like. More often than not, they think I'm in a constant state of communication with the Other Side. They assume it's as if I'm walking down the street and can see thought bubbles hovering over the living that say, "dead mom," "dead brother," "dead grandpa." But no, it doesn't work that way.

Even some of my close friends have jumped to the conclusion that because of my gift, I must have all the answers. They'll ask if Spirit can give me the lottery numbers or whether I can make a collect call to Heaven anytime I please. I promise you, I don't and I can't.

The truth is, I'm very much like any other twenty-five-year-old girl and I actually live a very normal life. I enjoy watching my guilty pleasure reality TV shows at the end of a long workday. I love my fiancé, Tyler, and I always look forward to our next weekend adventure in and around San Diego, where we live. I spend nights scrolling Pinterest for inspiration for our upcoming wedding. And I have an unhealthy obsession with froyo (okay, so maybe that one's not as normal, but no harm in treating yourself every now and then, am I right?).

The only difference between me and my peers is that I'm also juggling the responsibilities that come with speaking to dead people along the way. Although to be honest, I don't normally refer to them as dead people; that's just my ice-breaker line. The reality is they aren't dead at all. Their souls are very much alive.

Now, don't get me wrong. There are definitely ways in which my gift has changed my day-to-day life. For instance, I do believe I have a broader perspective on the daily struggles we all face. I can't tell you how many times I've delivered messages from Spirit only to realize, "Wow, my shit is really not that big of a deal."

Having this ability has completely transformed my outlook on life. Working with people who are grappling with grief has made me less likely to take things for granted. I try not to sweat the small stuff because I know there are millions of people who are going through a hell of a lot worse than I am.

Connecting to Spirit has taught me the importance of telling the people you care for how much they mean to you. It has ingrained in me the need to say "I love you" to Tyler every night before we fall asleep. If you were to ask Tyler, he'd tell you there's no such thing as going to bed angry in our house. Whenever we get in an argument, we work out our crap that same day because we know we are never guaranteed tomorrow.

Still, I'm human, so it does become somewhat of a balance. On one hand, I want to let myself experience all that I came to Earth School for (more on this later). That includes going through all of life's ups and downs and having a range of emotions. Like everyone else, it's through this human experience of life that I'm going to evolve and grow. But, at the same time, I do try to remind myself that it's not *that* stressful to plan a wedding. At the end of the day, there are far more important things in life.

Another gift that mediumship has given me is the fact that I'm no longer afraid of my own death. There is no doubt in my mind that it will be a peaceful transition. I also understand that when it's my time to go, it's my time. To be honest though, I probably fear the "what-ifs" a lot more than most people do. I know that may seem ironic considering I'm so sure that the afterlife is nothing to fear. But the thing is, doing this work has made me acutely aware of how quickly things can turn on a dime.

In comparison to the average person, I'm also much more familiar with the many ways that one can die suddenly. This work has opened my eyes to the fact that all it takes is a split second for things to go wrong. Which is partly to blame for why I often get overwhelming anxiety when I'm in the car. It can be excruciating for Tyler to have to drive with me (thank goodness he's so understanding). He's now used to hearing me say a prayer to the angels every time we get in the car. I ask the angels to place a bubble of white light and protection around the vehicle to keep me and those around me safe. To be honest, I feel as though my angel bubble provides better coverage than my car insurance (but don't worry, I have both).

So, while I'm not afraid of death, I am concerned about situations that could leave me paralyzed, confined to a hospital bed, or unable to communicate. However, I also understand these things are ultimately out of my control and that if they're meant to happen, they will. I've learned that every challenge serves a purpose for our soul growth, and yet I'm still human. That human side of me sometimes forgets to see the big picture. Therefore, I still struggle with fears, anxieties, and irrational beliefs. Maybe you can relate?

Which brings me to one of the most important things that being a medium has taught me: we all have battles. You never truly know what someone else is going through. Because of this, it's so important to be as kind and compassionate as possible with everyone you meet.

WHY ME?

"Why me?" That's the big question. I've been doing this work for many years now, and yet I still think about this sometimes. I mean, I'm so normal in every other way. But the more time passes and the more I see how much good my gift does for others, how much healing it offers to people who really need it, the more I think, "Well, why *not* me?"

I've learned from Spirit that some of us are handpicked to do this work professionally and to share it with others. I just happen to be one of those people. Translating messages from loved ones above to their friends and family members who are still here on Earth is my purpose. It's what I signed up to do well before I was even born (we'll get into this in Chapter Five).

But I also believe that we all have the innate ability to communicate with Spirit. While some people might have a very difficult time accessing this skill—and, likely, never will in this lifetime—we all still have the capability to do so on a deep, soul level, far in the depths of our subconscious mind. It just happens to come more easily for some people, like me, and some of us are called to develop and strengthen it like a muscle. But, even with that, I still have to make the *choice* to connect. And, to be honest, it took me a while to make that choice.

Your Burning Questions

Once people found out that I was a medium, they started asking me a lot of questions. I get it, because I still have questions too. While I *do* have insight into some things that most people do not, I always tell people, there's a lot I still don't know.

Having said that, one of the reasons Spirit communicates with us is because they want to share information. Not all of it though; that won't happen for me or anyone else until the day we cross over to the Other Side. But to the extent that the information will help us through life and grief, Spirit does want us to have some answers.

Throughout this book, I'm going to answer some of the questions I get the most: people's burning questions about death, the afterlife, and being a medium.

I don't have all of the answers, but I will always be honest. Stay tuned for more boxes like this throughout the book, where I will answer all of the questions I'm frequently asked in the best way I can.

IT'S OKAY TO HAVE DOUBTS

In the years I've been working publicly as a medium, I've noticed that people have become so much more open to the idea of an afterlife and the ability to communicate with those who have passed. More people are willing to open up their minds a little bit and give the idea of this possibility a chance. This is a beautiful transformation to witness, and I'm so grateful to play even a tiny part in it.

Because I have had firsthand experience communicating with Spirit, I know it's for real. I have received mountains of evidence. But I also understand that many people are skeptical, whether for religious or any other variety of reasons. I mean, *I* was skeptical for a long time despite the fact that I was the person doing the channeling! In general, I think it's a good practice to question things, so I actually *encourage* a healthy dose of skepticism when it comes to mediumship and our ability to connect with souls in Heaven. My only warning is that, in my experience, when people are *too* skeptical they can build a wall of sorts around themselves that blocks their energy and makes it harder for their loved ones to get through.

This work is all about energy, so skeptical energy builds up resistance against the Spirit energy that is trying to communicate. This makes it more difficult for Spirit to get through to you, whether it's by communicating directly with you through signs or through a medium.

Really, working with a medium isn't that different than any other conversation or interaction you might have (okay, except for the whole communicating with dead people part of it). I'm sure you've had the experience of walking into a room where the energy feels hostile. It probably puts you on the defensive or makes it difficult to communicate effectively or articulately. Same thing here.

So, yes, be skeptical. But also try to be open to possibilities you might not have considered, both as you read this book and in your own life.

1

Growing Up Gifted

1

I Talk to Dead People

Long before I discovered I could talk to dead people, I knew that I was an empath. Or at the very least, I understood that I could feel other people's emotions as if they were my own. I was what most people would call an old soul.

Back in grade school, I was the kid who would sit in the passenger seat talking to my classmate's mom about her divorce while my friends and I were being carpooled around our Northern Virginia town. Almost like a mini therapist! While all the other kids were sitting in the backseat playing with their Nintendo DS, there I was up front, having a deep conversation with a forty-year-old mom like I was her peer instead of the ten-year-old kid I actually was. At the time, I didn't really think much of it. Feeling other people's pain was just what I did and who I was. In fact, I don't think I could have even explained what I was doing at the time.

It wasn't until a couple of years ago that I learned there were signs that I was different from an even earlier age than that. My mom told me that she has a vivid memory of me playing on the landing of our staircase one day when I was about four years old. As she came up the stairs with a basket of laundry, she heard me talking. "Are you playing make-believe with your imaginary friends?" she asked.

Apparently, I looked her right in the eye and responded, "No, Mom. It's not make-believe. Look! They're here. They're my angel friends! Don't you see them?"

Aside from my angel friends and playing the role of tiny therapist, my childhood was pretty average. I was the third of four daughters. My mom is a conservative Catholic Hispanic woman with the cutest Costa Rican accent. She was always a bit of a worrywart, while my dad was more laid-back. Although my parents are divorced now, they were married for twenty-five years and did their very best raising their kids together.

My mom and I had a lot of big, blowout fights during my adolescent years. I struggled with anxiety and had a hard time focusing in school. In retrospect, I wonder if that was a manifestation of my gifts that I didn't yet know how to use boiling to the surface. In that way, I was always sort of the black sheep in the family, even before I started talking to dead people. I was more outspoken, more rebellious, and more of a troublemaker than my sisters. I was just a little…different in ways that were tricky to put your finger on.

Are Mediums and Psychics the Same Thing?

Some people will tell you that all mediums are also psychics, even if all psychics aren't mediums. I disagree with that. I believe there's an overlap between psychic work and mediumship—but they're not the same, and I definitely consider myself a Spirit medium, not a psychic medium.

Psychics tap into either your energy or their own intuition to get an idea of what's happening in your life and around you, as well as what could be coming up in your future. Psychics work energetically on a person-to-person level, as they blend within your aura (aka, the human energy field). As messengers for the Other Side, mediums have to energetically raise their vibration to make contact with Spirit. It's kind of hard to explain, but mediums and psychics work on different energetic levels. I don't predict the future, or any of that stuff. Sometimes Spirit will bring up things that are on the horizon or in motion for the person they are communicating with, but that's not me predicting the future in the psychic sense. It's just that Spirit can see what's going on in your life, and they are sharing that information with me.

It is a fine line, though. Because of mediumship, I have definitely honed my intuitive sense as well. I can pick up on, feel, and sense things, but mediumship is still a completely different field from psychic work. My communication as a medium doesn't come from a psychic or intuitive place—it comes from Spirit. While I do have an intuitive sense, I never want to rely on it in my work as a medium.

To me, psychic information can't be validated in the same way that communication with Spirit can—and that's what's so powerful about working as a medium. Most of the time, my clients know exactly who is coming through for them based on the information I receive and the way in which that information is presented. There's no room for questioning or doubt. Psychic work doesn't always account for influences like free will, divine timing, and the fact that things can change. You typically don't receive instant validation in the way that you do with mediumship, and I think that's what the majority of my clients need.

GAY, CRAZY, OR GIFTED?

Around the age of fifteen, I began to realize that my empathic tendencies for the people surrounding me were accompanied by an overwhelming sense of feelings, flashes of images, and voices that I would later learn were Spirit communicating.

I would get choked up and emotional every time I was around a certain classmate at school. For a while, I wondered if I might be lesbian. "What is happening?" I wondered. Did I have feelings for this girl? It was all very confusing. It wasn't until a few months later, when I found out this classmate had lost her mom as a child, that I understood what was really going on.

As high school went on, I found that friends, acquaintances, and even teachers would randomly start talking to me about their loved ones who had passed away. I don't mean that I asked people questions and they opened up to me. I mean that people would come up to me and start sharing intimate details about their lives out of nowhere. It was strange, and I couldn't figure out what it was about me that made people tend to do that.

Now I understand that the reason this happened—and continues to happen—is because Spirit knows that I'm a channel and they have the ability to "coincidentally" lead their loved ones to me, in hopes that I will act as a conduit to deliver messages from above. But, of course, I didn't know that at the time. What I *did* know is that when these people told me stories about their childhood or about loved ones they had lost, I somehow heard, felt, or sensed the end of the story before they finished telling it. At first, I shrugged it off as a coincidence or a lucky guess. I figured that perhaps I had already heard the story but forgotten about it on a conscious level.

After a while, these "lucky guesses" evolved into hearing voices in my head. These voices, which came to me in the form of my own thoughts, told me information about the people I was speaking to. It wasn't a creepy voice. It sounded like my regular mind chatter, but in some ways it felt different. I had to actively work to surpass the incessant thoughts and, even then, I often wasn't successful. For a while I wondered if maybe I had a brain tumor. I can vividly remember typing into Google, "What does it mean to hear voices in your head?" You can probably guess how that search turned out for me. I now felt like a bonafide crazy person. And, remember, this all happened while I was in high school, a time when all you want to do is fit in. I wasn't about to tell my friends at the cafeteria table that I was hearing shit or that I felt like I was losing my mind.

During my junior year, I went to a psychiatrist. While I didn't exactly divulge the fact that I was hearing voices, I did admit to feeling anxious, distracted, and having shifting moods. The doctor tried to put me on medication. To this day, I'm so thankful that my gut told me prescriptions weren't the right path for me. While there are many circumstances where I do believe that medication is necessary for one's health and well-being, I've also learned there's a fine line between mental illness and being in possession of a gift or ability. (Of course, you should still always seek out medical advice.) But while I knew not to take medication, I was still convinced that I could be going crazy or that it was possible I had some sort of cancer or disease that was causing hallucinations.

I had to figure out what was going on. I didn't really have anyone to talk to about what was happening with me, so I kept searching. After a while, I stumbled across a YouTube interview with a few mediums who explained how their gift works. It was only then that I realized they were describing my exact experience. Finally, I had an explanation for what might be happening! In some ways, this gave me a glimmer of hope because I had stumbled upon a group of people that I could actually relate to. But, in other ways, it was all still very weird to me and hard to wrap my brain around.

Once I figured out that Spirit might be trying to communicate with me, it began to happen with more and more people. It was almost as if, without realizing it, I had swung open the door to the Spirit World and slapped down a giant welcome mat in front of it. On one hand, I was curious and trying to figure it all out. On the other hand, I wanted to shut Spirit out so that I could still fit in and not be judged by my friends. Some nights before bed I prayed that I wouldn't hear or see anything. I begged Spirit to please not show up at the foot or the side of my bed. I didn't want to see anything outside of my mind's eye—the thought of that was terrifying to me. This continued throughout high school.

Even as I started piecing the puzzle together, I still didn't talk to anyone about all this. The idea that I might be a medium felt like a dirty little secret to me. There were a lot of reasons for this, including the fact that I'm a very logical and rational person. While I didn't know what to make of communicating with dead people, it seemed like the only explanation for what was happening.

But I needed more validation. I went to a few mediums for private readings, secretly hoping something would come through to confirm my suspicions. This actually did happen in each visit. All three of the mediums that I saw brought through my own loved ones and, in the course of that, told me, "*You're* supposed to be doing this work. Spirit's acknowledging that you have a gift and that you're meant to share it with others."

I was worried that my mom would have a heart attack if it got back to her that I was channeling dead people. Mediumship was definitely not aligned with her Catholic beliefs; she would have told me it was coming from evil spirits. To be honest, I had some fears of my own. What if this *wasn't* coming from a good place? More and more, I understood what was going on, but there was a part of me that didn't want it to be true because it would drastically change my normal life—and I liked normal.

Every now and then, when I knew it wouldn't get back to my family and friends, I shared things with people that I felt, heard, and sensed from Spirit. Often, the person I was talking to started to cry. "How do you know that?" a lot of them asked. My answer was always the same: "I'm not really sure." Still, it was all very hush-hush, and I kept these conversations on the DL as much as I could. Other strange things started happening around this same point. For instance, I looked down at the clock one day while I was driving and randomly thought of my grandfather, concerned as to whether or not he was okay. Later that afternoon, I found out that he had passed at the exact time I had glanced at the clock and thought of him.

Shortly after high school graduation, I went through a three-month period where my whole body swelled up. I was misdiagnosed with rheumatoid arthritis. It was so bad that it got to the point where I could barely even walk. The doctors tried to put me on low-dose chemo and arthritis meds, but I refused because I read that those medications could make your hair start to fall out as a side effect. I didn't want to be in pain, but I also didn't want to be the girl with bald patches on my first day of college! So, instead, the doctors put me on prednisone and other steroid medications, which caused me to gain twenty pounds. Talk about crappy timing.

Here I was getting ready to head off to college and, honestly, I thought I was dying. Clearly, something was seriously wrong.

Do You Know When People Are Going to Die?

The answer to this one is easy: oh God, no. Again, I don't have all of the answers—not even close! Every now and then I might get a sense in my gut or heart that something is off with someone who I care about or that their time might be coming, but I never really know. It's not that clear.

For example, the week before my grandma passed away, I couldn't shake a weird feeling that I should call her. Feelings like this are Spirit talking, although sometimes it's easier to recognize that in retrospect.

I know that I am not alone in experiences like this. I've talked to plenty of people who aren't mediums that, for example, wake up in the middle of the night and just *know* that their loved one is gone, even if there is no logical reason to think that's the case. A lot of us have the ability to feel that moment of transition.

But at the same time, we're all still human, and we all sometimes worry about the people we care about—even when they're just fine! Knowing the difference between our genuine spiritual connections to people and the paranoid thoughts in our heads can be difficult. So don't jump to the worst case scenario every time you have a strange feeling or bad dream about someone in your life. At least give them a call first!

LET'S DO THIS, SPIRIT

That same summer between high school and college, while I was still struggling with the mystery illness, I was working at a major aerospace and defense company. I was based in their Maryland office, but they sent me to work at one of their Virginia locations for a week. On my last day there before heading home, a senior-level engineer in his sixties came over to my cubicle and started making conversation. Let's just say things got awkward real fast.

He randomly told me that he knew certain things about life after death based on what he's read in the Bible and that he also knew for a fact that his father was in hell. Immediately, my heart started racing and I began to sweat, I couldn't catch my breath, and my face felt really warm, then quickly turned bright red like a tomato. You know, all of the sensations that usually occur when Spirit starts to make an entrance—or when you have a panic attack.

"Tell my son I'm in Heaven," I heard. "I'm not in hell! There is no hell. I'm in Heaven. Please tell him!"

"Oh, my God," I thought. I had just met this guy, and letting him know what I was hearing would mark the first time that I ever gave someone who was a complete and total stranger a full-blown reading. And it had to be for this guy, of all people?! Not to mention, this was all going down while at work.

"Hey, look," I said. "I don't know exactly what's going on with me. I think I have this ability that some would call mediumship. I don't know how you feel about mediums or what the Bible says about them, but I'm sensing some things. I'm not sure if you're comfortable with this, but would you mind if I tell you what I'm getting?"

He looked taken aback but told me to go ahead and share.

At that point I told him, "Okay, well, your dad is showing me you as an eighteen-year-old boy, walking into a white shed in your family's backyard and finding him dead, lying next to a motorcycle."

I continued to describe what I was seeing in detail, as well as other things that came up, such as the fact that this guy was one of five kids and had been in the navy.

I explained, "Your dad is acknowledging why you feel like he would be in hell or this horrible place, because he's saying that he was not a good guy. It feels like he had been mentally and verbally abusive to you. He wants you to know how sorry he is for the man and father that he was. Now that he's on the Other Side, he's realized where he went wrong."

I watched as this man turned stark white and started shaking with tears coming down his face. "Young lady," he finally said, "There's no way you could know any of these things. I've never told anybody. How do you know this?"

"I told you," I said, "I think Spirit is communicating through me."

"I don't know." He shook his head. "I don't know what just happened or what I believe now. But I think you just changed my life." He gave me a hug before clocking out for the day. Luckily it was after five o'clock on a Friday, so most people were already gone. Otherwise, I probably would've gotten fired, considering how inappropriate this whole scene would have appeared to HR, what with me talking to dead people on the job and all.

Tears streamed down my face as I left the building that day. This guy's life wasn't the only one that had been changed; mine had too. I knew in that very moment that I would be doing this work for the rest of my life. Finally, I didn't have any more questions and, just like that, I had all the validation I needed. This experience proved to me that, wherever this information was coming from, it was real. It was more than just a lucky guess or an uncanny ability to read people. Understanding this allowed me to start letting go of fear and worry about what people would think if I shared what I was hearing, feeling, and sensing.

I've never seen that guy again—I don't even know his name—but I still think about him every now and then. He opened the door for me to comfort so many people who really need to know that *yes!* Not only are their loved ones okay, but they are also still right here.

And you want to know what? That validation I was needing? As soon as I received it, that mysterious disease of mine went away. Just like that. No more rheumatoid arthritis. The doctors told me it must have been an arthritic virus, while my mom said it was a miracle. Maybe. But I doubt it.

I think what actually happened is that suppressing my gifts manifested in the form of physical illness. Since that time, I've talked with a lot of other mediums who also experienced various forms of strange sickness that couldn't be explained. Once they truly embraced their gift, they also experienced miraculous recoveries just like I did. As soon as they opened up to Spirit, *poof!* The illness disappeared, as if by magic. It's like the illness is a wake-up call to be your authentic self (although, of course, not all physical illness is brought on by gifts, so, again, be sure to see a doctor). It makes sense: communicating with Spirit is all about energy, so if you are blocking that energy, it can manifest as a physical blockage.

Things started to change quickly. I made the choice that if I felt or heard something, I was going to share it in that

moment. I fully accepted the fact that, whether I could understand it or not, Spirit was talking through me.

2

Monica the Medium

I spent the rest of the summer before college and my freshman year at Penn State studying the ins and outs of Spirit communication however I could. I read books about mediumship to understand the communication process and fine-tune my connection to Spirit. Through all of this, I began to accept myself and what I could do more and more.

I think it helped that I came into my gift during the time of life when I was in the mindset of a student. I started channeling my academic energy into mediumship instead of the advanced geometry class that I couldn't get through despite the fact that I took it two semesters in a row. I felt like I could be learning things that would actually help other people instead of trying to bend my brain around math that just didn't make sense to me.

Even though I was working hard at expanding my gift, I continued to keep things a secret. I didn't want to scare off my roommates or new friends at Penn State, so I spent my freshman year of college quietly honing my gifts, while also keeping them to myself.

How Does Spirit Know Which People Are Mediums?

I like to use the analogy of trick-or-treating to help explain this. Imagine yourself as a kid on Halloween night. You're excited as can be, running around in the darkening night with your pillowcase just waiting to be filled with candy. What are you looking for as you go from house to house? Porch lights that are turned on, of course! Spirit works much the same way—they look for the lights that are switched on. My belief is that those of us with the ability to connect to the Other Side have our own little spiritual "light" about us that Spirit can see and recognize as a channel to the physical world. Then they go up and knock on the door, so to speak.

But it can even go a step further. If you were a lucky trick-or-treater, you might remember those special houses in the neighborhood that were known for giving out full-sized candy bars. I'd bet you made sure to hit those houses first, if you could. Spirit does something similar. Not everyone with the ability to channel Spirit necessarily wants to do so. Others are at the beginning stages of their mediumship journey and not yet ready, and some might not be in a physical or emotional place to deliver a message. So, Spirit can sometimes try to guide their family and friends to a specific medium—or, point them to the house most likely to give out full-sized candy.

The summer after my freshman year, I finally decided to be more open with others about my gift. It was like the flood-gates opened from that point on. I switched my light on full blast, Spirit saw this, and my ability to communicate with them only got stronger and stronger as I made sense of it over time. I took mediumship workshops and meditated daily. I did readings for anyone and everyone just to get more experience. It feels weird to call it practice, but it was. The more I shared with people, the more validation I received that the information I was receiving was really coming from Spirit. As I moved further away from fear and doubt, I was able to start enjoying the process. I got to the point where I could just let things happen and it felt like everything had finally clicked. I now understood that I wasn't crazy at all—I was *supposed* to be doing this. When Spirit came (which was *a lot*), I could feel the shift in energy really quickly, almost instantaneously. My heart started to race, my face flushed, my ears turned bright red, and my breath felt labored. Then the nagging words and thoughts started to come. Sometimes it can still be tricky to distinguish what's coming from me and what's coming from Spirit, but the more I did it, the more I could distinguish between the two by the feeling. It's a weird, trippy thing that just kind of happens and is hard to put into words.

The more readings I did, the more I developed my own "Spirit Dictionary" and learned the ins and outs of interpreting Spirit's signs and symbols. It was a lot like working a muscle—the more I practiced communicating with the Spirit World, the stronger my gift became.

COMING OUT OF THE MEDIUM CLOSET

I've met some mediums who remember seeing and talking to dead people from the time they were a little kid. Then there are people like me. Looking back, I think it's probably not an accident that I really came into my abilities at the point in my life where I was leaving home and going off to college, where I could be freer. I feel like timing is everything and I was supposed to go through more "normal" experiences in life before opening up and coming into my gifts. Had I been seeing dead people swinging off the monkey bars during kindergarten recess, I can almost guarantee you I would've been scared shitless and probably would have cut off my connection to Spirit completely. I needed to live a little bit of life and figure some things out first. There's also the fact that I would never have been able to do what I do when I was still living under my mom's roof because she was so against it at first.

When I finally opened up to Spirit, I felt so free. The only thing I can really compare it to is when people try to act straight, even though they know at their core that they're gay. I've always been a medium. I was born this way. It's just that I didn't choose to fully accept that part of me until the timing was right for me to be comfortable with who I was.

Despite being more open about who I was and what I could do with my friends and some of my family, I still continued to hide my ability from my mom for a while. I knew I had to tell her, though, so I came up with a whole plan for breaking the news. I kid you not, I even started to create a PowerPoint presentation for her. I know that sounds extreme, but it was the best way I could think of to walk her through what my gift was all about. My plan was to sit my mom down, take her through each of my points, and explain my situation to her as gently as possible in hopes that she would come to terms with who I was without freaking out in the process.

Sadly, the plan got totally botched. One day while I was home from Penn State for the summer, I was sitting in my room giving a spur-of-the-moment reading to a girlfriend over the phone. (And, yes, I can give readings over the phone—it works pretty much the same as it does in person.) I was trying to be quiet because I was in my family's home, but I didn't account for the fact that my mom had a tendency to eavesdrop. I should have figured she was standing at the door with her ear pressed against it, listening to the whole conversation.

When my friend and I finished talking, I walked downstairs and saw my mom sitting at the kitchen table, crying with her face in her hands. The second I saw that, I knew she had heard everything.

"I'm sorry," I told her. "I didn't want you to have to find out this way. I had a whole plan to sit you down and walk you through a presentation to explain."

"What is going on?" she asked. "I thought I knew my own daughter!"

It was pretty much the worst way a conservative Catholic mother could possibly find out that her kid was talking to dead people.

I sat down with my mom and did the best damage control I could. I explained what had been happening over the past few years and how scared I had been to tell *anyone*, let alone her.

It was a tough day for my mom. She was worried I was possessed, and I had no idea how to calm her down and make her understand the truth of the matter. For the next few days, we didn't really talk about the elephant in the room, but it felt like she was almost angry at me. None of this was fun, but I knew that it was coming from a place of love. My mom believed what the priest at her church had to say, and, according to him, I was possibly communicating with dark spirits. She started praying for me every night.

I was frustrated and did my best to shut it all out. In general, there is so much misunderstanding about mediumship and what exactly it is that people like me are doing when we communicate with Spirit. I didn't want to feel attacked.

Things were pretty awkward between my mom and I for a while. I avoided her phone calls when I went back to school because I didn't want to hear crying or a lecture. It seemed like every conversation we had was a hard one. Finally, when people my mom knew began to have readings with me, she started to slowly come around. "Marlene," they would tell her, "your daughter has brought me so much comfort and healing. There's no way her connection comes from a dark place... what I experienced was beautiful." As my mom heard more positive and reassuring feedback from people she trusted, she started to slowly open up her mind to my gift and view it in a slightly different light. It was a slow progression, and I think it wasn't until my mom got to witness me give a reading first-hand that she really started to get it.

I'm going to flash-forward a little bit and tell you about a big moment my mom and I had several years later, when she was in the bathroom during intermission at one of my live Messages from Above events. Apparently, a few different people came up to her and told her how amazing she was for raising a daughter with such an incredible gift. As the night went on, she saw the comfort I offered to people in the audience, many of whom had gone through really tragic losses, including the loss of a child.

Later that night, my mom told me how proud of me she was and gave me a big hug. She even wanted to take a photo with me after the event. I love that picture of us, with my mom standing next to me, looking so proud. It was a very sweet moment, and it really shifted things for her. It cracked me up when, not long after that, my mom asked me if I had any messages for her. I told her what I tell everyone, which is that it doesn't work that way. With my closest friends and family, I can't be a clear channel because I already know too much and bias tends to get in the way.

But, just like everything else in life, there are some exceptions to every rule. Ironically, in those really rough first few weeks following my coming out, one of my mom's cousins who died before I was born came through. I shared some details with my mom that made her emotional. "You couldn't have known that," she said. Obviously, that single incident wasn't enough to sell her on what I was doing, but I think it was the first thing that made her go *hmmm*.

As far as where we stand today, I think my mom will always have some worry or concern about all of this because she loves me. She wants what's best for me and wants to make sure I'm safe, healthy, and okay in every way. I know that, at the end of the day, her fear mainly stems from her religious beliefs and desire to protect me. But I also think she now understands that there's something to this whole medium thing, whether she (or the church) likes it or not.

Is Mediumship Hereditary?

People often ask me if mediumship is hereditary. It can be! Sometimes the gift is passed down to one or more of the medium's kids or nieces or nephews. Other times, it skips a generation entirely. I definitely feel like this ability runs on my mom's side of the family. Which is interesting, considering how much the whole medium thing freaks her out. If you asked my mom, she would tell you there's no way this gift runs in her family. But, from my perspective, I can tell you that my mom is super intuitive. She gets these gut feelings that, in my mind, are far more than just a mother's intuition. Obviously, this isn't the same as talking to dead people, but there is undeniably an element of intuition to mediumship.

I've also been told that my mom's grandmother used to have dreams about people right before they passed away. She just sort of knew things and was very connected. I've heard about other people on that side of the family who also had a natural inclination when it came to connecting with Spirit in various ways. However, being such hardcore Catholics, I'm sure they've naturally suppressed these gifts. Many of them would tell you that none of it is real or, my favorite, that it's "the devil's work."

As we'll discuss, so much of connecting to Spirit has to do with whether or not you're open to the idea of it. So, in my family's case, I think they could have very well been doing this work if they were willing and it didn't conflict with their religious beliefs.

HELLO, WORLD!

With my mom now in the loop, I decided to publicly own my gift on a level that I never had before. That October, I shared a "coming out" post online. I wrote:

A lot of you may already know, but for those of you who still do not, I am ready to announce that I am a medium. I was terrified and scared to tell the world about what I do. Fear of what people might think of me is something that constantly worried me when I would contemplate whether to be open about being a medium. It seems people are very accepting of [mediums they've seen on TV], but would they be accepting of nineteen-year-old me who also has the gift of connecting with people who have passed away? I didn't know, and I still don't know, what the response will be. I'm sure I will lose a lot of acquaintances, maybe even friends because of what people will think of me. At this point, I really don't care. Judge me, hate me, unfriend me. I want to be open and true to myself, and if you don't accept that, then okay. This is my passion, and it's what I'll be doing the rest of my life, so I'm excited to finally be open to everyone about it.

The minute I clicked Post, everything I was doing felt real in a way it hadn't before. Like it was official or something. Although my friends and family had already known I was a medium for months, this was the first time I had owned what I was doing to the world in a larger way. In many ways, that gave me a great sense of relief. The weight of living with such a huge secret for years was finally lifted off of my shoulders once and for all. I felt like a butterfly breaking out of its cocoon, finally getting to flap my wings and soar, finally getting to do what I love through sharing my gift, and finally publicly recognizing who I am and what my purpose is.

A few acquaintances stopped talking to me, but not anyone who I really cared about. I started to realize that the trickiest part about coming out as a medium wasn't so much losing people, but having to regain their approval. It felt like I had to prove myself to a lot of people in my life all over again. Or maybe I had to prove to myself that people still approved of me and liked me, even though there was this thing about me that was really different.

I felt this a lot with my sisters, who I have a very close bond with. I know that they love and support every part of me, but I think they wondered what was going on with me for a while, and that was difficult to navigate. When I told them, "Hey, I'm pretty sure I have this gift," at first they were like, "Yeah, right, Monica. Are you nuts?" I felt like I had to prove to them, no, really! This is real. It was a big deal for me the first time each of them saw me do a reading because that's when I was able to witness their realization that this really *was* for real. I particularly recall being at the mall with my sister Vanessa and giving a spur-of-the-moment reading to one of the cashiers. "Oh, my God!" Vanessa whispered as we walked out of the shop, "It's not like I didn't believe you. But, wow! Now I really get it. What you just did for that woman was amazing."

On another occasion, I was traveling through London with my younger sister, Joanna (who, at the time, was the most skeptical of my three sisters) and we popped into a stall at Camden Market where I gave a spontaneous reading. Ironically, I was actually there to shop for a new notebook to use for readings because I've always liked to write as I channel Spirit during one-on-one or small group sessions.

The gentleman working the stall was in the midst of showing me their selection of handcrafted journals and notebooks, when the gleam of the gold wedding band on his left ring finger caught my eye. In that moment, I heard, "It's been a few years now, but my husband still wears his ring. He can't bear to take it off."

Naturally, I was nervous to say something to a complete stranger on the streets of London, but I knew in my heart that he needed to hear from his wife. I told him about my gift, and while skeptical, he was open to hearing what I had to share. I'm so glad he was, since his wife proceeded to come through with loads of evidence and healing messages. She wanted him to know how thankful she was for all of the sacrifices he had made while she was sick with cancer. She expressed how proud she was to watch over him from Heaven and to get to witness him taking on the role of "Mom" in addition to being such an amazing father to their five-year-old daughter (whose physical description and personality she described perfectly). She also acknowledged her living mother by name and brought through details and facts no one else would've known. As the man wiped away tears, I noticed that Joanna's eyes had widened. This was the first time she had seen me give a reading.

When I went to the register to purchase the journal I had picked out, the man refused to let me pay, telling me it was the least he could do in exchange for the gift he had just received. Of course, I later dedicated the first few pages of that journal to write about what had happened. I did not want to forget that beautiful reading!

When we left, Joanna told me, "Honestly, I didn't really believe that your medium stuff was real. I didn't think you were lying to people, but I thought you were lying to yourself. But now that I've seen it, there really is no other explanation for what you're doing."

I had similar experiences with a lot of my friends. It was like everyone had to either experience Spirit come through to me with a message for them or have a moment when they witnessed it. I can't tell you how many times I heard something along the lines of, "To be honest, Monica, I thought you might be a little bit wackadoodle, but now I realize this isn't all just in your head."

At certain points, it was a challenging process to go through, and then it evolved to the point where everyone at a party would line up to take a turn for their reading. It was an interesting evolution to go through.

Does Spirit Know All of Our Secrets?

This question is usually accompanied by some version of, "Does Spirit always see us?" Don't worry; I promise Spirit isn't watching you in the shower. They respect your privacy. The bathroom and any hanky-panky you might be up to? Those are both off-limits as well.

But your feelings, emotions, struggles, and the things you keep to yourself in this life? That's a different story. Spirit does have a sense of all-knowingness. They know about the things you might have kept a secret from them before they crossed over, and they know what you are going through in the physical world today. They can see it all: the good, the bad, and the ugly; the ups and downs; your inner struggles; and, yes, even your secrets.

Here's the thing, though: there is zero judgment in the Spirit World. They have no negative perceptions about even your deepest, darkest, or dirtiest secret.

JUST YOUR AVERAGE COLLEGE KID

Once I publicly owned my gift, everything started to happen really quickly. I was constantly giving spontaneous readings—to the girl typing her essay next to me or the guy in line at the coffee shop. I was so open that I just couldn't resist. Out of the forty thousand students at Penn State, without fail, it was always the girl who had just lost her boyfriend or the guy whose mom had just died that sat next to me in the library or coffee shop. In other words, the people who needed it most always found me without even realizing it.

"Hi, sorry to interrupt…" I found myself constantly saying before launching into a reading. Word started to spread like wildfire, not just on campus but throughout town as well. People wanted me to talk to their roommates, to their moms, and at their gatherings. Before I knew it, I had a six-month waiting list.

All the while, I continued to strengthen my connection with Spirit. At this point, I've met enough developing and established mediums to understand that my scenario isn't necessarily the norm. Often it can take years to develop your gifts. But I decided to push myself and Spirit, and I was able to improve in a matter of months. "I want names," I told Spirit. "I want more validation." If I was going to do this—and, by now, it was clear that I was—I didn't want to be just *any* medium. I wanted to be the best I could be. I wanted to be as strong of a channel as possible for the Other Side.

It was a crazy time. I was juggling my PR communication classes at Penn State, work as a medium, and my job for the same defense contractor I had worked for throughout high school, which I was able to do remotely from my dorm. My boss had made it known that they were more or less ready to offer me a job as soon as I earned my degree. Basically, I had a very stable and predictable life set up for myself.

At the same time, I found myself channeling Spirit for people more and more often and with greater and greater clarity. I started to question this traditional path that had once seemed so comforting to me. I knew that if I were to dive into mediumship full force, I would potentially be giving up a lot of security. But it was also clear to me where my heart was leading. There were a lot of unknowns, though, and that was scary. I struggled with the idea of throwing away all of the hard work I had put into establishing that path for myself and what I would be giving up if I were to shift my trajectory.

"Screw your job," people were telling me. "Start doing the medium work as a business. You are amazing at it, and you love it!" Through this encouragement, I began to realize that my mediumship was turning into a career in and of itself despite the fact that I had been doing all of these readings for free up to this point. I finally hit a breaking point where I realized something had to give. There was no denying the fact that the readings were more fulfilling than the technical work I was doing up until that point. It was risky, but I finally decided to follow my heart and take the leap.

I quit my job and started doing readings for forty dollars a session. At first, I struggled with the idea of accepting money for something that was a gift from God and that wasn't even really coming from me—but, rather, was coming *through* me. In the end, it almost felt like I came to an agreement with Spirit that it was okay to simultaneously help people and financially support myself.

Almost immediately, I was booked solid. I started getting calls to do both one-on-one and group readings all over

Pennsylvania. I couldn't keep up and even got to the point where I was ditching my classes to give readings. While plenty of other kids were skipping classes when they were hungover, I was doing so to help cover my tuition. I paid for college myself and have always been a go-getter. I identified with working hard, dating back to my days as a babysitter and working at Cold Stone as a freshman in high school. And I *was* working hard. That just looked different for me than it did for other kids my age. If I was going to give up the "safe" choice of a full-time job lined up for me to take a risk on being a professional medium, I was going to go at it full force.

I think it's because of this hard work that I grew and accelerated so quickly as a medium. It didn't take long before I became known as Monica the Medium. You gotta love alliteration!

It wasn't all smooth sailing from there, though. Word travels fast in a small town, and there were a lot of people who went out of their way to be rude and sometimes even downright cruel. I once got kicked out of a party because some frat boys got word of what I do and jumped to the conclusion that I must either be a fraud or a witch. I got a lot of flak from complete strangers, which was very difficult. During that time, my oldest sister, Jessica, said, "You keep saying you want to do this work for the rest of your life. If that's the case, then you're just going to have to accept the fact that this is inevitable. No matter how long you do this or how much you prove yourself through your readings, there are always going to be people who don't believe and hate on you. Those people will forever try to tear you apart. You either have to accept that now, or decide if it's not the right path for you."

Are Mediums Frauds?

There are definitely mediums who are frauds, just like there are lawyers, doctors, and bankers who are frauds. It's not an industry thing—it's a people thing. As with any other industry, there are going to be some bad eggs in the world of mediumship as well. While some of us are literally hand-picked by Spirit to do this work and share it with others, remember that each and every human here in the physical world has free will. That's why there *are* quacks out there, and that's also why the Spirit World can't just stop those con artists from taking advantage of grieving people. It sucks, but that's just part of life.

What bothers me is that people tend to make generalizations about mediums and how mediumship works. They might say that, as mediums, we should know *everything*, and if we don't then we're a fraud. It just doesn't work like that, though. Mediums are human and we can only work with the information we are given. Additionally, Spirit can only communicate with us based off of our personal frame of reference. For example, Spirit can't give me the name of an illness I've never heard of before. They can only use *my* Spirit Dictionary and signs and symbols that I've developed over the years (we'll talk more about this soon).

Skeptics and naysayers try to cast doubt on mediumship by implying that mediums just throw vague generalities out there or research their subjects prior to the reading and pull off a con that way. They might say that mediums let the sitter fill in all of the blanks or that they read a client's body language. Whatever the accusation may be, I'm sure there are many people who do things like that. But there are also mediums who are legitimately gifted, yet are put under this same umbrella.

In my opinion, one of the most difficult things about doing this work is that you have to have a thick skin. This took a while for me to develop. When I was first coming out of the mediumship closet, attacks and doubters really got to me. I spent a lot of time feeling defensive and crying. I felt bullied and hurt.

I don't feel like that anymore, though. Today, I feel like it's not my job to prove myself or to make other people believe in what I'm doing or the information I have to offer. In fact, it's not even any of my business if people choose to believe me or not. I've learned that, for some skeptics, it doesn't matter how much evidence you bring through. They'll always find a reason or explanation as to why it's not true. It's not worth me losing sleep over. All I can do is focus on the people who *are* open to my gift. That's where I want to put my energy.

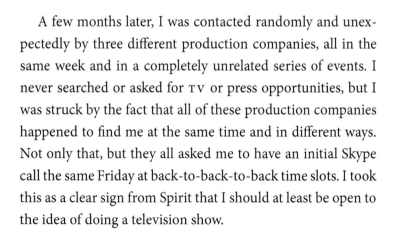

A few months later, I was contacted randomly and unexpectedly by three different production companies, all in the same week and in a completely unrelated series of events. I never searched or asked for TV or press opportunities, but I was struck by the fact that all of these production companies happened to find me at the same time and in different ways. Not only that, but they all asked me to have an initial Skype call the same Friday at back-to-back-to-back time slots. I took this as a clear sign from Spirit that I should at least be open to the idea of doing a television show.

As soon as I finished these meetings, I called my sisters and said, "You guys, I have this weird feeling that I'm going to have a television show and it's going to be with ABC Family." They thought I was completely naïve and totally ridiculous. "This stuff never goes anywhere," they told me.

Still, I knew in my heart that it was going to happen. Sure enough, flash-forward a month, and I was out in Los Angeles, taking thirteen meetings with a variety of production companies and networks. I was only twenty at this point, and I was doing this all on my own.

During my interviews with all of these different production companies, I gave a lot of spur-of-the-moment readings. Here I was with these high-up executives, watching their eyes pop out of their sockets as Spirit came rushing through and they realized I was legit. I think it was the readings that really made them want to develop a show with me. The power of what I was doing was undeniable.

In the end, I received talent offers from about half of them. But I knew in my heart that Lionsgate was the production company I was meant to work with. During the meeting I told them, "Honestly, I think I'd only want to do a television show if it was with ABC Family." They kind of laughed at me, and their answer was something along the lines of, "Sorry, sweetheart. We're excited to sign a talent agreement with you, but we don't even know if it's going to get a pilot, let alone a full season pickup. And we definitely don't think it'd be with ABC Family." This response was fair enough. At the time, ABC Family had done maybe one or two reality shows over the years. Reality just wasn't their jam; ABC Family was all about the scripted shows. Still, Lionsgate told me that if we got to that stage, they would pitch the show to everyone. They also cautioned me not to get my hopes up, because it probably wasn't going to happen, especially with ABC Family.

What do you know? Flash-forward a few more months and ABC Family (which later changed its name to Freeform) ended up being one of the networks to make an offer on the pilot, and then picked it up for a full season. *Monica the Medium* was one of the first reality shows to air on the network, and the very first to ever get a second season.

3

Life in the Public Eye

The irony isn't lost on me that for so long I was afraid of what people would think if they knew I talked to dead people. And now, here I was, starring in a reality television show about being a medium, putting myself out there for the whole world to see.

Monica the Medium debuted on ABC Family on August 25, 2015, in a prime slot directly after *Pretty Little Liars*. By the time we went to air, it had been more than a year since my initial meetings in Los Angeles. According to Hollywood standards, though, that's actually considered a quick turnaround. My meeting with Lionsgate took place in March 2014. That September we filmed the pilot. We had a full-season pickup by January 2015 and began filming in March.

SEASON ONE

Although the premise of *Monica the Medium* was a glimpse into the life of a girl navigating college and mediumship, season one didn't actually film on campus at Penn State. We weren't allowed on university property because the A & E show *Paranormal State* had filmed there previously. Penn State felt the show had given them somewhat of a bad reputation that they didn't want to build upon. Instead, we filmed downtown and in other campus-adjacent areas. Basically, we were everywhere in the small town that wasn't part of Penn State's campus. Not surprisingly, we attracted a lot of attention. Suddenly, my life was under a microscope; it was hard to be incognito with a television crew trailing me.

The crew filmed me as I lived my life as a typical college student and did a mixture of readings in my home office and traveling to my clients. There were also plenty of spontaneous readings when I was out and about, where I would approach people I felt drawn to. I got a bit of flak from some of the mediumship community about this. Some argued that it wasn't ethical to go up to strangers in a place like a restaurant and give them an on-camera reading. At the time, I was still figuring out how to set boundaries with the Spirit World and how to shut off the connection while off the clock—but you also have to remember that this was a television show about a medium. Producers and viewers alike expected there to be readings. My weeknight routine of watching Netflix with my dog Luna might have been thrilling to me, but for some reason the producers didn't think viewers would be as interested. So, when I was out and about filming, I intentionally let my light switch flicker on and allowed myself to sense Spirit. Luckily, Spirit has never guided me to anyone who wasn't open to hearing the messages—but, nonetheless, mediumship ethics were and are still always my number one priority.

Even if it was cut out of the episode due to time constraints, I made sure to receive permission from each and every person I gave a reading to before bringing through any messages from Spirit. In some circumstances, producers even made me hold off from approaching someone until they first signed an on-camera release and, if we were filming somewhere that was particularly loud, were mic'd up.

The other thing to note is that a single one-hour episode stemmed from an entire week or more of filming. There were many times I went to the mall or out with friends and didn't give a reading, even though it might appear to viewers that that's literally all I did 24/7. Often, those more mundane moments just didn't make the cut.

Anyway, I'm incredibly blessed to have had such an amazing opportunity and platform to share my gift. I have so many memories of good times with our awesome crew, and I loved the people I got to meet and give readings to. Yet, at the same time, there were challenges that I didn't exactly see coming. Filming in public brought on terrible anxiety for me. People yelled at me as the cameras followed us walking through downtown State College or in the local stores. They called me a fraud, a bitch, and even told me I was fat. I never drank when I knew I would be giving a reading, but sometimes Krista and I told the producers that we were going into a restaurant to use the bathroom, then proceeded to quickly take a shot of the *other* kind of spirits just to combat the nerves that came with the staring, pointing, and yelling from bystanders.

Of course, not everyone was like that. A lot of people were very nice and went out of their way to welcome and accept us with open arms. Still, after the first season, it was clear to me that I didn't want to do the show if I had to continue filming it in Pennsylvania. I never really felt like I belonged in that small town. Not to mention, I had always dreamed of moving to Southern California (three years was enough time to show me that I couldn't handle the harsh winters in State College). The crew was over it too—all those Californians had had enough of the cold!

Where's the Funniest Place You've Given a Reading?

Over the years, I've definitely given readings in some strange, sometimes even downright awkward, situations. Once, I was trying to relax at the steam room in the gym. Imagine me, in nothing but a towel, sweating profusely in thick clouds of steam. Out of the corner of my eye, I see another person has joined me in the room. Immediately, I hear Spirit trying to come through. "Excuse me! That's my daughter! Would you mind?"

I have to admit that I *did* mind a bit. I could barely even see the girl through the fog of steam, and I wasn't sure how she'd react to a half-naked stranger tapping her on the shoulder. It's a bit more intimate of a setting than I would prefer.

But her father was insistent, so I crossed my sweaty fingers and hoped she'd take it well. Luckily, after she got over her initial surprise, this woman was overjoyed to hear from her dad. I talked to her for about twenty minutes, until I had to stumble out of the steam room to get a glass of water. Connecting to Spirit tends to make me thirsty under the best of circumstances, so the humidity definitely didn't help matters. But later, I was happy that I'd taken the chance, knowing that the girl got to leave understanding in no uncertain terms how much her father loved her.

Another time, during a night out at Penn State, I delivered messages from Spirit to a girl through the wall of a bathroom stall. Although, that time I was partially to blame since I was the slightest bit tipsy. As I mentioned earlier, I don't ever drink when I know I'll be channeling Spirit. In fact, I won't even have one sip the night before my live events because that's how careful I am about my energy.

But when it's a spur-of-the-moment thing and I've had a glass of wine, sometimes it can actually make the reading stronger. Just like a drink can make it easier for many of us to hit the dance floor at a wedding or approach that cute guy at the bar, the same goes for delivering messages from Spirit. No matter how confident I am in my connection, I'm still human and sometimes second-guess or question what's coming through. With a little liquid courage, I'm less likely to hold anything back (although, luckily, I've gotten to the point where I pretty much have no filter while completely sober too). For ethical reasons, though, if I've had more than one drink, channeling of any sort is out of the question.

REACTION TO *MONICA THE MEDIUM*

From a ratings perspective, the first season of *Monica the Medium* went over great. We had an awesome time slot, our ratings were good, and our audience grew larger throughout the course of the season.

Of course, not everyone loved it. Before *Monica the Medium* even started airing, online trolls and bullies tried to tear me apart. I learned how to thicken my skin early on, which helped as the season progressed. There will always be naysayers when it comes to this stuff, and I had to accept that if I was going to share my gift on such a public platform.

The show was also another hurdle for my mom and me to clear. When I first told her about it, she seemed very apprehensive. I remember her asking me, "What is everyone going to think? Are you sure you want to do this?"

I think she was concerned about how her family would react to this public display of my channeling. My mom didn't tell a lot of people in her Costa Rican family about the show until word finally started to spread on its own. I mean, my mom is one of eight kids and I have a massive extended family, so news gets around. I'm pretty sure there were some whispers along the lines of, "*Ooohh,* what's happening with Marlene's daughter?"

In the end, it all worked out. I think it was good for my mom to get to watch and see more and more of the positive impact I was having. It allowed her to understand me and what I do in a new way and on a different level.

Does Spirit Ever Annoy You?

Over the years, I've learned how to better control my gift so that I can fully be "off the clock" when I'm not work-ing. But I always joke that when I'm in the shower, it's almost like a telephone booth for Spirit. This is especially true on days I'm hosting a Messages from Above event, because I'm in such an open, receptive state. I'll be tak-ing a shower and will start sensing loads of dead people, even if it's still several hours before the event. From an energetic standpoint, it makes sense because water is an energy conductor. But, still, if they're going to bother me in there, I wish they would at least make themselves use-ful and pass the shampoo!

I know this might sound like a contradiction because I already told you that Spirit isn't watching you in your more private moments. And that's true: they're not trying to catch you naked. Your shower is safe. I promise that Spirit is never a peeping Tom. They're not watching me in there either, but they're definitely chatting my ear off!

In all seriousness, though, I don't mind that they bother me in the shower leading up to an event because at least I know that someone's planning on showing up! Plus, I'd much rather Spirit "pop in" mid-shampoo instead of just as I'm about to fall asleep at night. Yup, bedtime is another popular time for the pushy spirits. I once had Spirit come through to say, "Real quick, I wanted to let you know that my daughter will be in the audience tomorrow night. Hoping I'll get the chance to come through for her! Look out for old man Odin with the missing front tooth and scally cap."

> I told him, "Look, Odin, I understand your eagerness,
> but you'll have to get in line like everybody else. This isn't
> a restaurant. There are no advance reservations. Now,
> please let me sleep!"

SEASON TWO

The second season of *Monica the Medium* featured me and
my best friend Krista moving out to San Diego. We took some
classes at the local community college, but I was already pretty
set on dropping out (sorry, Mom). I knew I could always finish
my Penn State degree online later down the road if I wanted
to. A lot of people in my life thought I was making the wrong
choice because I was so close to being done, having already
completed three out of four years. But I knew I had already
found my purpose, and another year of school wasn't going
to change that. My dad understood, though. I will never forget him telling me, "Out of every hundred people, I'd say it's
smart for ninety-nine of them to take the traditional college
path and get their degree. But I think there's always an exception. And I feel like you may be one of them." I knew that was
my dad's way of giving me his blessing to leave school, and I'm
so glad he did.

As a result of all of this, the focus of *Monica the Medium*
shifted more to Krista and I meeting boys and finding roommates. It also showed my journey as I started to establish my
business and host more events.

The difference between season one and season two was like
night and day. The people I encountered in San Diego were so

much more open to and accepting of what I was doing. People weren't whispering or making rude comments. Plus, it was a much bigger city, so I had more space and less scrutiny. I had so much more fun filming the second season.

From a business perspective, things were a bit bumpier this time around, though. During season two, ABC Family switched over to Freeform, and, with that, the network was moving into a new, younger, and hipper direction. This meant that a bunch of new shows were coming onboard. It was a very competitive environment, and there were a lot of time slot changes as shows were shifted and bounced around. Whereas season one aired at eight o'clock on Tuesday nights, season two aired at ten o'clock on Mondays. In the world of television, this is a pretty crappy time slot.

Still, our ratings were steady. After we wrapped for the season, Freeform went back and forth about whether or not they were going to renew *Monica the Medium*. We came close, but in the end, Freeform decided that while our ratings were good, they weren't as great as they needed to be to move forward. That's the nature of television. The network has to make money from their ad sales, and for that to happen, advertisers want to know that a show is an undisputed success. The other extenuating factor was that Freeform was new to the reality show market. I think they were still working on cracking that formula while we were on the air.

Like I said, I know that everything happens for a reason, including the cancellation of the show. I was mainly sad because I was going to miss the crew so much. They had become like my family, and not being with them all of the time felt like a loss. I also loved having the type of platform *Monica the Medium* gave me and being able to share my gift in that way. So many viewers sent me letters and messages, telling me how much the show helped them heal and open up to the signs from Spirit. That made all the hard days worth it.

But I'll be honest. There was also a certain sense of relief when we got canceled. Working as a medium requires a lot of energy. Television doesn't think about scheduling from this standpoint because it's a business. To them, it's black and white: if Monica gives X amount of readings a day, we can film in X number of hours per day. Business does not account for the mental, emotional, and physical exertion of mediumship.

Also, having the spotlight on you brings a lot of pressure with it. Long shooting days and early call times are exhausting. Often, we filmed for ten to twelve hours a day. It wasn't like we were filming *Jersey Shore* and there was a whole group of people to split camera time between; it was literally my name in the show's title. My roommates were included, but 99 percent of the show fell on my shoulders, and that was a ton of pressure. Not only did I feel like the crew's salary was reliant upon me but I also felt responsible for the editors, the finance department, and a whole bunch of other peripheral players.

One day during our lunch break (side note, craft services was a *major* perk of filming—I mean, who can say no to free food?), I accidentally stumbled upon a thick folder that had a directory of the different departments and the names of at least one hundred people I didn't even know who were working on *Monica the Medium* back in Los Angeles. That knowledge brought with it even more pressure. I knew that if I didn't put 110 percent into the show every single day, not only was I letting myself down but I was letting everyone else down too.

In the end, I consider the show to be a huge win. It was an amazing opportunity for me to get to share healing and hope with hundreds of thousands of people across the world. Not to mention, it led me to my future husband! I met my fiancé, Tyler, on a blind date during an episode of season two. People always ask, "Was it really a blind date?"

Yes, it was as real as it gets! One day while we were filming a party at our house, I told my roommates that I really wanted to meet "an East Coast guy who lives in San Diego." Later that night, my roommate, Kirsten, met Tyler at a bar in Pacific Beach off-camera. When she found out that he grew up in Pittsburgh and had been living in San Diego for the last few years, she said, "I think you'd be perfect for my roommate! Please let me set you guys up."

Kirsten got Tyler's number and called him the very next morning. "How do you feel about going on a blind date with my roommate?" she asked.

Tyler figured, "Why not?" He had never been on a blind date before and is always down for a new experience.

"Okay, perfect!" Kirsten replied. "Oh, and by the way, I hope you don't mind if it's filmed for TV."

That's when Tyler (understandably) pumped the brakes and said he'd need to sleep on it. The next day, a producer called Tyler up and somehow managed to convince him to give it a go. All the producer told him about the show is that it featured a college girl in San Diego. Little did he know this girl also talked to dead people!

Long story short, the blind date went well, but it surely wasn't love at first sight. Our relationship progressed slowly, but over time turned into the soulmate connection I've always dreamed of. To this day, Tyler and I go back to that same restaurant every year on the anniversary of the night we met.

Even though *Monica the Medium* didn't go past those two seasons, in my mind the experience was still perfect. I met the love of my life, and the show allowed me to grow my platform, share, and bring healing to people—but not to the extent that anything ever became overwhelming. It's not like I've ever been bombarded by fans at the airport. I still get to live a normal life in a way that I don't think other mediums on TV can. This relative anonymity makes it easier for me to share with the people who are open to what I have to offer. At the end of the day, that's what matters most. It's the reason I have this gift in the first place.

A Word from Tyler: What It's Like to Date a Medium

People always assume that dating a medium is somehow a different experience from being with any other girl. The truth of the matter is that it's really not. I think there's a common misconception that Monica is different from other girls our age in every way because she can talk to dead people. In so many ways, Monica is completely normal, aside from the fact that there is this superhuman part of her with abilities that most people can't understand. She's not weird or odd, and she fits in just like anyone else. I promise you that if you didn't know any better, you would assume Monica was just like you. Until you witness her do something amazing, which, if you hang out with her for long enough, she inevitably will do.

But, in all fairness, I understand why people think this. If I'm being perfectly honest, at first I thought Monica was a little bit odd myself. The night of our first date, Monica gave me a reading (who the hell does that on a first date?!), and I remember calling my brothers after the fact and telling them how weird our meeting had been. But as I got to know Monica better, I began to respect everything she does and stands for.

A few weeks after we met, I lost one of my childhood best friends. Monica brought through messages from him that erased any and all doubts I might have had about where he was and whether or not he was okay. From that moment forward, I knew that Monica was the real deal.

I am so proud to be with Monica. She brings so much happiness and healing into other people's lives. I have experienced her gift firsthand and, also, have witnessed so many happy tears as the result of conversations she has had and messages she has given to complete strangers. I have no choice but to support Monica in everything that she does. She really is amazing.

LIFE AFTER *MONICA THE MEDIUM*

When *Monica the Medium* came to an end, I decided to focus on all of the things I'd wanted to do while the show was in production but hadn't had the time or bandwidth for. Most exciting was launching my Messages from Above events, which allowed me to share my gift in the way I've always wanted to—onstage before a live audience so that the messages from Spirit could reach even more people. I also really enjoyed the opportunity to start raising money for various causes through charity auctions and sweepstakes and began my podcast, *Wine & Spirits with Monica the Medium.*

A Note to People Who Attend Medium Events

For me or any other medium, channeling Spirit at events is always an unpredictable process. Sometimes thirty spirits come through, and sometimes thirteen do. You never know, and I have no control over the process. I let everyone know up front that I'm just the messenger, and I can't guarantee who will come through on any given night (that's true for readings of any variety).

It's never a good idea to come to an event with the mindset that you *have* to get a reading. In fact, I encourage people to go into events expecting that they won't get a reading and to enjoy it as a more general healing experience. The bottom line is that Spirit always comes through for the people who need it the most, not who want it the most. At the end of my events, I always jokingly remind people, "I promise that your mom still loves you. Just because she didn't come through tonight, doesn't mean she loves you any less."

It's tricky because when you're grieving, of course it feels like you need these messages the most. But you have to remember that loss affects everyone differently, and you have no idea what the other people in the room are going through. I get that it's human nature to want to hear from your specific loved ones. The problem is that if you get too stuck on that, you will miss out on all of the other bits and pieces of other people's messages that might very well directly apply to you as well.

It's impossible not to notice that my Messages from Above events often end up having themes. For instance, on some nights I notice there are a lot of dads coming through, and then I might realize that Father's Day is approaching. Obviously, this is not a coincidence. It's safe to assume that a lot of people are missing their dads around this time of year, so Spirit collectively comes together to help heal and offer peace. On other nights, there might be a lot of people in the audience who have lost children or who have lost loved ones to something specific like suicide or cancer, and a big group of those souls come through. Some nights are lighthearted to the point where everyone is laughing at departed sassy grandmas and hysterical dads, whereas other nights are filled with tears and tragic stories. It's almost like Spirit organizes itself around certain themes so their messages have maximum impact and touch the people who need to hear them most.

I can't tell people enough that they are never at an event on accident. That's the way Spirit works. You are in a specific audience because you're meant to be, and because something is being offered for you to learn or heal from.

In fact, most people receive validation and healing messages through the readings of others.

A woman recently contacted me to share her experience with this. She explained that she was born with a missing chromosome, which led her to face many challenges in life. She had gone through more than thirty major surgeries and two near-death car accidents, and she couldn't help but wonder, "What's the point? What is my purpose on this Earth?" Family members often told this woman that she had a tremendous impact on the people in her life, but she struggled to accept this. Then she decided to attend one of my events and heard a message that changed her entire outlook. She said:

> *Monica channeled a kid who had an extra chromosome and, already, I'm listening intently. She said that he impacted and inspired so many lives and that's what all of my friends say about me. I felt as if Monica was talking about me. Then she said that when he transitioned into Heaven, he no longer had a disability, and that he was, in fact, a whole person. That gave me so much peace, joy, and strength to carry on. I started crying uncontrollably because before, I felt my whole life had been a mistake and now I know that I'm here for a purpose. My family friend turned to me during the reading and said, "She's describing you." There's no doubt I was meant to be there.*

Along with all of this, it's a profound experience just to be in a room where so much healing and communication is happening. That alone can change a person's entire perception on life and death. I've seen many skeptics turn into believers by witnessing an event, regardless of whether Spirit specifically came through for them or not.

I've also branched out into the world of teaching other people to learn how to strengthen their own ability to connect with Spirit. I teach a six-week online course called *A Beginner's Guide to Connecting to Spirit,* and have thoroughly enjoyed the opportunity to mentor others. In addition to my specific work with mediumship, I love working with empaths who feel the emotions of others like I do. I also just finished creating a sixty-two-card oracle deck, *The Empath Oracle,* to help fellow empaths develop tools to manage their energy and find balance. Of course, writing this book has been another way I get to share healing with others. Shifting my focus along all of these different avenues helps me avoid burning out and gives me a variety of creative outlets. It also allows me to share my gifts in ways that can help people, even if it's not through a one-on-one interaction.

SETTING BOUNDARIES (SORRY, NO PRIVATE READINGS)

These days, I don't give any scheduled private readings unless it's to raise money for charity or for one of my free reading giveaways. I still do spontaneous readings when I can and also surprise winners with free mini readings on my podcast from time to time. In the years before and during *Monica the Medium,* I was giving readings six or seven days a week. Honestly, that's a recipe to start resenting the gift I've been given and a quick road to burnout. I even got to the point where I started to dread giving readings because they took so much out of me. A lot of this has to do with the energy it takes to connect to Spirit, but the emotion of it all took a toll on me too (#empath). Readings sometimes left me feeling sad for days after the fact because I got so energetically and emotionally sucked in.

Don't get me wrong: I am still just as in awe of and grateful for this gift as ever, but I also understand that if I want to act as Spirit's middleman for the rest of my life—and I do—I have to find the balance between providing healing for others and maintaining my own mental health and well-being in the process. For me, the only way to do that is to eliminate private readings and to share my gift with more people by channeling in front of larger audiences or on episodes of my podcast. That way, even if a person does not receive a direct message from Spirit, they are still receiving healing through the messages given to others. This frees up my energy and allows me to help others in different ways.

I have learned to create very firm boundaries around this that apply equally to everyone—from my best friends to family members and even celebrities. I've had people assume they're entitled to a private reading with me just because they have millions of followers on Instagram or because they're willing to pay me tons of money. I politely tell them that no, there are no exceptions. None of this is about money or fame. When it comes to Spirit, every single one of us is on equal footing.

The truth is that I could give a couple of private readings a week and be perfectly fine, but this presents another problem: who am I to pick and choose who is most deserving of a reading? By the time I stopped offering private readings, my waitlist was more than six months long. It stressed me out to see how many people were waiting and knowing there was no way I could get to them all. The list included friends, distant relatives, acquaintances, and strangers who desperately wanted a reading. I knew that if I left myself open to doing scheduled private readings at all, I'd feel pressured to take on more than I could really handle. I'd land right back in the same cycle of exhaustion and mental drain. So, for me, doing private readings came down to an all-or-nothing choice. Maybe one day my thoughts will change on this, but for now, this is where I stand.

When I first accepted my gift and came out of the medium closet, I was walking through the world with no clue how to manage my ability—which basically meant that, as I like to put it, my "light switch" was always turned to "on." No matter where I was, Spirit would come through. I went about my everyday life being pulled here and there by Spirit, giving readings all the time. Over the years, I've learned that *I* control the gift, not vice versa. I get to choose who I connect with and when. As I like to say, "My energy, my schedule." These days, I'm able to turn the volume down and even flip the switch to off.

Even if you're standing next to me on a train and have just suffered through the worst loss imaginable, there's a strong possibility I won't pick up on anything. At the very least, that's the case about 99 percent of the time. I'm grateful for that because, otherwise, I think I would have burnt out really quickly and not been able to continue doing this work. As I mentioned before, on days when I have a big event, there are times a Spirit will break through some of those boundaries.

But that's only because I'm already opening myself up to sensing Spirit in preparation for the evening ahead.

One of the most important things I teach those who are coming into their own gifts is how to set boundaries and maintain control. They can't allow themselves to give, give, give. This is one of those things that is usually inherently tricky for mediums because most of us are givers by nature. We want to help everybody, but we also have to take care of ourselves by allowing ourselves to shut it off. Otherwise, we'll go crazy, get exhausted, and burn out.

But every now and then, a strong Spirit will still get through. This rarely happens, but when it does, it's usually for a good reason. And, honestly, it's also usually when I'm in the mood to connect. I've noticed that it happens in situations when I'm by myself with time to kill. For example, during long Uber rides or while I'm waiting at the DMV. It's as though I allow myself to flicker the light on and see if anyone is out there waiting on the porch.

Sometimes my empathic nature plays a role in this too, and readings slip in that way. The other morning I was in the Starbucks drive-thru line like I am more often than I'd care to admit (cold brew = life). Usually, by the time I get to the window there's a line of about ten other cars behind me. On this particular morning, though, there wasn't a single other car to be found.

As I pulled up to the window, I noticed that the barista seemed a bit standoffish. At first, I thought it could just be your run-of-the-mill, early morning tiredness. But as soon as I looked into the woman's eyes, I instantly felt a flood of intense pain and grief. I decided to flip the switch on to see if that pain was related to a loss. Sure enough, the woman's little girl came through, and I was able to give her a spontaneous reading.

"That's my mommy!" I heard in my thought's voice. "I was only two years old when I passed."

The barista's daughter communicated how her mom had put everything on hold to be there for her while she was sick, and how she's now a single mother carrying all of the stresses that come with providing for two children, while simultaneously trying to process feelings of anger and guilt.

This sweet little girl wanted her mother to let go of worries such as, "Should I have taken her to a different doctor? Should I have stopped treatment sooner to fully let her enjoy her final months?" The young daughter communicated that every choice her mom had made was the right one, and that she is so thankful to have had her as a mother in this lifetime.

As the healing messages continued to pour through and this child expressed her goofy and sweet little personality, I saw the barista's demeanor instantly begin to soften and a smile spread across her face. I could see layers of grief slowly peel away and a blanket of comfort come over her. The woman thanked me and told me that, for the first time since losing her daughter, she now felt hope, knowing she has a guiding light watching over her. I'm grateful to Spirit for always putting things into perspective for me. What started out as an interaction with someone who I thought was merely lacking customer service skills, turned out to be a grieving mom who was understandably going through some things. This is why it's so important to be kind. Everyone's facing their own struggles. You never really know what someone else is going through.

This woman and I were both in tears as we shared this time together. It felt like the whole world had stopped, and I truly believe that Spirit played a role in that. Interestingly, I was able to speak with her for ten minutes before another car appeared behind mine. I don't know about your local Starbucks, but at mine it's unheard of for it to be that empty at eight o'clock on a weekday morning. I'm sure it was no coincidence that it was so quiet on this particular morning. Spirit is amazing that way. They're able to set up a series of circumstances that allow them to come through when we need it most. In this instance, I have a wonderful vision in my head of a whole army of souls blocking the Starbucks drive-thru with a wall of energy so that this woman could receive some much-needed messages from her daughter.

II

The Big Picture

4

The Mechanics of Mediumship

've told you a lot about my background and coming into my gifts, but I still haven't really explained how this whole channeling thing works, at least for me.

People always tell me how lucky I am to get to talk to my own deceased family and friends all the time. The reality though, is that it doesn't work that way. I get to use my mediumship gifts for everybody else, but not for myself or the people I am closest to. Whenever I know too much about a person or situation, it creates a bias that makes it too hard to make the separation between what I already know or might want to hear and what's *actually* coming through from Spirit.

Every now and then, I'll have a strong visitation dream or receive a message from a loved one through automatic writing or meditation. But even those instances are very rare. For the most part, I connect with them in the same way that I encourage all of you to (we'll talk about this in Part Four of the book).

Luckily, when I communicate with Spirit on behalf of others, it's much clearer.

Can You Connect to Any Dead Person You Please?

A question I get asked all the time is, "Can you connect to *anyone* in the Spirit World? Like, if you wanted to have a conversation with Elvis, could you?"

Ha, I wish! But nope, doesn't work that way. As I've said before, Spirit comes through for those who need it, not for those who want it. And I certainly don't need to talk to Elvis (though it *would* be cool!). Put me in front of an immediate family member or close friend of Elvis, then you betcha, he'd probably come through. But for me, or just anyone? It's unlikely. Remember that it takes a tremendous amount of energy and effort from Spirit to lower their vibration enough to connect with a medium. Then, as a medium, I have to raise my vibration enough to meet them in the middle and communicate. This process is unlikely to happen just because I want to know if Elvis really did meet Marilyn Monroe.

Generally, the key to a strong connection with Spirit is the love and closeness they feel with someone here in the physical world and the need of that person to hear a message from them. This means that eventually, it becomes just about impossible for any medium to connect with certain people. I think it's safe to say that there's no one left here on Earth who desperately needs to hear from Cleopatra. The simple fact of the matter is that spirits from past generations have already been joined by everyone they love and have no reason to connect with a medium (and no, unfortunately, curiosity is not a good enough reason for Spirit to connect). This is one of the reasons I recommend you remain wary of a medium that promises you they can connect with anyone.

CHANNELING SPIRIT

Especially now that I intentionally turn my light off as I go about everyday life, I usually know beforehand when I'm going to be in a situation where I want to start channeling. Over the years, I have developed a whole process to prepare for communicating with Spirit. If I'm going to be channeling at an event or doing a reading, I will usually fast in the time leading up to it or only eat something light because that makes it easier for me to raise my vibration to connect. I also drink lots of water, both because connecting is easier when I am hydrated and also because the process of channeling Spirit makes me as thirsty as our bulldog Chubba after a brisk walk around the neighborhood.

I do a meditation to clear and quiet my mind, and then say an opening prayer in which I call in my angels, spirit guides, and loved ones to help me connect and be the strongest, clearest channel I can be. I ask for God's protection and that only energy of light and love step forward. With my vibration raised and light switch turned on, I'm ready to open the door to the Spirit World and see who's there.

If I'm hosting an event, I usually find that there's already a line of dead people waiting to communicate. Even though this is always my experience, every time I can't help but wonder, "What if this is the night when nobody shows up?" (Hence, why I let it slide when the dead crash my shower or bath time; at least I know that *someone* plans to come through!) Despite this irrational anxiety, the truth of the matter is that Spirit is always not only there, but starts to gather hours beforehand. They are excited and ready to talk. I work with a punctual crew.

At this point, I'm ready to channel, and I start with what I like to think of as an interview process with Spirit. I have learned that in the midst of their excitement, often Spirit can be a little all over the place, so I make them follow my specific communication process (or at least I try to since they're admittedly a bit stubborn at times).

First, I go through my process of identifying Spirit, which can happen in a few different ways. Spirit might appear on either my right- or left-hand side, which tells me whether they belong to that person's maternal or paternal side of the family. Or I might visualize a family tree in my mind's eye and Spirit brings me to the part of the tree where they connect to the person I'm channeling for, in order to communicate their relation to them. All of this happens very, very quickly.

Look, I'm the first one to say that I wish Spirit could simply hold up a cardboard sign that reads something like, "I'm cousin Jo, twice-removed from her mother's side of the family. I passed away from lung cancer in December of '84, just shy of my fifty-fifth birthday. I'm about 5'4" inches tall, a bit heavier-set, short curly gray hair. I'm a frequent gardener, I never step outside without wearing my red lipstick, and I love long walks on the beach."

Unfortunately, that's not the case. While Spirit can and does communicate an incredible amount of identifying information and clear messages, it's usually not conveyed in fully formed sentences the way most of us are used to speaking with one another. Spirit primarily communicates through flashes of images, sporadic words or sounds, feelings, and physical sensations. When I deliver Spirit's messages, it's *my* interpretation of what I'm hearing, feeling, seeing, and sensing.

I'll sometimes hear specific phrases or names in my thought's voice, but typically I'm *not* relaying sentences from the Other Side word-for-word. Instead, I'm doing my best to put together all those puzzle pieces to interpret the information and translate it into the more human terms that you'll hopefully understand.

When I communicate with Spirit, there's a mental back-and-forth during which I ask questions and they bring through the information they're able to give me. Throughout all of this, I'm using The Clairs, which are the senses through which a medium connects and communicates with the Other Side.

The Clairs

I primarily connect through some combination of the first four Clairs on this list, but all six of them are in my rotation.

1. **Clairvoyance** (clear seeing)—This is how Spirit shows me things in my mind's eye, similar to how you might experience a daydream as a little movie playing or pictures flashing through your head. It's not like HD television. I wish. A lot of the time, these images are a bit fuzzy.

2. **Clairaudience** (clear hearing)—When I hear information, it's in the form of my thought's voice, not another person or Spirit's voice. To do this accurately, I have had to learn to separate my own thoughts from what is coming through from Spirit. Sometimes I hear names, and other times Spirit brings forward random words or phrases that serve as evidence or validation to the person they are communicating with.

3. **Clairsentience** (clear feeling)—Spirit loves to communicate with me through feelings. I'd say this is probably my strongest clair. Sometimes I feel emotions that Spirit experienced at a point in their physical life, and other times I take on the emotion of what the person getting the reading has felt in the past or is currently going through. Clairsentience is also used to communicate through physical sensations. It's one of the ways Spirit can tell me how they passed. I'll feel a pain in my chest if someone died from a heart attack. Other times, if someone passed from Alzheimer's or dementia, I might feel like my mind has gone blank. In cases of overdose, I tend to feel nauseated or lightheaded.

4. **Claircognizance** (clear knowing)—Sometimes I just know things. I jokingly refer to this as "Spirit vomit."

It's when things just come out of my mouth and I have no idea why or where they stem from. Have you ever answered a question in class or in a trivia game but have no idea how you know the answer? It's sort of like that.

5. **Clairalience** (clear smelling)—This happens when Spirit communicates through scent. I might get a whiff of cigar smoke if your grandfather regularly smoked cigars, or I'll smell gasoline if Spirit was a mechanic or had a passion for working on cars.

6. **Clairgustance** (clear tasting)—This is when Spirit communicates through taste. Over the years, I've asked Spirit to only use this Clair with me if it's something pleasant (as you can imagine, tasting blood is...not so great). I might randomly taste your mother's freshly baked sugar cookies or your father's favorite deep dish pizza. Remember how I eat lightly leading up to any readings? Because of this, I occasionally have to pause to get clear on clairgustance messages before I deliver them, to make sure they're truly coming from Spirit, and that it's not just me getting hungry!

I know many other mediums who only use one sense; for example, they might exclusively see, hear, or feel things from Spirit. Personally, I've learned how to simultaneously use multiple senses over the years and rely on a combination of The Clairs. This provides me with more opportunities to receive information and leaves less room for misinterpretation. The more information I can give the person I'm reading for, the more easily they can verify who they are communicating with on the Other Side and receive the utmost healing from the experience.

SPIRIT DICTIONARY

What I call my Spirit Dictionary consists of a variety of signs and symbols I've gotten over the years that I now know how to interpret. It's basically the shorthand of Spirit communication. My Spirit Dictionary makes it much quicker for Spirit to bring through information that I can easily receive and interpret. A lot of mediums have their own version of this, but no two dictionaries are ever going to look the same because Spirit works off of each of our unique experiences and frames of reference. Spirit might show me something I've been through or someone I've known to communicate the message they're trying to get across.

Other signs and symbols are developed by working with Spirit over time and are a combination of how Spirit likes to communicate and how I will best receive information. Remember how I said that I can tell if Spirit is related to a person's paternal or maternal family line based on which side of me they appear? I cracked that code by doing enough readings that, at a certain point, I put the pattern together. Once I realized that, I set the intention that Spirit would only come to me on the left side when they're related to the dad and on the right side when they're related to the mom. This is a good example of how Spirit and I work together to figure out how to communicate with each other.

These signs and symbols can come to me through any of the Clairs. My Spirit Dictionary contains many sounds, feelings, and physical sensations. Spirit will use what's most accessible for me, then I piece it together and interpret it as a message for the person who needs to hear it.

If I receive a message that's not already part of my routine frame of reference or in my Spirit Dictionary, then I'll either not be able to interpret the information or Spirit will try to give me something close. For instance, I might get my symbol for a "Mar" name if your mother's name was Marlee.

There have also been many times when Spirit has tried to communicate something that I'm completely unfamiliar with; perhaps a hobby I've never heard of, or a rare illness. Furthermore, sometimes a symbol will come up in a reading that I do recognize, but I'm not sure what to do with it. In both scenarios, I do my best to simply describe what it is I'm seeing, hearing, and feeling rather than jump to interpret it.

I once got an image of an old neighbor of mine and was completely confused since normally I would interpret that as Spirit's way of identifying themselves as the client's neighbor. This time, I saw my neighbor while I was in the middle of describing the client's late father. Turns out my client's late father had the same first name as my old neighbor! I was glad I didn't focus on trying to interpret the image and instead just described what I was seeing. I've learned that I've just got to trust myself and Spirit during this process. Sometimes there are moments in readings where I see the client's face glaze over a bit, obviously thinking hard, before they admit they don't understand or connect with something I've shared from

Spirit. I always tell them the same thing—to keep the information in mind because it'll probably make sense later! And it usually does, even if it takes days, weeks, or months to make the connection.

One of my favorite examples of this happened at an event a couple of years ago, when I was bringing through a woman's brother. During the reading, Spirit wanted to communicate that he was watching over his daughter (this woman's niece) and could see everything she was up to while away at college. Following that message about his daughter, I kept seeing something about plunging a clogged toilet. I knew it must be significant since I could hear Spirit laughing as if it was the funniest prank ever. The woman shook her head no and assured me that she didn't have a clue what I was going on about. The next day she emailed to tell me that after the event was over, she called her niece to pass on all the messages her niece's father had come through with. She told her niece about the plunger, only to find out that at the exact time she had been getting the reading at my event, her niece had been plunging her clogged toilet for twenty minutes at her college apartment. With this, her dad was able to convey the message that not only was he looking out for her while she was away at school but that he also had the time to pull a few jokes.

With all of the different aspects that come along with the process of channeling, you can probably imagine just how *much* information I'm receiving from Spirit during my events. It's the reason why I get a huge burst of euphoric energy in the thirty minutes or so after an event—a lot like I would imagine professional athletes feel after a big win—followed by a big emotional, mental, and physical crash and burn. By the next day, it's a full blown Spirit hangover, as I like to call it.

SPIRIT GUIDE SUPPORT

We will talk about spirit guides in the more general sense in the next chapter, but for now just understand that each one of us has multiple spirit guides who serve specific functions. For example, you might have one spirit guide who helps you with health issues and another who helps with family or career issues.

I have what I call a gatekeeper guide. I like to think of this specific spirit guide as the bouncer at my readings. Just like a bouncer would do at a club, my gatekeeper guide helps line up Spirit at the door before I go onstage at an event. I imagine my guide saying, "Before you go inside to chat with Monica, I'm gonna need to give you the ground rules. This is how it's gonna go, and if you don't adhere to that, we're going to have to ask you to leave." Thanks to my gatekeeper guide, Spirit already knows the lay of the land and how I work before they begin to come through.

I also ask my spirit guides to encourage Spirit to bring through the lighter side of their personality to the greatest extent possible because it helps raise the vibration of the room and makes the people in the audience more open and relaxed. I am here for all of the sassiness, sarcasm, and laughter that Spirit wants to bring. Some nights are still heavier than others, but I work with my guides to do what I can to lift the energy in the room. I love the occasional dad that jokingly warns his daughter's boyfriend that he's keeping an eye on him or the grandma that surprises her grandkids by letting them know she's seen them rolling joints in the basement.

People are always shocked when I bring through the specific names and details of their loved ones, but I think it's the way their personalities come through that really validates how real this connection is. I mean, if someone was an asshole on Earth, they're no longer that way once they get to Heaven. But their little quirks, mannerisms, and ways of speaking still come through loud and clear. I love when I'm able to really blend my energy with theirs and convey the true essence of a person. For their loved ones, that is the part of it that tends to be the most comforting, confirming, and powerful. Spirit might as well hold up a big, blinking sign that reads, "Yes, it's really me!"

Can You Control Which Spirits Come Through?

Part of communicating with Spirit is honoring the process of who wants to come through and needs to speak. Just because you don't necessarily want to speak to Aunt Sally, I can't turn her away if she comes through in your reading. I mean, that's just rude.

I would say that 90 percent of the time, the Spirit that a client is specifically looking to connect with does come through. Sometimes, others push their way through too, though. You might want to dedicate your entire hour-long session to your mom, but many times other people will pop in as well, even if you're not as interested in hearing from them. Spirit has a better view of the big picture than you do, so they may realize that you still have things to work through with their loss that you are completely unaware of.

For example, someone might think, "Screw my father. He was a drunk, and I don't want to hear from him." That's not going to stop him from coming through. In my experience, no matter how resistant the person getting the reading is at first, they'll generally be in tears by the end and come to the realization that they *did* need to hear from their father but just didn't consciously know it. They needed that relief, closure, and peace.

And other times, Spirit needs *you* to be the messenger for someone else. I'm not going to lie, though. I have had some awkward moments during readings when, all of a sudden, a neighbor's husband pops in and takes up almost half the reading. This doesn't always feel fair to me, but that's how it goes. So, even though that message may be meaningless to you, chances are your neighbor desperately needs to hear from her husband and Spirit realizes you have to be the conduit for that if, for example, your neighbor isn't the type to seek out their own mediumship reading. Your loved ones are willing to step to the side and allow this to happen because in Heaven, the human emotions like jealousy and anger don't exist. Everything is for the greater good.

ACCURACY

With the help of my Clairs, Spirit Dictionary, and experience navigating the ins and outs of Spirit communication over the years, I'm now at a point in my gifts where I'm able to be pretty accurate in conveying messages from the Other Side. I would say that approximately 90 percent of the time, the messages I bring through are clear and correct. But I still can't be right on the nose 100 percent of the time—no one can. Mediumship will always require a certain element of interpretation because channeling Spirit isn't a black and white process. It involves a combination of elements. That definitely leaves some room for misinterpretation. It's a little like traveling through a foreign country where you (kind of) know the language, but your travel companion does not. You're doing your best to translate for them as necessary and accurately relay what people are saying, but some things might get lost in translation.

There are other factors that play into communicating with and interpreting messages from Spirit too. Some spirits just so happen to communicate much stronger than others. I'm not entirely sure why that is, but I've found that the chattier they were here on Earth, the stronger they communicate from the Spirit World and vice versa; it's also true that your loved ones who were shier and more reserved here on Earth may well also be shier coming through from the Other Side.

It's not just Spirit that can affect the accuracy of a reading. As the medium, sometimes there are aspects in my own life at play that make me not as clear of a channel as I might usually be. There was a time in college when I was going through a difficult breakup. I was dealing with so much personal pain that I just couldn't connect. I had to reschedule all of my readings and take some time off to process my own emotions. The emotions and energy of the client can influence things as well. If someone comes into a reading closed off or upset, it lowers the vibration in the room and puts up walls, making it more difficult for me to connect with their loved ones. These are just a few of the many ways in which the strength and accuracy of a reading can be impacted by things that are beyond my control.

The way I look at it, there is plenty of room for misunderstanding and miscommunication even when two humans are talking face-to-face here on Earth. Sometimes it's because we're not listening well enough. Other times we're so focused on what a person is going to say next that we're not fully taking everything in. In certain conversations, some things might go right over our heads. All of this can also happen when communicating with the Spirit World.

What if Spirit Spoke a Different Language on Earth?

On the Other Side, we all speak the same universal language. It's kind of like the language of love. Therefore, I don't experience any sort of communication barrier with people who spoke a different language than I do here on Earth.

The only thing that can get a bit tricky to interpret are cultural differences. Since a Spirit who lived in a different culture might want to acknowledge things that aren't exactly a part of my frame of reference, it can sometimes be difficult to interpret things like that super specific foreign cuisine that your Russian grandmother always cooked or that Japanese board game that you played with your dad as a child. I can still do my best to describe what Spirit is showing me, though, even if it takes a bit more explanation. For example, I might not be familiar with Borscht, a Russian beet soup, but I can describe the visual I'm getting of your grandmother cooking soup and chopping up beets.

As with any other job, it's important to keep growing and expanding as a medium. I mean, I love to travel regardless, but I also feel like seeing as many cultures as possible expands my frame of reference and allows Spirit to show and tell me even more in future readings. I like to revise and update my Spirit Dictionary as often as I can.

CLEANSING COMMUNICATION

A lot of times, people talk to me about readings that I have done for them in the past. While I'm so glad that the information I was able to bring through stuck with them, I usually don't remember the reading myself. I purposefully cleanse my energy after every event and reading because if I don't, I end up carrying around a bunch of information, energy, and emotion that isn't mine. This can be draining to hold on to.

There are a handful of readings that I will never forget, but these are the exceptions. I usually only remember a reading when it particularly hits home with me or triggers something personal that I can relate to. Some readings teach me lessons that I don't want to forget; I want to carry them forward with me for the rest of my life. In those cases, I journal about the readings so that I can refer back to what a soul or experience had to teach me.

Every now and then I'll channel a Spirit who's come through in a past reading, but I usually don't realize it. The energy might feel familiar, a lot like if you were to run into someone you've met briefly before but don't really know. Usually this isn't the case, though, and I actually prefer not knowing that I've already channeled a particular Spirit. That allows me to be in a clearer state and to be a stronger channel. I won't start to wonder, "Did this come through last time?" or "What was said?" Questions like these can serve as another form of bias.

For the most part, this isn't an issue since I normally can't remember the readings after the fact. In this way, it's a lot like day-to-day human conversations. If you think about your own life, my bet is that you talk to so many people every day that your brain releases most of those conversations over time. It's just a select few meaningful ones that stick with you over the long run.

How Do I Find a Medium?

Obviously, there are many different ways to locate a medium, but if you don't have a referral from a trusted source, here's what I would recommend.

Try searching online until you can locate a medium who has a significant enough number of reviews and testimonials that you can get a good gauge of their style and ability.

After you've identified some options, carefully check out that person's website and photos. Some red flags might be if a medium has a laundry list of services to choose from, like psychic readings, past life regressions, angel card readings, astrology readings, the list goes on and on. That doesn't necessarily mean they're not gifted, but it might mean that they're spreading themselves thin. It could also be an indicator that mediumship isn't necessarily their strength.

I'm not trying to get too woo-woo on you, but in addition to all of these more logistical things, remember that on an innate level we are all connected, and we all have intuition. Connect with and trust your gut on this. If it is telling you this is your person, go for it; if not, listen. You want to find a medium who is a good energetic match for you, so this stuff counts.

Finally, don't go broke for a medium. Some will charge more than others based on experience, and experience is great! But I promise that you can find a gifted medium in your price range. You just might have to look a bit harder, but it's worth it.

THE ETHICS OF MEDIUMSHIP

Listen, we all know that there are certainly plenty of fakes, frauds, and con artists who pass themselves off as mediums. There are fakes, frauds, and con artists in a lot of fields. But I feel like illegitimate mediums are particularly problematic because mediums are already dealing with something that is largely intangible and that not everyone believes in. The fakes give all of us genuine mediums a bad name.

Some people might consider my profession somewhat strange, but to me it is very much a profession. Underlying every single thing I do in my practice as a medium is a sense of ethics. Ethical practices are crucial in all fields, but *especially* in mediumship because we are dealing with people who are in such a vulnerable state. This topic is so important to me that I have dedicated an entire lesson to the ethics of mediumship in my online course.

I'm also very aware of the fact that mediumship is entirely unregulated. Anyone can set up a website, book clients, and market themselves as a medium. There is no medium license or quality standards they must meet. If you find someone claiming to have a certificate of some kind, you might want to look at them with some healthy skepticism. It certainly helps to go through a course, as many gifted mediums have done, but often the only thing that is required to get a certificate is enrollment and participation in a course. With my own course and students, I don't offer any sort of certificate or stamp of approval. I would never even think of doing so unless I had a rigorous process for my students to go through first that allowed me to gauge whether or not they were ready to share their gift professionally.

Despite all of this, I do take it upon myself to follow my own strict ethical rules, and encourage other mediums to do the same. I know that is what our clients deserve, and I want to help set the standard for the community.

I jokingly call myself the medium with no filter. I say it how it is, and it's not always butterflies and rainbows. So much of the art of mediumship is in the way a message is delivered. As we've discussed, a lot of the information mediums channel is open to interpretation, but we also have a responsibility in how we deliver it. I am unfiltered so that messages are translated in the way Spirit wants them to be, so they are the most accurate and pack the strongest punch to the person they are meant for. But I try to do this with an underlying tone of professionalism, graciousness, and sensitivity to the people I am reading for. The way in which these messages are delivered is crucial, because the experience of connecting with loved ones who have passed is so intense and impactful.

Here's an example. Some of the signs in my Spirit Dictionary have double meanings. When I see a rainbow, it might serve as validation that Spirit has been using rainbows as a simple sign from above or it could be Spirit's way of acknowledging that they were part of the LGBT community here on Earth. A medium without strong professional ethics might see this and just blurt out, "So your son is telling me he was gay," when, really, this sign simply represented a way that this Spirit sends hellos from the Other Side. The problem isn't the message itself because love is love and Spirit offers nothing but encouragement for same-sex couples, but the fact that it might not be true. It may simply be a hello from Heaven that has been misinterpreted, but it might leave a mother wondering, "Did I even know my son? Does he think I would have judged him?" The client will likely leave the reading feeling worse instead of better based solely on the medium's misinterpretation. That is why, in my opinion, mediums should ask for further clarification from Spirit as necessary before passing on messages.

When I find myself confused, I will be as honest and up-front as possible with my client in explaining how the process works. I will let them know what I'm seeing or hearing, explain what that might mean, and the areas in which there is room for misinterpretation. To do this requires taking ego out of the process. I don't care how my clients view or judge me; I just want to do right by them and by Spirit.

Like I said, no medium is ever going to be correct and accurate 100 percent of the time, but it's up to us to practice and hone our gifts and our process so that we can offer the clearest channel possible. We never want to muddle messages and leave clients believing something is true when it's not. Mediums should let their clients know when they can't explain something. There have been times I've had to say, "I'm so sorry, but I'm not sure what this means. You'll have to take this information with you, and hopefully it will make sense later."

It's important that mediums don't try to make things fit. Yes, there are times I may not know how to interpret the information, but you might have a clear understanding of what it means (I always say you know your loved ones better than I do) and so we're able to agree on what Spirit was trying to convey. For instance, I once gave a reading in which the man coming through kept showing me Tito's vodka, so I assumed this meant it was his favorite drink. It turned out this man's name was Tito—*that's* what Spirit was trying to communicate. I walked her through my Spirit communication process, explaining how the name Tito wasn't part of my Spirit Dictionary and that Spirit had shown me the closest thing to try to communicate the information.

I call it lazy mediumship when a medium delivers information they've misinterpreted, and rather than explain what
has happened or follow-up with Spirit to ask them to communicate the message through a different clair or symbol, they
attempt to just stitch it together into one cohesive explanation
that encompasses everything. It just doesn't work like that.

For example, a medium might tell you, "I'm feeling like
there's an uncle who's coming through for you." You respond
by saying, "Um, no, but I have an aunt who passed?"

If the medium then says, "Oh, yes, an aunt, of course!" and
just makes it fit with no additional questions asked, that's a
red flag.

While it could be that they misinterpreted the information
coming through, the medium still should've paused to clarify
with Spirit and not just immediately agree to what the client
says. Maybe the client has an uncle-like figure, such as a mentor or a coach, who has passed, or maybe it was the uncle of a
friend and the client was meant to pass along a message. The
client may even have an uncle on the Other Side who they
forgot about and wouldn't have been able to validate until
talking to their family later on (believe it or not, I've seen this
happen many times). Regardless, the medium has now jeop-
ardized the messages that Spirit was trying to communicate
by prioritizing their desire to always be right.

Mediums should always have a positive impact on their
clients' lives, even in instances where they have to deliver sensitive information. Sometimes the client is connecting with
someone who they had a tense or unhealthy relationship
with or maybe they lost a loved one to especially traumatic

circumstances, such as a murder or suicide. I have learned that these circumstances can require a different approach, from the words and tone I use to the privacy of the reading. Mediums have to feel a sense of protection and responsibility for their clients. If you ever sit with a medium who doesn't give you this vibe, I strongly recommend that you continue looking for the right medium for you.

The more experience a medium has, the more likely they are to be able to walk that fine line between delivering information that is unfiltered and accurate, while still remaining compassionate and sensitive to their client's well-being in the process. A good medium will be acutely aware that they have a responsibility to both Spirit and their client to communicate accurately and clearly.

Also, remember that mediums do not have all of the answers. We don't know how everything works. No human is meant to have all of the answers or a complete grasp of the big picture. It is only in Heaven that we gain that sort of perspective.

Will Spirit Tell Me About Future Events or Health Issues?

The answer to this question is: sometimes. Spirit has a responsibility to let us go through our own life lessons and to check off the experiences we need to have. Because of this, they can only give us messages that might impact our decisions or future if providing that information serves a larger purpose.

Part of being an ethical medium means being mindful about all of this when I interpret messages. My main goal is to do no harm. I never want to scare or even worry the person I'm reading for.

Once I had a mother come through and tell her daughter (who was only in her thirties) to get a mammogram, despite the fact that breast cancer didn't run in her family and it wasn't related to how her mom had passed. I had to be mindful to word the message as carefully as I could, while still conveying what Spirit said. When I told the woman, she responded, "Oh, yeah, it actually crossed my mind the other day that I need to get one done."

I told her not to worry, and that this message was probably her mom's way of validating that she knew her daughter's thoughts and was aware of what was going on in her life. "But she still wants you to always stay on top of your routine checkups," I finished.

The daughter didn't panic, but she did get a mammogram. A couple of weeks later I found out that this woman had discovered she had breast cancer. Not only did her reading give her so much healing but it also potentially saved her life.

In situations like this, I feel like it was either never in the daughter's soul contract (we'll go over soul contracts in Chapter Five) to pass from breast cancer or that it wasn't her time yet. What I do know is that this message helped encourage her to go to the doctor's office and likely spared her from having to undergo an even longer course of treatment. It was also delivered in a way that didn't cause panic to set in.

There are more mundane examples, too, about things like moves and career changes. Still, these are things that have the ability to change the course of a person's life or relationships, so I have to be so careful about how these messages are phrased and to always make it very clear that just because Spirit gives advice or a suggestion, it doesn't mean you have to follow it. I always phrase potentially life-changing messages as guidance rather than a warning and remind the person I'm reading for that they have free will.

GIVE YOURSELF TIME BEFORE TURNING TO A MEDIUM

While there are things I can do to help enhance my connection with Spirit, there are also things my clients can do. The first is to give it a bit of time. Back when I gave private readings, I had a rule that my clients had to wait at least three months after losing a loved one before they could even schedule their reading with me.

I didn't put this rule in place because Spirit can't come through any earlier than that. I've had Spirit come through within twenty-four hours of their death. But it's still good to give our loved ones some time to get adjusted on the Other Side and to go through the transitional period that occurs there (we'll talk about this in-depth in the next chapter). In a way, they have to learn—or, more specifically, remember— how to communicate all over again, in a new way. It's sort of like starting a new job. You need a bit of time to adjust and familiarize yourself with how things work.

This doesn't mean that you shouldn't talk to or otherwise communicate with your loved ones in those early days. You absolutely should. But as far as asking for messages or signs at that early point, I usually encourage people to tell their loved ones something along the lines of, "It's okay for you to take all the time you need. When you're ready to communicate, I'll be right here, ready to receive from you."

It's also good for those left behind to allow themselves some time to begin going through the natural grieving process. If they go to a medium when they are too heavy in their grief, chances are they won't get as much as they could out of the experience. This can happen for several reasons. Maybe the client is so close to a recent death that they aren't open to hearing from other souls in Heaven who also have a reason for coming through. Even if the soul they want to connect with does come through, people often either can't hear or can't process the information they are being given. It could be that they're still stuck on one particular issue or just that the general fog of grief makes it difficult to take in information. In cases like this, sometimes Spirit won't come through because they *know* their loved one isn't yet ready to hear what they have to say. Grief can make us cloudy in ways we're not consciously aware of—but Spirit always knows.

Most of all, I think it's best that people allow some time to pass between the death of a loved one and their first visit to a medium so that they don't feel like an outside source is the only way they can connect with Spirit. Going to a medium or any other external source should not be the only way to find a bit of relief, to get through the day, and breathe a little easier. For as difficult as it is, this is a process that has to be learned and practiced, it's not something that someone else can give you. In the long run, seeing a medium too soon after a death will only make things harder.

I often joke that I've seen people turn into medium junkies. I'm kidding when I say this, but it's also a serious thing that I see. I've had a couple of people fly in from all over the country to attend multiple Messages from Above events in different places. I've even had more than one Spirit come through with messages along the lines of, "Mom, please don't spend any more of your money attending mediumship events. I promise that readings aren't the only way you can connect with me. I've come to you time and time again, and I'm with you every day."

I understand why people become attached to mediums as the channel to their loved ones, but it also makes me sad. *Everything will happen in due time*, and it's important that people find other fuel to keep them going in times of loss outside of mediums alone. This seems like a good place to add that if you happen to come across a medium who is pressuring you to see them on a regular basis, run. Same thing if a medium ever tells you that there is negative energy or a curse attached to you. You should never be reliant on a medium; seriously question anyone who tells you differently. This is a major red flag.

I am serious when I say you don't need a medium to connect with your loved ones, whether that medium is me or anyone else. You just have to trust that your loved ones are always with you, know that they are safe and at peace, and allow yourself to continue to feel their love and receive their hellos from Heaven in the form of signs. I'll give you some tips for doing this in Chapter Eleven.

Having said that, I understand the appeal of mediums and the type of information we can offer. It's more clear and evidential than what most people can get on their own. I'm aware of the comfort it provides more than most people are because I've seen it firsthand time and time again. But I *don't* like to see readings taking over people's lives or witness it turn into an unhealthy addiction. After all, one of the primary messages Spirit has for us is to keep moving forward. They don't want their death to leave you stuck in grief and in the past.

It's also important to realize that there is only so much new information Spirit can bring through. It's because of this that when I was doing private readings I had a rule that people could only get two readings per year max, and that they had to wait at least six months between readings. You have to allow enough time to go by and life to ensue for new things to happen that Spirit will be able to validate. There has to be space for new births, new marriages, new challenges, and new victories. Also, since Spirit can only work off of my frame of reference, they are only able to provide so much information about their passing and so much closure before it all starts to seem a bit repetitive. The same goes for any medium you see on a regular basis.

TIPS TO OPTIMIZE YOUR READING WITH A MEDIUM

Medium readings involve three people: the medium, Spirit, and you. During your reading, there is a three-way connection going on, even if you are not actively doing the work. You can think of yourself as an energetic conduit that both the medium and Spirit will interact with. Because of this, you will want to do whatever you can to keep your energy levels as strong and as vibrant as possible for the reading. Following are some general tips for doing that.

- Balance any skepticism you might have with a sense of openness; too much skepticism can create energy blockages, making it difficult for Spirit to come through.

- Don't drink alcohol or do drugs in the twenty-four hours before your reading. This lowers your vibration, which can affect the energy of the medium and make it much harder for them to connect to your loved ones.

- Freshen up on details about your loved ones who've passed (and those still living too) for validation purposes. It helps to know the first and middle names of your family members on both sides, their personalities, illnesses, how they passed, important dates (deaths, birthdays, anniversaries), what they did for a living, their favorite hobbies, and so forth. This will make the reading flow easier, and the whole experience will be more worthwhile for you.

- In the weeks leading up to your reading, start to ask your loved ones to come through. This sets the intention that you're planning to communicate with them, and they appreciate the invitation. That being said, a legitimate medium shouldn't need you to bring anything to the reading like an object or photograph. Personally, I communicate with Spirit through a direct soul-to-soul connection; I don't rely on holding your deceased grandpa's wallet to form that connection. When a client pulls out certain objects it can even create bias within the medium, and make it more difficult for them to connect. Same goes with wearing anything that might offer details about who you've lost. For this reason, I sometimes prefer phone readings because I can't possibly be influenced by a person's physical appearance or reaction to things. If you insist, you can carry something in your purse or pocket, but I recommend you don't show the medium unless they bring it up during the reading. It might not come up (especially if it's not part of their frame of reference), but when it does, it's always an extra special nugget of validation.

- Get a good night of sleep before your reading. You'll want to be well-rested and clear headed during the session.

- Try to release as much stress, anxiety, and nervousness as possible beforehand. I always say that the more relaxed you are, the easier it is for me to channel Spirit.

- Don't feed the medium! If you go off on a drawn-out tangent after every message a medium delivers, you'll end up giving more information to them than they give to you. Try to stick to only yes or no responses to any questions they ask. You don't want to leave the reading questioning or doubting whether or not your loved one came through for you, or if all the medium brought through was based on information you gave to them. Let the medium do the work. After all, that's what you're paying them for.

- That being said, don't make bets with Spirit, as I call it, or you may leave the reading feeling disappointed or even doubting the connection, even in instances when Spirit did come through for you. For instance, I've had people come into a reading with the thought, "Okay, Sis, I'll only believe that it's you coming through if you bring through that memory of us in third grade when we went to the zoo with Mom and she bought us Popsicles." Spirit typically can't communicate a highly specific, detail-laden memory from your childhood like that through the medium's signs and symbols in their Spirit Dictionary.

5

The Soul's Journey

know I'm starting to sound like a broken record at this point, but let me begin this chapter by reminding you once again that I am just like you. I'm not God, and I don't have a crystal ball or all of the answers. I don't have access to all of the ins and outs about how the universe works. I've definitely had skeptics grill me on this and suggest that because I don't have all the answers, it means that what I do isn't for real. It just doesn't work that way, because I'm human too. Just like you and everyone else, I'm here in Earth School, learning lessons and evolving every single day. I won't know exactly how it all works until that day when I'm on the Other Side. Knowing every last detail would be like having the answers to a test before taking it. We're not supposed to have a complete understanding of it all until the day we return to Heaven. Our journey here on Earth is all the better and more productive because of the things we don't know right now.

Having said that, over the years I have learned and consistently heard some things from Spirit through my readings and from my own spirit guides in meditation. When I researched further, I found that other mediums were sharing some of these same concepts based on their own readings and work with Spirit. All of the information we receive is not the same, but a lot of it is. As with anything else, all of the information from Spirit comes through our own lens and frame of reference, which leaves some room for different interpretations.

What follows in this chapter is not gospel but a good gist of some of the fundamental ideas about the afterlife, Spirit, and our journey here on Earth. These are the things that resonate in my heart, gut, and soul as truth. They just resonate in a certain way that feels *right*. Maybe they will for you too.

WHAT'S YOUR VIEW ON GOD?

I do believe in God. You can call God a Higher Power, Source, whatever feels right to you. I don't view God as an individual entity, but rather as being made up of universal energy and connecting all that there is. Spirit has described it in a way where they make it clear that they *feel* the presence of God. They *feel* and *know* God's pure and unconditional love. They don't describe it as meeting an individual person. Think of God as an overarching energy that makes all of us one. To be honest, I only use the term "God" because it's so familiar to me and my upbringing. But it would probably be more accurate to refer to God as Source or Universal Energy.

What About Religion?

I often get asked about where I stand with religion and how mediumship fits into that. Although I grew up Catholic, I no longer practice Catholicism or any other religion. But I do still believe some of the things I learned in Catholicism, as well as some concepts I've picked up from other religions. While I'm not religious, I do feel like mediumship has made me more spiritual than I ever was before. I believe in Heaven, God, angels, and the afterlife way more now than I ever did when I was part of an organized church.

Having said that, I do feel like religion serves a purpose for a lot of people. From what I've learned through Spirit, some people are meant to be in specific religions for this lifetime. A certain faith can be a part of a person's journey and growth. From a larger perspective, religion is also meant to teach us how to love one another despite our differences. This lesson applies to why we experience all kinds of differences, whether that be ethnicity, skin color, or sexual preference.

My work with Spirit has shown me that there are bits and pieces of each religion that hold some validity. There is not one "correct" religion, but little aspects of every faith that, when pulled together, make up what is actually the truth.

However, once on the Other Side, people aren't practicing different religions. Everyone's in the same place regardless of religion, gender, sexual orientation, race, and so forth. God is not going to reject you because you were Jewish instead of Christian in this lifetime. Spirit has communicated that we don't worship in Heaven, nor are we part of a specified faith. Yet, we do feel and recognize the overwhelming love that comes from Source, God, or whatever you'd like to call it.

EARTH SCHOOL

Oprah Winfrey once said, "Consider the world, this Earth, to be like a school and our life the classrooms." Based on what I've learned from Spirit, this quote pretty much nails life and our purpose in a nutshell.

This planet is completely dedicated to our soul's learning and education. From the moment we are born, we begin our Earth School curriculum. Every day of our life, we are attending classes and learning. We are here for the opportunity for our soul to grow, evolve, and learn. This curriculum includes certain understandings and insights that our soul can achieve only through having a human experience.

THE SOUL AND THE HIGHER SELF

In my opinion, the most important thing to understand first and foremost is that each of us has a soul. Our souls are ever-evolving and eternal. The soul exists long before this iteration of our human life and lasts far beyond it. There is nothing temporary about the soul.

The soul (or spirit; for the most part, these terms can be used interchangeably) can be anywhere and everywhere in ways that might be difficult to wrap your head around from the perspective of our physical experience on Earth. If our loved ones in soul form want to be with us, they are with us. All they have to do is think it, and *bam!* they are there, just like that. They can also be in more than one place at a time. Say your father died and you have four siblings. In soul form, your father can be with all of you at once (and other places too). Obviously, souls are great multitaskers!

Our soul is pure, invisible energy, so we require a physical body to travel through Earth School. No matter how attached to it we are, our physical body is simply a vessel. As part of that, we need our brain to interpret the information we receive here and our emotions to express how our soul feels about the information we are receiving. Our body allows us to encounter lessons and interact with others in ways that we can't in that pure soul form we exist in on the Other Side.

You can imagine it like this: your body functions a lot like a car. Your soul sits inside it as you make your way down the road to your destination (Heaven). Once you reach the end of the road, you get out of the car, and the car is no longer significant. When we come to the end of our curriculum in Earth School, our soul hops out of its now-unnecessary physical body and continues on.

Here's where the soul thing gets a little tricky: within our soul, we also carry our higher self. Our higher self is the part of our soul that remains in Heaven, even when we've made the choice to return to Earth School. It's the part of you that stays purely connected to the divine and is not influenced by your earthly experiences (whereas your soul can be influenced by these experiences). You can think of the higher self as always having one toe firmly planted in Heaven.

Is There a Hell?

Not once have I ever had a Spirit come through and communicate that hell exists in the afterlife. In fact, I hear the exact opposite: "Tell my loved one I'm in Heaven! There's no such thing as hell. I'm not in a bad place. There's only peace and love here."

The fire and brimstone and red devil with horns and a pitchfork that are often featured in religious perspectives of the afterlife do not exist according to the spirits I've connected with. These stories always scared me when I was a kid, and I can't tell you how much of a relief it was to hear that I wasn't hurtling toward eternal damnation. The truth about the afterlife couldn't be any more different. The most important thing you need to understand about the Other Side is that it's based in love and growth. Here, there is no place for pain anymore. Plus, everything I've heard tells me that God is forgiving and loving, which doesn't exactly fit with dooming someone to an eternity in the fiery dungeons of hell.

But what about the people who've committed the most heinous of acts? What about the Hitlers of the world? Where do they go when their time comes? These are usually the questions I get right after the initial sigh of relief that there's not a hell. So here's my question for you:

where would you draw that line? What actions deserve forgiveness and a chance to grow, and which mean a soul is eternally ruined? When you really think about it, it becomes more complicated by the second. The choices that people make on Earth are impacted and twisted by thousands of moments and interferences. But we are also given free will, which means we must take responsibility for our own actions. So, what does that mean for the afterlife?

From what I've gathered from Spirit, there's no hell, but there *are* levels on the Other Side. If you live your life focusing on kindness, compassion, and generosity, you are raising your vibration to become closer to the Spirit World. When your time comes, you enter a level of Heaven that is of the highest vibration. What that means is that you are close to or have reached your highest and most evolved self. You're also as close to the love of God as you can get. You will have contributed essential lessons and teachings to your whole self, and you will feel complete and totally at peace in the afterlife. Others who have done serious wrongs in the physical world vibrate at a critically low level on Earth and in the afterlife. They enter the Spirit World knowing they failed to reach their soul's purpose during their lifetime. They will review every misstep, every cruel act, every moment their soul turned away from goodness and light. It will be incredibly enlightening but also a tremendous amount of work for them in Spirit form. They can, and do, work hard for what can be a long time to learn the lessons they failed to accept on Earth.

Especially for those who have been hurt by someone or who have lost a loved one to violence, it can be hard to imagine the perpetrator reaching Heaven. Try to remember that, in the physical world, it is difficult to see or understand the big picture. We are all carrying feelings of resentment, grief, and pain. In this state, it can be nearly impossible to find forgiveness. But in the Spirit World, we are freed from these negative emotions. There is only forgiveness and the sincere wish for everyone to find their best selves. The best way I can describe it is to say that in the afterlife, those at a higher vibration, closer to their whole self, know the peace brought to them from reaching that state. How could they not want that for all souls?

(I should also note here that these levels are not physical places. It's not as if Spirit has to take an elevator to visit their friend who's one level below them. It's more of an internal level that involves the state a soul is in and the work that is required of them when they reach the afterlife.)

It's alright if you struggle with this concept. There are things we cannot or are not meant to fully understand until we enter the Spirit World ourselves. For the time being, focus on your own soul's journey. Don't panic if you make a misstep every now and then. Confront it, make amends, and move forward. Don't be afraid to set your sights as high as they can go for your soul's growth. You can make it there!

THINK OF IT LIKE A CLEMENTINE

Understanding the difference and relationship between the soul or spirit and its higher self can be mind-bending. It's one of the most common questions I get as a medium, and I've found that the easiest way to explain the difference is through the analogy of a clementine. In fact, I've even started bringing clementines to my events to help people understand how this all works!

Clementine

Think of a whole clementine as your higher self. The higher self is the purest part of your soul that will forever and always remain on the Other Side, and is always connected to Source. This clementine contains all of the consciousness, memories, experiences, and personalities of every lifetime you have ever lived, each of which is represented by an individual Spirit or, for the purpose of this analogy, a segment of the clementine.

Segments

Now that you've visualized the whole clementine as your higher self, imagine you've pulled apart one segment from the clementine. Essentially, this segment represents the part of your higher self that has decided to journey down to Earth School. Through this process, you became an individual Spirit and entered into your physical body. Your soul has its own unique traits but, at the same time, shares some common characteristics with the other parts of your higher self. When you die, your soul will rejoin the other segments of the clementine, which have lived different lifetimes and have had different experiences. But from what I've gathered, rejoining your higher self does not mean your individual identity is erased. It's not as though your segment gets absorbed by the clementine and you lose your individuality. Your Spirit continues to live on for eternity.

To be clear, there aren't a bunch of other pieces of your clementine walking around right now. This is *your* turn to go through Earth School, to live, grow, and collect the lessons your higher self needs to know. The segment of my higher self that is Monica won't return to Earth School again but will take on and share the lessons of every other segment of my clementine that goes to Earth School, both before and after me.

The higher self allows a medium to still be able to communicate with a person's deceased grandmother, even if a part of that granny's soul has chosen to come back around for another journey through Earth School. While this grandma rejoins her higher self on the Other Side upon her passing, the individual essence of who she was, still is, and will always be, remains. She won't ever disappear, and she can communicate through a medium in the same way that any other Spirit does.

How Old Is My Loved One on the Other Side?

I was never good with numbers in school, and I'm still not great with them as a medium. In general, I get an age range or a sense of what point in life Spirit was at when they died. But sometimes Spirit describes themselves around the age when the person I'm reading for best remembers them. For example, even though my grandma passed in her early nineties, most of my memories of her are from when she was in her late seventies. So, when I've gotten messages from other mediums in which my grandma comes through, they usually describe her physical appearance as the way she looked in her seventies.

Spirit gets to come through however they want to. Most of the time, though, Spirit comes through as you remember them, as they like to remember themselves, or at the age of their passing.

I always joke that we get to be the best version of ourselves on the Other Side, and it's true. For instance, I've had many men who were balding prior to their death come through bragging about the full head of hair that has now been restored.

In readings, Spirit presents themselves in physical form because that's how they can resonate and connect with us. But on the Other Side, they are actually pure energy (sorry, guys, there's not actually a literal full head of hair waiting for you in the great beyond). The way Spirit physically portray themselves to me and to their loved ones is more of a representation of their total peace with themselves. When you cross over, you will recognize your loved ones in their true form—it is their purest, most beautiful state and the way you actually know them best. From one soul being to another.

SOUL CONTRACT

Soul contracts are one of the fundamental ideas that come through from Spirit in almost every reading. Over the years, I've seen how this idea brings people (myself included) comfort and clarity.

Our soul contracts dictate those lessons we will learn here in Earth School. When we are still in pure soul form (before we are born), each of us signs up for our Earth School curriculum. We identify those areas in life that will help us grow and evolve. You can think of these items as your soul's to-do list or the Earth School syllabus.

We put this contract together with the help of our spirit guides and members of our soul family (both of which we will discuss shortly). Together, this spirit team figures out the lessons that are most important for you to learn during your upcoming lifetime. These lessons involve going through a certain set of experiences—the good, bad, ugly, and everything in between. Our soul contract is not all rainbows and butterflies because, if it was, how could we hope to learn and evolve in any sort of significant way? For many of us, it is through our challenges that we grow the most.

Sometimes I talk to people who are shocked to hear that, at some point, they signed up to go through traumatic events. *What? Who would do that?* The answer is that, potentially, *you* would. This is not for the purpose of suffering or karmic punishment but for the growth of your soul. Again, whatever pain and suffering you might temporarily experience here on Earth is just a blink of an eye in the ultimate timeline of your soul.

I find this piece of information especially helpful during those moments in life when things seem particularly hard or downright unfair. I remind myself that any challenges and suffering I go through are by my own design and ultimately for my greatest good. It helps me look at difficult experiences from a completely different perspective than I would otherwise.

Whenever I have this discussion with people, it usually turns into a conversation about fate versus free will. I'm not saying that everything you do in this lifetime is predestined. We all have unplanned circumstances arrive in our lives, and those usually happen when we don't pay attention to our gut feelings or as a result of the red flags we choose to ignore. We all have free will, which we can exercise at any point. Sometimes this means we find ourselves in challenges or painful situations that are *not* part of our soul contract. Though, even then, we're still gaining wisdom.

If you were to sit down and really journal or think about your life, you could probably begin to get an idea of things that are likely part of your soul contract. You can see patterns emerge in the lessons you've encountered over the years. You can see how challenging times have changed you. In doing this, you might even have a moment in which you gain some clarity or your soul remembers, "Yes! That's what I'm here for."

I think the concept of soul contracts is also very healing for those who are holding onto guilt surrounding a loved one's passing. Think about your most recent drive home after a long day of work or school. Maybe you took the highway, or maybe you chose the backroads. You might've been driving eighty in a sixty mile-per-hour zone or chose to stop along the way for a bite to eat. The choices you made (your free will) and the route you took may have resulted in completely different experiences (you got stuck in traffic, fined for speeding, hit a deer, whatever the case may be), but the *destination* remained the same. I promise you the same goes for this journey called life. So for those of you who constantly replay and dissect every last moment leading up to your loved one's death or who feel like there was something that should've or could've been done to prevent it, I urge you to put an end to the unnecessary torment.

Most people's soul contracts involve lessons that result in some sort of enhanced self-knowledge, self-growth, and self-mastery. Of these, self-mastery—which I define as the total knowing, acceptance, and transcendence of your true self—is the biggest goal and the trickiest thing to obtain, so it can take us multiple journeys to Earth School to accomplish. There are many different lessons that a soul might strive for. Maybe it's overcoming anger or jealousy; it could be learning self-love or faithfulness; maybe you want to master compassion, patience, or even joy. All of these things might take multiple lifetimes to master.

Inherent in this is the idea of reincarnation. While the Spirit with the identity and memories of our loved ones exists eternally, other parts of our souls are likely to return to Earth School (in the form of a new Spirit; remember the clementine analogy) time and time again over multiple lifetimes to continue learning, growing, obtaining more experience, and ultimately mastering whatever lesson it is that we've set out for ourselves to achieve.

Do Kids Have a Stronger Connection to Past Lives and Spirit?

Aside from talking to a medium, we can get a lot of validation from children about topics like Earth School, past lives, and reincarnation. Now, this is not to say it's okay to go badgering your child for answers (please don't do that). But there have been several news stories over the years about kids who've led their parents to a location that is somehow tied to a past life or who knew information they couldn't have possibly known in any way that can be explained outside the context of past lives.

Generally, I don't allow children under twelve to come to my events, but I made an exception at an event in Seattle one time, after a mother explained to me that her daughter, Grace, was a very mature old soul who could handle it. At the time of the event, Grace was about nine, but her mother told me that, since the age of four, Grace had been telling her, "You're not my mommy."

Whenever they would drive past a specific home in their town, Grace insisted that they needed to stop and park the car to go see her "real parents." It got to the point where Grace's mother decided it was worth looking into. They were able to go inside the home and meet the couple who lived there.

While Grace did not recognize them, she *did* recognize the home and stated that this was where she used to live. She took charge, showing the owners and her mom around the house. She knew all about the home, including the old boiler heater in the basement and the big tree and rose bushes in the backyard, which she said she had helped plant. Prior to touring the house, Grace had gone on and on to her mother about all of the pink paint and pink furniture within the home. The female owner stated that she and her husband had been painting over all the pink paint since they had purchased the home.

It gets even more wild. After the visit, the mother shared this information with Grace's father. He then asked what address she was referring to, and when she told him, he said, "Oh, my God. That's the home I lived in as a child."

It became even more real when Grace told them that her father was actually her brother—but that she had passed away as a child.

The mother went on to tell me that this experience felt like a healing journey that she and her daughter had to go through together, and that it taught her to really open up her heart and listen to Grace.

Not only do kids often have more access to subconscious memories of their past lifetimes but they're also a lot more connected to Spirit in their day-to-day lives. In my own work, I see all the time how children are so much more open because they haven't yet been told by their family or society that "It's not real." Most children have not yet suppressed Spirit in the way that many adults have. I would say the prime ages for this are between as young as eighteen months up until four or five years of age. It's around the time kids start going to school that they begin to shut this connection down. I know many mediums who say things like, "I've been communicating with the Other Side since I was four years old." I believe these are the people who never grew out of that innate connection to Spirit we are all born with.

As I've said, I very, very rarely do readings for family or close friends, but every now and then, something pops through. A few months ago I was texting with my future sister-in-law, Marissa, who was pregnant at the time with her second child. I was feeling a lot of anxiety around her and getting the sense that she was feeling especially stressed about her pregnancy. I called her up and asked what was going on. As we were talking, I could sense her grandma, Helen, who she was very close to, trying to come through.

Helen brought through validation that it was really her and then told Marissa that she was with the soul of her unborn child. She said that everything was going to be okay. Then she started talking about Marissa's son, Trevor, who was just a few months shy of turning two. Helen said that she often sings Trevor lullabies to put him back to sleep in the middle of the night. She then communicated to me that if Marissa were to show Trevor a picture of her, he would somehow express recognition of who she is.

Shortly after we got off the phone, Marissa sent me a video of her showing Trevor a picture of her grandmother (who she's always called "Gram"). "Do you know who this is?" she asked him. A huge smile spread across his face. "Gram," he replied. It was a little hard to make out at first, but he then followed up with "Helen," which is her name. His whole face lit up, and it was clear to us that he knew who she was.

You may very well have a story like this in your own life. Lots of people do, because kids are more easily able to access, interact, and communicate with the Other Side. I'm sure that's exactly what I was doing that time on the stairs when I told my mom I was playing with my angel friends. Who knows? You may have even done the same as a child. I think so many of our "imaginary friends" aren't really imaginary at all.

If you happen to notice this ability to connect in your own child, my advice to you is: don't discourage it. Be open-minded and allow your child to talk through their experiences and to share what they want to. Allow them the space to explore it rather than shutting down the connection by telling them it's not real. At the same time, if your child is frightened by any of their experiences, remind them that they are in control and that they can ask Spirit to go away anytime they please.

I'm not entirely sure about what happens once we have learned all of the lessons we are meant to and are done incarnating here on Earth. My impression is that you reach a point of enlightenment and get to determine a new role to take on the Other Side. You might become a spirit guide or some sort of teacher or counselor. You will be put in a position where you can share your wisdom with other souls. You may take on a specific role, such as assisting people who have gone through quick or violent deaths in their process of transitioning back into Spirit.

As for whether or not this role lasts for eternity or evolves over time, I am not sure. Heaven is not bound by time, so things like this can be difficult to interpret from an earthly perspective. Plus, as with everything else, we are not meant to have all of the answers here and now.

WHAT HAPPENS WHEN WE DIE?

Transition is the moment at which we leave our physical body and our soul returns to Heaven. Spirit always describes this as an incredibly peaceful experience, which is easy to imagine. In that moment of transition, you return to a sense of wholeness and are greeted by your loved ones, spirit guides, and angels. It has been described to me as a feeling of euphoria and unconditional love, regardless of how a person dies. Also, at that moment of transition, any of those human emotions that are associated with Earth—such as resentment, anger, fear, or judgment—dissipate. There is only love, beauty, and peace.

This holds true for everyone, even those who were scared to die. Every single time Spirit has discussed this topic, they've said the same things: "I was not afraid." "I did not suffer." "I only felt peace." "I was greeted by those I loved." Some of them reference God too.

Not long ago, I did an automatic writing session, during which I asked to be shown an individual Spirit's transition process so that I could share the experience in more detail and from a Spirit's firsthand perspective. While I'm sure the experience varies for each Spirit and is influenced by the circumstances of their death, hopefully this gives you a little more insight into what happens when we die:

The first moments outside of my physical body were so incredibly freeing, it's hard to put into words. I felt lighter than I ever did while on Earth. In what felt like an instant, there I was, hovering over my physical body. I could see my mangled car from a bird's-eye perspective. I had a clear 360 view of what was happening and could hear the sound of sirens from fire trucks and ambulances approaching the scene.

When they arrived, my car was already engulfed in flames. I saw the firefighters working as quickly as possible and witnessed them using their tools to pull off the door to my truck. EMTs lifted my severely burnt body out of the driver's seat and onto a stretcher. Without needing to be told, it was

clear to me that my physical body was no longer of importance. I heard one of the EMTs yell that I still had a heartbeat,
and I watched as they did everything in their power to keep
me alive. All of this was happening as I was already in Spirit
form, free of any pain or suffering.

Angels appeared by my side from the very moment I transitioned. Let me just tell you, they are far more magnificent
and beautiful than anything you've seen in the movies or sto-
rybooks. Words did not have to be spoken, as I could receive
their wisdom by simply being in their presence. Their love and
light flowed through my soul and fueled me with feelings of
all-encompassing peace. They put me at ease and made me
feel safe.

This transition to Spirit was indescribable. I felt childlike
and was overjoyed to learn that life does exist beyond the
physical. I was in awe at this discovery that who I know as
myself would never die, even as I was watching my physical
counterpart do just that.

The EMTs were not able to save me. I watched as they
announced my time of death. In that moment, I felt concern
for my closest family and friends, but that was very quickly
replaced with a sense of knowing that I would be reunited with
them one day. I now knew that they too would exist beyond
this earthly lifetime, and that the essence of who they are would
remain. My own awareness of all of this was still limited, but
with each passing moment, I received additional insights
about my new reality in the form of instant impressions.

Death was not scary. In fact it was electrifying, exciting,
and freeing all at the same time. My soul could fly like a bird

soaring through the sky. I could go anywhere I wanted to; all I had to do was think, and I could be there.

But before I could play around with my newfound freedom, there was some routine business the angels wanted me to attend to first.

At that point, my grandparents, who had passed before me, appeared out of nowhere. It's strange, because although they did not have a physical body, I could recognize them and see them as I knew them to be while on Earth. My nanna looked like she was thirty years younger! And Gramps was rocking the same beloved 'stache he used to have back in the day. They were smiling, laughing, and holding hands.

"Sarah, you're here! Nice of you to join us!"

I'm thinking to myself, "Here? Where's here? I'm still hovering over my dead body. Is this supposed to be Heaven?"

But nonetheless, I was overcome with joy at getting to see my grandparents. I felt so welcomed and loved.

Along with the angels still surrounding me, my grandparents looked at me and said, "Are you ready, dear? They're waiting!"

Not knowing what I was about to embark upon, I felt a rush of excitement. It was like an adventure and I couldn't wait to see what happened next.

That's when a tunnel of the brightest, most electrifying light appeared just ahead of us. I felt so drawn to this light, there was no avoiding its lure. My grandmother ushered me to follow her, and in an instant I was being pulled up the warmest flow of light. The angels were right behind me. On the other end of that tunnel, I felt enveloped by pure love. I was greeted by what seemed like a hundred angels singing.

You'll understand what I mean when you get here one day, but it all feels so familiar. Almost like you never left. It's not so much a place but rather a state of being where you feel so at ease. All my human insecurities and emotions were immediately washed away and replaced by a sense of forgiveness and love. Any and all the fears I had before my death disappeared.

I immediately felt connected to the wisdom of universal energy, or what most people would call God. I felt comforted and warm. I felt so at peace. I felt safe and filled with everlasting joy.

My grandparents and angels then brought me to my spirit guides. I knew who they were without any introductions. It's amazing how quickly you're filled with a sense of all knowing upon returning to the afterlife.

I then got to witness a life review, which contained the most beautiful moments I had experienced in my earthly existence. I was brought back to my own birth. I saw the happiness I brought my parents and siblings. I witnessed all the years of my life flash quickly before me. In a way, it's very much like a highlight reel of your favorite movie.

With this life review came a clear understanding of all that I had gone through during my time on Earth. My Spirit self did not hold any judgment toward my human self. If anything, I had more compassion toward the parts of myself that I never approved of while on Earth. I immediately had a much greater understanding of who I am and why I did the things I did.

I got to witness the ways in which I had spread peace and love during my lifetime. I got to see things from the perspective of those I was closest to in the physical world. I learned of ways in which I could've done more to help others, or even myself. I realized where I had gone wrong and saw glimpses of where I could've been a better person. I no longer had such a limited perspective. Removed from my body, I now had such a vast understanding of the universe and the purpose of life.

As my life review came to an end, I was once again greeted by my guides and other loved ones who had passed before me. To say it felt like one big family reunion is an understatement.

In the midst of all the excitement, I could hear the thoughts and prayers of my loved ones left behind. I could feel their pain and love for me. I also knew of those who couldn't care less of my passing, but I did not judge them in the slightest. Even with knowing what my death was doing to my loved ones still on Earth, nothing could take away the joy I felt on the Other Side. As difficult as it was for my family, I knew they would survive. If only they knew how okay I really am. But they'll learn for themselves when it's their own time. Until then, I'll be by their side. That's the best part of all this. I can be wherever I want to be in the flash of a moment.

I'm not dead. In fact, I'm more alive on the Other Side than I ever was on Earth.

By the way, I'm not sure who this Spirit that I was connecting to during this particular automatic writing session is. I don't personally know a Sarah who passed in a car accident. I'm assuming this Spirit (or multiple spirits communicating as a collective) came through as such for the people who will read this book. Also, I found it interesting that this particular

Spirit described how she watched the scene of the car accident after she had transitioned. This is definitely not the case with every Spirit. Many of them communicate that they're immediately summoned toward the light and greeted in Heaven. But I'm sure this process works a little differently for each soul.

LIFE REVIEW

When your physical body dies at the end of your lifetime and your soul returns to Heaven, you will undergo a life review. The life review happens once you've completed your journey to Earth School and is an opportunity to watch back through your life, not only through your own eyes but also through the eyes of those around you and who you have impacted.

The life review allows the opportunity to see your life through a fresh lens and new perspective. Through this, you gain a deeper understanding of the experiences and relationships you had on your most recent journey to Earth School. It will enlighten you about why you went through certain challenges, pain, losses, suffering, and heartbreak. The life review provides answers and serves as a transition between Earth School and Heaven.

During the life review, you will sit down with your spirit guides and review your soul contract. You will see what you were able to accomplish and check off of your soul's to-do list. It's a chance to celebrate how much you grew and developed over the course of this lifetime. Because of free will, there will probably be some things on your soul contract that you didn't check off this time, so a part of your soul will return to continue along your evolution. Again, this is where my clementine analogy and the idea of reincarnation comes into play.

In Heaven, you will continue to learn and grow by being assigned to certain roles or "jobs," but again, it's through the earthly experience that we gain the most growth, which is why ultimately a part of the soul decides to return to Earth School once again.

Can I Connect with Loved Ones on the Other Side Who I Didn't Know on Earth?

You may not even know who all of your "people" are while you're here on Earth—but they know you. I get a lot of messages from grandparents, biological parents of adopted children, and other relatives who the person I am reading for never even knew on Earth. They want to let you know that they feel bonded and connected with you, that they see your life and are there with you, watching over you. Sometimes they will offer answers for questions you can't resolve in any other way, like, "Why did my mom give me up for adoption?" It's so healing when things like this happen.

I've had cases where the person who I am reading for has an intuitive sense of this bond. Sometimes, they talk to the uncle who passed before they were born even though they never met him. Other times, the person is unaware that this loved one in Spirit ever existed. Either way, Spirit cares for that person all the same.

SOUL FAMILIES

Our soul families consist of our higher self and, generally speaking, our family, friends, mentors, and romantic
partners, as well as perhaps some coaches and teachers.
Basically, this is the collection of souls who, throughout
your lifetime here in the physical world, you felt either a
strong connection to or an instant sense of knowing. That
feeling you get when you feel like you've always known
someone who you've just met? They are probably part of
your soul family.

Before any of you are born, the members of your soul family group together to help construct each of your soul contracts for this lifetime. You figure out which areas on your
to-do list need attention, what lessons will be most beneficial
for you to learn, and how your earthly relationships can help
you achieve those goals. That person you dated who things
didn't work out with? The one who taught you about self-
love and inner strength? You may very well have agreed to
go through that experience together in order to ultimately
achieve growth and greater knowledge.

Members of your actual family are part of your soul family, especially your close family members, like your parents
and siblings. I believe that we also all have multiple soulmates
(who we may or may not end up in a romantic relationship
with) and that they are part of our soul family as well. Since
people always tend to think of soulmates as romantic partners, I prefer to think of them as soul connections or those
who we share a soul bond with. These are the people who we

are meant to cross paths with and to have experiences with during our lifetime here in Earth School. That might mean romantically, but our soul connections can also touch our lives as a coach, mentor, close friend, or in any other sort of relationship. They are here to help us learn and grow, as all members of our soul families are.

Generally speaking, your soul family stays consistent over lifetimes, although new people may be added here and there. For example, multiple mediums and people who do past life regression work have told me that my mom and I have lived many lives together in pretty much every type of relationship you can imagine. I've been her parent. We've been married. You name it, my mom and I have been in that relationship. I know it sounds kind of creepy, but you have to look at it from a higher perspective. I joke with my mom that this explains my lack of patience with her! We've been dealing with each other literally *forever*.

Once the members of your soul family return to Heaven after this lifetime, they continue to watch over you as part of your Spirit team. One really cool detail about this is that they also hang out with the members of your soul family who have yet to stage their cameo appearance here on Earth. So often, when I work with a pregnant woman, a deceased relative will come through to say they are with the soul of the baby before the mother has even met them. They will generally verify whether the baby is a boy or a girl unless they know there is a reason the parent doesn't want to find out yet.

What if My Loved One Who Has Passed Reincarnates as Someone New in My Life?

Let's say that your mom in this lifetime has died, gone to Heaven, and then a part of her soul reincarnates as your grandchild many years later. Would you know?

I get asked questions like this a lot. Sometimes Spirit will communicate this, but only if they know that it will bring you comfort or healing. As far as I can tell, Spirit usually refrains from providing us with this information if they know it wouldn't serve us. For instance, if you're the type who would freak out to look at your little baby lying on your lap and say, "Mom? Is that you?" then you're probably not meant to have that information. For other people, it's what they need to hear to move forward. I've had Spirit who was stillborn communicate that a part of their soul lives on through their sibling, who was born a few years later. This can be very healing, and even validating, for that child's parents who might've always wondered.

SPIRIT GUIDES

Spirit guides are souls who once existed here in the physical world but have lived enough lives and learned enough lessons that they now remain on the Other Side. Most of them have reincarnated many, many times and, through that, reached a level of self-mastery. They have spiritually evolved to the point where they are now able to offer guidance and support to you and, possibly, others who have been assigned to them as well.

These spirit guides help us along our journey through Earth School. There are several different types of spirit guides, but we all have one main or master spirit guide. This is the guide who is with us from before we are born to the moment we cross over and return back to Heaven. I believe our main spirit guide is usually with the parts of our soul that return to Earth School over the course of multiple lifetimes, but there are also situations in which our main spirit guide might switch from one lifetime to the next.

We've already touched on the fact that each of us also has a team of spirit guides that helps us out with various aspects of our lives as we travel through Earth School. This isn't an exhaustive list, but know that you have your own personal Spirit squad, as I like to call it. In addition to our main spirit guide, we each have a gatekeeper guide, who guards our soul's memories and personal record file. And as I mentioned earlier, this guide also helps mediums and other lightworkers, acting as the bouncer for our readings.

We also have messenger guides who help us out with little nudges or messages at various points in our life when we are in need of a sign from the universe that we are on the right path. You might have a synchronicity spirit guide who helps lead you to meet the right people or to go down the right path. Your feeler guide assists with a variety of physical and emotional issues, helping you feel the things that might otherwise block you from growing and evolving. We have a joy guide to lift our mood, especially when we are feeling low.

Their sole purpose is to bring a smile to our face when we need it most.

For the most part, our spirit guides don't come in the form of our loved ones who have crossed over, but occasionally—especially in the case of parents who have lost children through miscarriage, termination, sickness, or an unforeseen event—joy guides come in the form of babies who have passed on to the Other Side. As for the rest of our spirit guides, I'm not really sure why the vast majority of them are not related to us, but it could possibly be because they would bring some sort of bias with them.

In addition to this Spirit squad, many different helper guides pop in and out of our lives depending upon the type of assistance we need at any given moment. For example, there are romance guides, career guides, creative guides, health guides, and all sorts of other guides who focus on helping us through particular situations or events during which we need a little extra boost of guidance or support.

ANGELS

Our spiritual support squad also includes guardian and archangels. Angels are purely divine in essence and have never walked the face of the Earth. They are powerful beings of divine energy who protect us and make us feel safe and loved.

Guardian angels serve a similar function to that of our main spirit guide; each of us has at least two and sometimes more. Guardian angels are with us from the time we're born until the time we cross over.

Archangels exist at a higher frequency than even our guardian angels. You can sort of think of them as the managers of the guardian angels. They're at the top of the angelic hierarchy, for sure.

Our angels come to us when we ask them for help. That is the key difference between angels and spirit guides. Whereas our spirit guides are always with us, our angels tend to step up when we call out, pray to them, or specifically ask them to. Every now and then, our guardian angels are allowed to come in when we don't ask them to. This might happen in situations like a car accident that results from someone else's free will and when it's not yet our time to go. These exceptions are pretty extenuating and far and few between, though.

I love to call upon my angels when I need love, comfort, or guidance. They want to help us, so all we have to do is pray to them to ask for things like wisdom, a sign, or a little message. I've found that signs from angels often come in the form of repeating numbers or white feathers.

To receive and see these signs in your own life, all you have to do is open yourself up to communicating with your angels and asking for signs. Angel card decks are also great. All you have to do is shuffle them and ask the angels to give you the information you need for your highest benefit. Then pull a card and read the message.

Although angels tend to appear on their own accord only in dire situations, they are there for you to call upon at any moment, as frequently as you would like.

III

They Really Are Okay

6

Sudden Deaths

will begin each chapter in this part of the book with a channeled message that came through during an automatic writing session. I did this because I wanted to bring Spirit to you
in the most direct way possible. My hope is that these messages
will resonate with you. Even if just one sentence hits home and
helps you heal, I'm sure that's why you're meant to read it.

As you read these channeled messages, remember that
Spirit works off my frame of reference and can only give me
things I've seen or experienced in my own life. I interpret
what I'm receiving to the best of my ability, and then I do
my best to put it into plain English. So if you're wondering
why some parts of these channeled messages "sound like me,"
there's your answer. That being said, I can assure you I had
some amazing Spirit helpers working with me and through
me for each and every channeled message you will read in

this book. I did, however, ask Spirit to come through as a collective and to hold back specific information such as names, dates, and so forth so that these words can resonate with as many people as possible.

May these messages from above bring you peace, hope, and comfort.

You know, it's funny how grief works. One moment, things can feel okay—maybe even "normal"—and then the next moment it can feel as if the world has come crashing down on you all over again. Suddenly, any healing you thought you had achieved has dissolved into a sea of longing for someone you can't see or touch. I know I'm that someone you've been longing for, but you need to understand that I'm right here. My love, my laughter, and my spirit surround you like the oxygen you breathe.

I know this may not change your desire to physically hear my voice or feel my arms wrapping you tight in one of those big ol' bear hugs I used to give you, but please trust me when I say I'm not missing out on your life. I hear your thoughts. I see everything that you're going through. You don't have to worry or wonder whether I know about the big things you've been up to. I'm proudly watching over you, day in and day out.

If there's one thing I've learned from having left the physical world with no warning of my impending death, it's that you should live each day as if it's your last. I know it's such a cliché thing to say, but it's the truth. Enjoy this lifetime that you are so blessed to have. Don't take a single breath for granted. You never know if today is the day your time on Earth will come to an end.

Work hard, but only so that you can support your ability to live even harder. Travel the world. Go on an exciting adventure. Or simply stroll around your neighborhood, appreciating all of the sounds and sights.

Do whatever brings you joy (as long as it's legal...I will haunt your ass if you end up in a jail cell).

Say "I love you" to the people you care for. Make an effort to go beyond the surface and form truly meaningful relationships. Do your part to try and leave the world a better place than it was when you came into it.

It's true that I'm happiest when I see you happy. I feel all that you go through, and feeling your joy is the greatest gift you can give me.

Please know that you did no wrong. You couldn't have saved me. If you feel guilty for anything you said or did prior to my passing, forgive yourself. Because I already have. I have nothing but love for you. You can release any regret over words not said. I promise you, I've heard them all. Even if you've never spoken them aloud.

While all I want for you is happiness, I also understand that grief takes time. So take all the time you need. Be patient with yourself. Give yourself permission to feel what you need to feel. Remember that it's an ongoing process.

And until we are reunited one day in Heaven, just know that my soul lives on and is forever by your side.

UNEXPECTED PASSINGS

I consider sudden deaths to be those passings that happen quickly and unexpectedly. While suicide and overdose fall into this category, we'll specifically talk about those types of passings in Chapter Eight.

Sudden deaths might happen in a variety of ways and include events such as a car accident, murder, freak accident, haphazard occurrence, or even something biological like a heart attack, brain aneurysm, or other swiftly moving physical glitch. These are the deaths that seem to come out of the blue and can't be anticipated. The deaths that leave the ones who are left behind feeling like the rug has suddenly been pulled out from under them.

Here's the thing: we're all going to die one day (our physical bodies, that is, not our consciousness). As Benjamin Franklin once said, "In this world nothing can be said to be certain, except death and taxes." We all know that it'll happen at some point. But no one wants to believe that either they or the people they love will go in any other way than by passing in their sleep at an old age after having lived a long, healthy, and happy life.

So when a sudden death occurs, it's especially difficult for those left behind to come to terms with what's happened.

Someone they loved was here and everything was fine, then the next moment they were gone.

THE EXPERIENCE OF SUDDEN DEATHS

Sudden deaths are peaceful and do not involve suffering, even in cases where the death involves an accident that might appear particularly gruesome. There is no pain or suffering involved, no matter how it might look to those of us still breathing. As a human, this can be hard to wrap your head around, especially if you happen to have lost someone in a circumstance that we commonly associate with pain. How could that person *not* be terrified? How could they *not* be in pain?

The message that comes through in almost every reading is that, in circumstances like these, the soul has already transitioned even before the person was technically deceased. I can't tell you how many times Spirit has come through saying something along the lines of, "My soul crossed over before the impact occurred. I felt nothing!" or "Tell my mom that I had already left my physical body before the bullet even entered my chest."

This means that even if there was a period of time during which their heart was still beating or their brain was still active after an accident or some other type of tragedy, their soul was no longer in their body. Yes, their body may have still been alive, but their soul had already transitioned. So, for example, if someone died in a fire, you don't have to worry— they didn't suffer a slow death. They would've already been at peace before feeling any of the heat or pain. This is because our loved ones and angels are fully aware of our soul contracts and know when it's our time, so they swoop in to assist us with our transition.

One young woman who I did a reading for, Kelsi, received messages from Spirit that highlight this beautifully:

I received a spontaneous reading from Monica a few years ago. A few minutes into meeting Monica, she pulled me aside. "Your mother is here," she said. "She's saying, 'look at my baby girl!'" I didn't know it at the time but after my reading, my aunt (my mom's sister), who was also a little skeptical, said that just from that one phrase, she knew it was my mom. In the small time I had with my mom, she never called me by my name, only "baby girl."

My mom was in a bad car accident at the age of sixteen. She was ejected from the car and paralyzed from the back down. She was told she would never be able to walk again. My mom won a lot of money in her settlement, which was later questioned as a motive in her death.

When my mom was communicating with Monica about how she passed, Monica felt short of breath, as if she couldn't breathe. She said that there had been smoke and flames. This was all accurate. While napping, my mom found herself trapped in a house fire with no way to escape. Because of her paralysis, she needed someone to get her in and out of her wheelchair. No one was there to help, and my mom passed in the fire.

My family spent twenty-four years wondering if there had been any foul play involved. After all that time, Monica was finally able to reassure me there was not. It had simply been a house fire, and it was my mom's time to go. Knowing this gave me so much comfort.

Every year on the anniversary of my mom's death, I would talk to my now-husband about the fact that I can't think of a worse way to die than to be trapped in a fire and burning. I can't imagine the pain and how scared my mom must have been. There was no way for Monica to know about these conversations. Still, she said, "I know you worry about the way your mom passed and the pain she must have endured, but her soul transitioned before she felt any sort of pain. I promise you that she didn't suffer. She was immediately greeted by loved ones and angels. She wasn't afraid," Monica said. This made me feel so much better.

At the time of this reading, my husband and I had been together for five years but were not yet married. I knew an engagement was coming (or at least thought, it better be!). When I imagined our engagement and wedding, I often thought about how sad it was that my mother wouldn't be there to celebrate. Monica reassured me that my mom would be right there with me in all of those milestone moments. She wouldn't miss it. My heart filled with joy.

Monica went on to say, "There's a young man here and he's been waiting patiently." I knew immediately it was Tim, the sweet man I had shared my life with before I met my husband. He was respectful on the Other Side, just as he was here on Earth. Tim wanted my mother and I to have our time together first. Monica immediately validated the horrific way Tim was taken from us. She said she sensed he had been murdered and that she felt a blow to the head, followed by pain in her gut. At the time I didn't connect with the head trauma; all I knew was Tim had been stabbed in the stomach. There were still many unresolved questions around his murder. It wasn't until about a year after my reading that I found out new information about what had happened. It was only then I learned that Tim *had* suffered a blow to the head. How could Monica have known this? I hadn't even known! She brought through other facts that no one knew, which have since checked out, but that I unfortunately cannot share due to possible legal implications.

Tim said that he did not suffer. His soul was at peace before he would have felt any pain. He said that he was now in the most beautiful place. He was happy to see I had moved on and he gave his approval of the man I was with, saying what a great catch he was. My heart melted. "Would he just get down on one knee already?" Tim joked. I laughed as Monica told me this, and it felt just as if I was talking to Tim himself.

Monica asked, "Do you cut your boyfriend's hair?" It was so random, and Monica said that Tim was chuckling as he showed her this. I think it was his random way of letting me know that he really is with me. I'm sure he was chuckling because I do a horrible job of cutting my husband's hair, particularly in terms of straightening the back, but I always think to myself, "Whatever, he can't see it; I'm the one that has to stare at it!" I knew this was Tim's way of poking fun at me.

This experience changed me. It changed the way I look at life, death, and everything else. I cried tears of happiness for days after the reading. It was an unreal experience that I wish everyone had a chance to experience. I want Monica to know the impact she had on my life. I thank her from the bottom of my heart. There are no words to describe the joy of having closure and clarity.

In the case of sudden deaths, there are instances where the soul still experiences or witnesses the event for the purpose of learning, but even this occurs from a bird's-eye view outside of their body, as was the case in the automatic writing I shared in Chapter Five. But never once have I heard that a soul suffered on the way out. I've only been told, time and time again, that they are at peace, feel love, are unafraid, and are greeted by angels and loved ones.

I have connected with a handful of souls who *were* conscious at the time of the event and leading up to their official time of death, but in these rare cases, they communicate that their soul had chosen (and even wanted) to fully experience that particular death, with the intention of gaining a new level of understanding or a greater compassion for others. But even then, they show me that they were already feeling the comforting presence of their angels or deceased loved ones, and that any pain stopped in the instant their soul left the physical body.

The only difference in the experience of transition for those who pass as the result of a sudden death is that it might take a moment for them to become aware of and understand what has just happened. But even that happens nearly instantaneously.

This is important information that Spirit wants you to know, and one of the biggest reasons they come through. Those left behind can often become fixated on their loved one's experience of suffering or pain at the moment of death. It's easy to imagine that people who die in these circumstances experience a lot of fear and turmoil, but in 99.99 percent of cases, they do not. It is so important to Spirit that you know: *your loved ones did not feel what you are worried they felt.* You can release yourself from the torment of all of those questions.

I have found the questioning and torment can be particularly intense when the person left behind is experiencing some form of survivor's guilt—the wife who survived the car crash or the son that was able to get out of the burning house in time when the rest of his family could not. In these cases, there is almost always a sense of "Why did I survive?" and even more difficult, "How could I not have saved them?" These questions are a natural response to death, but our loved ones on the Other Side want us to know that there was no question of saving them—they passed because it was their time to go. You lived because you were meant to live. It wasn't your time yet. You still have more to learn and do in this lifetime. Spirit holds no grudges, nor do they feel any resentment. They feel only peace.

When I tell people this, I can almost see a physical weight lifting from their shoulders. It is those of us who are left behind that experience the pain, suffering, and loss of these events. The loved one actually involved experiences none of that. They are now at peace, and they want you to be, as well.

What Are Near-Death Experiences All About?

A near-death experience (or an NDE, for short) is when a person has an out-of-body experience that allows them to have a glimpse into the afterlife and experience what it's like to be in Spirit form. Most near-death experiences occur after a traumatic event where the person's physical body actually died for a few seconds or minutes, and then came back to life. However, many near-death experiences have also happened in less dire situations; for example, while a person was undergoing a routine surgery or was briefly unconscious upon impact in a crash.

While I've never personally had a near-death experience, I've had Spirit come through in readings to confirm other people's NDEs, to validate for them that it really did happen, and that they're not crazy. I've also heard and read stories about NDEs and wholeheartedly believe many of these experiences to be real. For some people, a near-death experience is part of what they agreed to go through in the physical world to learn, grow, and expand their perspective. They might come to a new understanding that there is still more for them to learn or do here on Earth. They might realize that now that they don't have to worry about death, they can really concentrate on the moment at hand or start living their life to the fullest. Sometimes it even serves as a wake-up call for people to make major changes in their lives, such as getting sober.

A lot of people who have lived through near-death experiences are meant to act as teachers by sharing their stories and messages. It turns into a purpose for them. Their experiences bring a lot of comfort to people who are afraid of death and who question what there is beyond this lifetime.

By sharing their story, those who have had near-death experiences can help others piece things together to gain a better understanding that the soul lives on. While hearing about one near-death experience alone may not alleviate the concerns of a person who is skeptical about the afterlife, hearing multiple similar experiences might help validate what waits for us on the Other Side.

Many NDEs include one or more "verifiable moments," where the person shares information about something that occurred here on Earth that they had witnessed while out-of-body and couldn't have possibly known otherwise. For example, exact phrases the surgeons had spoken as they were being operated on or being able to recount a specific meal a family member ate in the hospital cafeteria.

You might hear some variations from one person to another's near-death experience. This is because we all see things through our own lens, which is informed in part by what we've been taught and our personal background. However, there also tends to be a lot of commonalities between these stories. Many of the NDE stories I've heard include experiences that are very similar to things I've been told from Spirit and in readings over the years. They talk about a tunnel of warm or bright light and feeling wrapped up in love by that light. They have said they were greeted by loved ones who passed before them, angels, or even God. Some have even experienced life reviews and, as part of that life review, saw what they still needed to do on Earth and why they had to come back to their body.

A lot of these people talk about how the experience was so beautiful that they didn't want to go. They wish they could have stayed, but their fresh perspective made them realize why they had to leave and what their purpose was, or sometimes they're told outright, "It's not your time yet. You have to go back now." As with any other experience in life, there is always a purpose to and lessons within a near-death experience.

TIMING

No matter how out-of-the-blue sudden deaths may seem, they generally occur at the point a soul determined it should return to Heaven in their soul contract. Yet, there are also some cases when free will can come into play and change the script. I know it can be difficult to understand the dual nature of soul contracts and free will. Again, let me remind you that I don't have all the answers, nor will I until the day I cross over. However, the best way I can describe it is that our soul contracts set up the challenges we're going to face in this lifetime, the experiences we need to live through, and the lessons we need to learn.

Knowing this, there is a natural end point where we have experienced everything we were meant to, and only then are we ready to pass on. But we also go through these experiences in a way that is unique to us and make our own choices along the way—this can impact the exact timing and manner of our death, even if it's by just a bit. This comes up most often in traumatic circumstances like suicide, which I talk more about it in Chapter Eight. For example, someone with serious mental health issues may have their soul contract ending in middle age, but should they make the free will choice to end their life by suicide, then they will have crossed over years earlier than what their soul originally planned before coming into this world.

For the most part, though, I believe that even free will doesn't change the general timing of one's death (which is a window of time, rather than a specific date) much, regardless of the circumstances. The timing of our death is in line not with the life we live here on Earth but the precise *lessons* we are meant to learn, although this can seem, to us, unfair and illogical. For example, I once did a reading in which Spirit had survived a shark attack, the ensuing surgery, and a six-month recovery, only to pass away less than a year later in a car accident. From an earthly perspective, that seems unfair and even cruel. But from a big-picture view, it likely indicates the experiences during that time, and even the attack itself, were things the soul needed to go through in addition to being within that window of time for them to cross over, as established in their soul contract.

I've done a handful of readings in which a soul has communicated that their higher self, spirit guides, or God made a change to their soul contract, which resulted in another few years here in Earth School than they had initially planned for. As far as I can tell, situations like this are the exception, and not the norm. When it does happen, it's typically when someone else in the immediate family has passed away due to a decision made out of free will, thus shifting the soul contracts of themselves and those closest to them.

Like all deaths, a sudden passing always occurs in the way that's in the highest good for everyone involved. We might experience that as a more difficult variety of grief on Earth (because our souls are learning more from it) or easier than it could be otherwise (in instances where further lessons aren't necessary). Here's what I mean by that. In the case of quick, seemingly freakish deaths, I often hear from Spirit that they left Earth suddenly because their mom wasn't meant to have to sit by their side in a hospital room for a year watching her child suffer through a slow, drawn-out illness. Of course, the experience of losing a child quickly didn't feel in any way, shape, or form easy to the mother, but she was unknowingly spared from the alternative because it was in her highest good, and her soul didn't require the experience of a child's drawn-out death.

As much as the timing of a quick death might seem abrupt or haphazard to those of us left behind, the truth is that in the divine sense, the timing is exactly as it was always meant to be.

UNFINISHED BUSINESS

With any variety of death, but especially with unexpected ones, it can often feel to those of us left behind like a lot of things went unsaid and issues went unresolved. You didn't get a chance to tell the person how much you loved them, or you never apologized for that thing that happened many years ago. It leaves a lot of room for questioning whether or not the person you lost knows how you really feel and how deeply you care. I've seen this happen in my own family: when I was about fifteen, we were told that my grandfather had at least three to six months left to live. My younger sister wrote and sent him a letter, telling him how much she loved him, but he never received it because he suddenly died three days after he was diagnosed. My sister was upset that he never got to read what she wrote, but we are both now confident that he knew exactly what she said from the moment he passed.

Then, a few years later, my grandmother passed away. I had never told her I was a medium because I thought she wouldn't approve or understand. After she died, I immediately regretted this decision. I wished my grandmother could have known my true self. But then I realized I needed to trust the messages that come through from Spirit in almost every reading. In Spirit form, my grandmother now knew *exactly* who I was and how I shared my gift. These days, I have no doubt that she and my grandfather are proudly watching over me as I do this work. This might seem too good to be true, but we have to remember that the barriers we have in the physical world do not exist in Heaven. Spirit is the embodiment of love, acceptance, and forgiveness, and there are no secrets anymore. Know that your loved one is very much aware of everything you feel and want to say, regardless of whether it was ever spoken out loud or not. They are not holding on to any anger or resentment. As far as your loved one is concerned, there is no unfinished business. They have all the perspective they need. If you feel the need to be forgiven, you have been forgiven. If you've been holding on to guilt or regret, I promise your loved ones only want for you to let that go.

Diane's reading offers the perfect example of this. She said:

I attended a Messages From Above event in 2017. My daughter agreed to go with me, even though she wasn't a believer. The week before, I was begging my brother, who had been killed in action in Iraq several years ago, to give me a message at the event. My sister-in-law had also passed away, and their fifteen-year-old son (my nephew) moved in with my family following her passing. At the time of the event, I was embarking on a custody battle for my nephew with a close family friend. I wanted my brother to tell me that he wanted what I was fighting for.

As soon as Monica said, "I have someone's brother coming through," I knew it was mine. As she continued, "...one who was in the military and his death was a result of this," my daughter (who was not a believer) gripped my arm and said, "Oh my God, Mom." This was the beginning of my message. Monica said, "Were you in a fight that you haven't forgiven yourself for?" I started sobbing. I knew for sure my brother was with us. I had been carrying around so much guilt for the twelve years since my brother had died because we got into a big fight and had not made up before he was killed.

He wanted me to know how much he loves me, that he wasn't angry, and that he knows how sorry I felt for not making things right when I had the chance. He said that if he could go back in time, he would've also made more of an effort to resolve our issues. He reminded me that fights happen, and that our fight could never take away from all the good times we had together and the bond we'll forever share. He also said he was really happy that his son is with me. That through me, he will get to know more about his father.

There was so much more that Monica told me. Between knowing about the fight we were in and all of the other details that came through, my daughter is now a believer too. It was such an emotional release that I slept for fifteen hours straight after the reading and was finally able to release my guilt and forgive myself. My brother was right; he told me raising his son wouldn't be easy. But knowing that this is what he wants makes it that much more rewarding. Thank you so much for bringing my brother to me and for his reassurance that I am doing what he wants me to do.

What's It Like on the Other Side?

While souls are assigned different roles and continue their learning on the Other Side, they also get to have a lot of fun. In addition to being joyfully reunited with loved ones, Spirit has communicated to me that, in a sense, they're able to create their own "version" of Heaven. Whatever they want to do or wherever they want to be, they have the ability to make that happen. Remember, on the Other Side we're all pure energy and are no longer attached to a physical body that needs food, water, shelter, and whatnot (yes ladies, that means no menstrual cycles or period cramps every month—hallelujah!).

While we no longer have a physical body, Spirit shows me that they're still able to enjoy human-like experiences in soul form. I've had so many spirits come through to say, "I'm riding down the highway of Heaven! My passion for motorcycles has continued in the afterlife" or "Tell my buddy I'm drinking our favorite beer and that I still go fishing at our go-to spot."

How is this possible? The best analogy I can come up with is that it's very much like virtual reality (VR). If you've ever tried a VR demo, I'm sure you can understand just how real it feels (trust me, I know this firsthand—the realness of virtual reality is what caused me to break my ankle not long ago). Just like in VR, where you can put on a headset and be skiing down a mountain, flying through the sky, or exploring the streets of Paris instantaneously, so it goes in the Spirit World.

Spirit has also told me that they don't have the words to describe just how beautiful the Spirit World is. The colors are much more vivid, the music is even more beautiful, and the scenery is incredibly breathtaking. They tell me it is beyond even our wildest imagination. In addition to all of this, they're able to enjoy whatever they please with a mere thought and make it their reality. When they come through with these messages, it also serves as a representation of just how happy and at peace they are on the Other Side.

MOURNING THE THINGS THAT DIDN'T HAPPEN

In addition to grieving the person who has passed, those of us left behind can also spend a lot of time mourning all of the things that *didn't* happen. This is true with many forms of death, but especially in the case of an unexpected passing. "He never had a child" or "She just started a new job and was so excited!"

Soul contracts aside, know that your loved ones are continuing to have experiences in Spirit form. They are unlimited and without restriction. They can travel to places they've never been, see things they've never seen, and experience so many aspects of physical life in an even more amazing way.

Also, remember that, in a sense, your loved one has had many, many lifetimes' worth of experiences. Remember the clementine analogy? These other parts of their soul *have* had children, gotten married, worked at jobs they loved, and traveled all over, even if they didn't get to do so in this lifetime. Once your loved one returns to Heaven, they will once again "regain" all of these experiences. They will remember *all* of their lifetimes and *all* of their experiences.

They also understand why they chose to have or not have certain experiences in this most recent lifetime. They have fulfilled their soul contract and, for them, there is no feeling of missing out. There is only peace and love. Your loved ones have a great perspective on all of this and not even a slight sense of loss. They want you to know this so that you, too, can shed these concerns.

I promise you, your loved ones are not missing out on anything!

Do You Work on Missing Persons Cases?

I have worked on missing persons cases in the past and, even now, I try to do one every couple of years to help families in need of answers and relief. Having said that, while there are some mediums who specialize in these cases just like some surgeons specialize in neurosurgery, I am not one of those mediums.

There's a very real reason why I limit this work, and that's because it takes an enormous emotional toll and time commitment. It's important to understand that missing persons cases are not like a typical reading. With these cases, a medium works with families and investigators for months at a time. It requires a tremendous amount of energy, and it's really draining. The other issue about missing persons cases is that they create the type of bias I always try to avoid in my work as a medium. To determine if it's even the right case for me to take on, I have to be given a brief summary of the circumstances. I can't go into the situation with a completely blank slate. And knowing certain aspects of a case can create bias and room for error. I never, ever want to lead a family down the wrong path or devastate them further, no matter how good my intentions are. I am aware there are limitations to this gift.

Also, there are no guarantees. Sometimes a family isn't meant to find the answers, no matter how difficult and painful that might be and regardless of how much they want answers. The not-knowing is part of their lesson, part of their soul contract. In those cases, even the best medium in the world won't be able to access answers or provide closure. There have been plenty of times when I wish I could just snap my fingers and get an answer from God. But just like I'm never going to get Spirit to give me the winning lottery numbers, they can't give me information that we're not meant to have either. Even when it feels like it would really, really help. I have

no influence over the soul journey someone has chosen—nor should I!

When this is the case, Spirit knows it and will hold back
accordingly. I understand that there is some skepticism
about this. People who are already doubtful of mediums
think this is an excuse for why we can't always provide
concrete information. This isn't helped by some mediums
who go to media sources and claim they do have all of the
answers, only to be proven wrong in the long run. It adds
to the bad rap of mediumship and often worsens what is
already a very sensitive situation. But, remember, even
under more standard circumstances, Spirit doesn't communicate in a black-and-white way. And even under the
best circumstances, their communication is all about interpretation and putting together the puzzle pieces of what a
medium is hearing, seeing, feeling, sensing, and knowing.

There is always room for error and misinterpretation,
regardless of the type of reading. A medium could work
on a missing person case and hear, feel, or sense a boat-
load of information about the person who went missing and what happened to them. While an experienced
medium will know who they are communicating with
the majority of the time, there's always a chance that a
medium could misinterpret communication as validation
that the missing person is deceased, when, really, the
details may have been coming through from one of the
person's loved ones on the Other Side or through one of
their spirit guides. Remember, some mediums only get
signs and symbols. Others will only feel things. Most of
us don't see an actual dead person standing before us.
Therefore, sometimes it can get confusing as to which
Spirit is actually communicating the information.

As mediums, we have to be very careful about what we share and how we interpret information, and this is especially true in missing persons cases where the family may not know for certain whether or not the loved one has passed away. A few times I have connected to the soul of someone who was missing, thus validating that they had transitioned. But with these readings, I was extremely confident that I was speaking to the missing person who is now in Spirit, as opposed to someone else connected to them. Even then, I'll still give a disclaimer that there's always a slight chance I may have misinterpreted. I'll even tell the family that I hope and pray I'm wrong, because I so badly want there to be a happy ending.

About six years ago, at a time when I was still giving private readings, I met with a family who came for a group reading. As with all of my readings, I knew nothing about their situation or who they were trying to contact. The dad came through by name, described himself, and provided a lot of details about his life. But he showed me my question mark symbol, which, for me, means there are still unanswered questions surrounding his passing. He gave me the feeling that there had been an unresolved investigation. I told the family this, and that's when they informed me that their dad was missing. It was only then that I realized I was bringing Spirit through despite the fact that his family wasn't even sure he had crossed over.

The family told me that, in their hearts, they were sure he was gone. Spirit acknowledged the fact that it had been nearly two decades since he had crossed over. Nonetheless, his family was still spending thousands of dollars every year, going back to the location where he had last been seen in Florida and getting teams to dig through the surrounding woods in hopes of finding some type of remains or answers. At that point, I did get some details about his last day and the people involved. Some of this filled in a few of the missing blanks, but ultimately, he wanted his family to know that it was not part of their souls' purpose to have all the answers. As gently as possible, he told them, "You'll never be able to find the physical proof you are looking for. So please, stop searching. Give yourselves permission to move on from this and continue living your lives, with me by your side." He wanted to be sure the family knew that he wasn't angry, they weren't giving up, and there was nothing to feel guilty about. He promised them that once their time came, they would be able to see the bigger picture and understand why they were never meant to have the physical evidence they so desperately wanted.

When I do work on these types of cases, I gravitate toward the situations that I feel most strongly about and where I feel like I am meant to be sharing my gift. This is definitely not my specialty, though. I feel like my work and purpose is in helping the masses by providing a bigger, more clear picture of life after death.

THE POWER OF FORGIVENESS

Not only does Spirit want you to find forgiveness in yourself for anything you may be beating yourself up about but they also want you to forgive others. Sudden passings come in a lot of different forms, but one of the trickier situations to navigate are those deaths that happen as the result of another person's actions. I'm talking about things like murders, fights, drunk driving accidents, or drug-related deaths that the person who passed isn't ultimately responsible for. The type of deaths that seem to involve particularly dark, tragic, or traumatic circumstances.

These types of death are so difficult for those who are left behind because, on top of grief, they are often dealing with feelings like anger, resentment, and blame. Or maybe they feel these same emotions in less violent circumstances, such as toward a doctor after a surgery somehow went wrong, resulting in a loved one's death.

My Spirit Dictionary symbol for circumstances like this is a pointing finger. Whenever I see this, I know that the person I'm talking to is dealing with anger or pain as a result of blaming another person for their loved one's passing. Regardless of the circumstances, Spirit's message for people grappling with this is always the same: "I don't want to see you holding on to all of this frustration, anger, and resentment. It's not helping you heal, nor is it going to bring me back in the physical sense. I need you to know that I'm not angry at the person responsible for my death. In fact, I've found full forgiveness. I hope you can too."

As humans, we often feel the need to seek justice, whether it's through a legal battle or less official channels. We want to see the person at fault take responsibility, or we want a greater understanding of why that person made the choices they did. There are scenarios where it is right and fair that you seek justice: I have had a few clients who have experienced the death of a loved one due to domestic abuse and violence. These families worked not just to get justice for their loved ones but to potentially save future victims. I have also seen parents dedicate their lives to working against drunk driving, creating meaningful change that has helped countless others.

But other people become overwhelmed by anger, and they wither away under trauma and guilt. Here, it is important to remember that Spirit does not expect or need us to take on the responsibility of justice, especially if it comes at a great emotional or financial cost. Your loved one came into this life knowing how it was supposed to end, and now that they have crossed over, they are full of understanding for their family and feel only forgiveness toward the perpetrator. It was a part of the soul contract of both parties because there were lessons to be learned. In this lifetime, you will never understand why this had to happen—but it did. And your loved one knows that.

Many people who lose loved ones in situations like this end up feeling like their lives have been ruined as well. They become fixated and hold back from living their own life from that point forward. Although you might feel like you are honoring your loved one's memory by holding on to what seems like an injustice or by continuing to fight, that's not what they need from you. Sometimes pursuing legal action is an experience you're meant to go through as part of your soul contract, but should you choose not to do so, I promise you're not letting your loved one down. A few months ago, I gave a reading at one of my events to a man who lost his twenty-eight-year-old partner and soulmate to a random act of gun violence. His partner's overarching message was not to focus on finding all of the answers or spending days in a courthouse, but to, instead, find solace in the love they shared and memories they made.

What Spirit wants most is simple: to forgive.

That's right. Even if someone murdered your mother, father, brother, sister, spouse, or friend, Spirit wants you to find forgiveness. They already have. Not once have I talked to any soul in Spirit form who has not forgiven the person responsible for their death. They understand that they could have just as easily been that person. Any one of us can make a bad choice or a mistake and, trust me, we all have, whether in this lifetime or a previous one.

When we forgive actions like this, we free ourselves. Justice really isn't up to us, even though it might feel like it is. Your loved one doesn't want to see their death result in financial or emotional strain that might take years off of your life. You have their full permission and support in forgiving, moving on, and letting go. All they want is to see you happy and moving forward.

I love it when Spirit communicates messages like the one this client received. Every time it comes through, it's something people remember even years after the reading.

I won a contest for a free reading from Monica in 2014. That year, my mom had gotten hit by a bus and died on impact. I was twenty-two, lost, and really just wanted a way to connect with her. I had never been to a medium and didn't know if I completely believed in them, but Monica was from Northern Virginia and was close to my age, so I decided why not enter? Lo and behold, I won! In retrospect, clearly that was my first sign.

Monica described both my mom and the accident so vividly. The reading was surreal, and it felt almost as if my mom was speaking to me in person. The first thing Monica relayed to me after she had channeled my mom was that she was okay and I will be okay too. She said my mom was with my blind dog, a fact I knew no one would know. She told me not to hold on to the guilt and the anger I felt toward the person who took my mom's life, because it was an accident, and accidents happen. My mom said that she had forgiven the person and that this was all part of her soul contract. There was nothing that could've been done to prevent this. Through Monica, my mom told me all of the things I needed to hear. My mom said that she wanted me to continue living my life and to always watch out for my brother.

It's crazy because, in my heart, I always knew all of this, but it sounded so much clearer and more real coming from Monica. Years later, I still think about this reading and how much peace it's given me.

But How Do We Find Forgiveness?

Forgiveness is great in theory but a lot harder to pull off in real life. I've read for parents who have lost a child to violence, and they struggle with their anger toward the perpetrator. I have also seen friends and family upset—even when they try not to be—at their loved one for their overdose or suicide. But one of the biggest lessons I have learned from doing this work is that, to the greatest extent we can, we should all try not to judge other people based on a mistake they made. At the very least, we should make an effort to have some sort of understanding. Even if a person made a *huge* mistake, because we are all so much bigger than that. We're so much bigger than the harm we cause, our issues, our betrayals, or our deceits. None of us are perfect. That is part of our life and part of our soul. This applies to *everyone*. Even to the people who you might feel *have* to be exceptions to this rule. Nope. It applies to them too. Knowing this can help you find forgiveness and move forward.

I often think about how difficult it must be for the parents of school shooters. It goes without saying that situations like this are a nightmare for the parents who lose innocent children to these shooters, but it is also a nightmare for the parents of the perpetrators. While I've never done a reading for any of these parents, I *have* channeled a few spirits who have passed as the result of a mass shooting. Not a single one of them was angry at or held on to resentment toward the shooter. They understand that this manner of death was always part of their journey and soul contract.

Even with this, I can only imagine how horrible it must be to live with the knowledge of what your child has done. I'm guessing there is guilt involved anytime they feel themselves shift into a place of feeling love for and missing their children and their good qualities. I would guess there is a feeling of almost unbearable responsibility on top of all of this.

If I could tell these parents—and all of the families who have lost a loved one who did terrible things here on Earth—one thing, it would be this: even the most terrible act does not take away from all the good parts of the soul you loved and the good memories you had with them. They had beautiful attributes and positive characteristics too. We all do. You don't have to feel guilty about remembering and focusing on those parts of that soul that you loved.

In fact, that is exactly what you should do.

Death by Illness

Never in a million years would you think that I would be the one to succumb to a long battle with illness. When we got the diagnosis, we simply stood there, completely dumbfounded. We couldn't fathom how this was actually happening to our family.

Don't ever think for a second that you should've noticed the signs or symptoms sooner. Or that I would have survived had we tried another form of treatment. This was all part of God's plan. You've gotta trust me when I say that. I understand that it's not fair. Why did I have to get sick and die? I know you struggle with this question every day. But, at the very least, I hope you realize that a terminal illness is what my soul needed to experience.

It taught me patience. Gave me strength and courage. Forced me to let go of control and accept help from others.

It made me appreciate all the years my body was healthy. It opened my eyes to how much love I have for you and every single person in our tight-knit circle, who rallied together to help out where they could—who delivered dinners, drove me to doctor's appointments, and who brought light into my life during some of my darkest of days.

The lessons I got out of being sick are too many to list, but just as I have evolved and changed for the better, so have you. Just as the loss of me has helped shaped you into the resilient and empathetic human being that you are today, so did my illness. One of the highlights of being in Heaven is that, at any time, I get to watch what you're up to and see how much you have grown.

Know that I am whole again. Free from any pain or physical limitations. I'm more than okay, and I want you to be too. Live for me. Laugh for me. And remember that you are never alone.

PASSING FROM SICKNESS

No one wants to see someone they love suffer. For a lot of people, the illness leading up to a death can be just as painful as the death itself. "*Why?*" we want to know. Why did this happen? Why did this beautiful person have to suffer, and why did *I* have to suffer? It can be difficult to find an earthly reason to justify this type of scenario. But there *are* other earthly reasons.

We are all like dominoes, and each of us has an effect on everyone and everything else. There are many reasons why illness exists in the world and why it is something some of us and our loved ones have to go through. Illness can help us appreciate what we have in the moment; it can help evolve medicine, which works for the well-being of others; and it gives us perspective. It also serves a million other purposes, both large and small, that we won't understand until we cross over ourselves.

By now it won't be a surprise to you that people who die as the result of a long-term illness made the decision to do so before they were even here. Just as some souls choose to pass away from something sudden, such as a heart attack, other souls *want* to have the experience of dying from a certain illness. There is so much to be learned from going through this kind of experience. Not just for the individuals who are sick but also for those standing by their side. It often involves tough choices, suffering, and bearing witness to the downhill trajectory of someone you love. No one on Earth *wants* to go through this, but from the soul's perspective, you do. For as much as it hurts, remember how much you have grown from having gone through this challenging process, both in this lifetime and in the much, much larger scheme of your soul.

DEATHBED VISION EXPERIENCES

When you talk to hospice nurses who have a lot of experience being with people as they die, many of them will tell you that no matter how out of it their patients are, and regardless of whether they were an atheist or a believer in the afterlife, they often have a sudden moment of alertness at the end. They'll point or reach out their hand to the "unseen" or say the name of a loved one who passed before them. This has happened with several of my own relatives when they were on their deathbed (I wish I could share every last experience, but this book would be far too long).

This even happens in the case of Alzheimer's and dementia patients, who may very well not have remembered the person they're calling out for in the years prior to that moment. I feel as though the veil between here and the Other Side starts to thin and we become more open to seeing Spirit in these final weeks, days, and moments before we pass, much like how many of us are more open to connecting with the Other Side as children. Some patients will even say outright to the nurses or their relatives in the room that a loved one or angels are there to welcome them into the afterlife and help them transition to Heaven.

There's even a term used for these kinds of experiences; they're referred to as deathbed visions. As with near-death experiences, skeptics have tried to shut down the idea of deathbed visions and dreams with various scientific explanations. But the truth of the matter is that in the majority of these cases, it really *is* Spirit gathering in the room to greet and usher us through our transition. Spirit is there to welcome us with open arms, to provide us with a support system we already know and love. Even if this occurs in such a way that it isn't obvious to the people surrounding the person who's dying, it's still happening. And even in a case where someone dies young and doesn't yet have any friends or family from this current life to greet them in Heaven, they still have a team waiting for them, including angels, spirit guides, and members of their soul family from past lives.

In most experiences of deathbed visions, the person dying communicates that the deceased loved ones are there to "take me away." They'll often say things such as "I have to go now" or "They're ready for me!" Other times, they experience their deceased loved ones gathering in the form of a visitation dream or a series of dreams in the weeks leading up to their passing. These dreams seem more vivid and real (because they are) than any other dream they've had throughout the course of their lifetime.

I've heard stories in which the person who was dying seemed okay or was told they still had six months to a year to live. Then, suddenly, they got up to "get ready for the party." A man who I met at one of my events told me that his mother got dressed, put on her red lipstick, and even placed her hair in curlers the day before she died. He explained that she had dementia, and how this was the first time in at least six months that she had made any effort to get dolled up. The doctors said she still had several months left to live. This man's mother looked him in the eye that day and said, "Honey, I'm leaving now. I'm going somewhere beautiful, you don't have to worry. I've been told there will be a welcome feast and celebration once I've arrived!" He knew in his heart that the doctors were wrong about the timeline and made sure to let his mother know right then and there how much he loved her. She passed away less than twenty-four hours later.

That's the other chill-inducing aspect of all of this. These deathbed visions usually won't occur *unless* that person is close to dying. There have been many instances in which someone who no one would have guessed was going to die anytime soon expressed that they had a vision that a deceased loved one had come for them, only to pass away shortly after.

I've given hundreds of readings in which Spirit has validated that these deathbed visions did, in fact, happen. Most often, this message comes through when the person receiving the reading witnessed the moment and had always wondered whether Grandpa was just being loony due to his meds or if Grandma had truly been present at his bedside, waiting for her husband to join her on the Other Side.

Once we transition, we are released from any pain we may have suffered throughout the course of an illness. I have had many souls come through and tell me that, for as much as they fought throughout the time they were sick, in the end they knew their soul was ready to let go and be at peace. They might not have been able to express this to those left behind while here on Earth, but they still felt it. Think of how beautiful that moment must be when, all at once, the pain completely disappears and your loved one is restored to wholeness. They can move freely once again; there are no more aches and pains, side effects, or symptoms.

There is only peace. That, and also lots of dance parties— think Meredith-Grey-and-Cristina-Yang-type dance parties (if you know me, you'll understand my need to include a *Grey's* reference at least once in this book).

In all seriousness though, I've had Spirit communicate many times that they're now dancing on the Other Side, to really convey this idea of being fully restored. Just the other day, this message particularly resonated with a woman that I gave a spontaneous reading to while in an Uber. Shortly after

the Spirit showed me my symbol for dancing again, he communicated that while he was here on Earth, he underwent
a double limb amputation following a severe case of septic
shock. His daughter validated that not being able to get down
on the dance floor (something he was largely known for—he
even majored in dance during college) was one of the things
her father had struggled with most after losing both of his legs.

WHY THE DYING OFTEN WAIT (OR CHOOSE NOT TO)

People often ask why their loved ones hold on for as long as
they do or pass at the specific moment they do. While the
general timing of passing is already established in our soul
contract, I do believe that this is where the power of free will
most frequently comes into play. Some souls choose to hold
on until all of their loved ones can gather at their bedside.
Often, it doesn't make any logical sense how that person had
the strength within to hold on until that point. Other times,
souls transition at the singular moment when their loved one
who has been there round-the-clock steps out of the room to
grab a snack or answer the phone. Either way, in addition to
using their free will, I also feel that, on a soul level, that person
knows what is best for both themselves and the people they
love—whether it's hanging on or letting go, allowing their relatives to be by their side or passing alone.

The time and scenario in which our loved one passes might
not *feel* like the right way to us, but the soul always knows.
I've had Spirit communicate that they crossed over when
their family and friends weren't by their side either because

it was going to be too difficult for those people to witness or because it would've been too hard for that soul to let go and leave had they been there. Both of these factors come into play, but there is always a purpose.

I am always struck by the beauty of stories about people who give their loved ones permission to let go. Sometimes we give them that permission without even consciously realizing it. A couple of years ago, I met a woman who told me about her visit with her mother the night before her mother's death. At that point, her mother had suffered from various diseases and multiple strokes that had caused significant brain damage, leaving her bedridden and unable to communicate very well. When she did speak, it was usually gibberish, with the occasional "yes" or "no" thrown in. However, that night, out of the blue, she had a moment of complete clarity and asked her daughter, "Is it okay if I leave? Your father is here waiting for me."

The woman was shocked by her mother's sudden awareness and couldn't believe she had just uttered a coherent sentence, let alone the fact that she was referencing her father, who had passed away many years prior. In that moment, the woman thought that her mother believed her husband was still alive. But because she did not want to upset her mother by telling her that her dad was deceased (and assumed the lucid moment was merely a random glitch), she told her, "Sure, Mom! If you would like to leave, go right ahead. But be sure to tell Dad I said 'Hi.'" All the while, this woman knew that her mother couldn't go anywhere without one of the home nurses hoisting her out of bed and into her wheelchair.

It wasn't until she was getting ready for bed that night that the woman had realized what her mother had really been asking her. And, indeed, her mother passed away the very next morning, even though the family had been told she still had at least another six months left to live. Sometimes a soul just needs to know that it's okay to go, that they won't be letting their loved ones down. I also think this relates back to one of the lessons we are supposed to learn in the physical world. In these moments, we gain perspective not just on what we need, but on what our loved ones need. We don't want to lose a parent, but we also don't want them to suffer anymore. We want peace for them. Death after a long illness can give us this perspective and provide us with the compassion to give this gift to someone we love despite our own deep feelings of loss.

Is It Okay to Find Love Again?

One of the messages I've repeatedly received from Spirit is that they want their significant other to be open to finding love again. Regardless of what your partner may have communicated to you prior to passing, you have their full support to resume dating whenever your heart is ready and even remarry if you fall in love with someone new. Even if your girlfriend, boyfriend, or spouse was the most jealous person in the world here on Earth, I promise you that now that they're in the Spirit World, they no longer feel that way. They have a fresh perspective that we do not, and they realize you deserve to love and to be loved. If you haven't realized it by now, Spirit wants nothing more than for you to be happy. Not only that, but sometimes finding love again serves a purpose for the rest of the family too. More often than not, our stepparents, stepsiblings, half-siblings, and so on are all part of our soul family, and are people we were destined to have experiences with in this lifetime.

All of this often leads to other questions: "Are we still married in the afterlife? Who will I be with if I've remarried?"

Any time I give a reading to someone who has lost both of their parents, grandparents, or any other couple who was married for a long period of time, they come through showing me the symbol of two hands holding each other, which for me means that they are still together and are reunited on the Other Side.

Just to clarify, though, relationships on the Other Side don't look like they do in the physical world. If a person has remarried or fallen in love again after the death of their spouse, they'll be reunited with both of those people once they're all in Spirit. Once they cross over, it's not as though they have to choose between their two (or more) spouses or partners. They're not on an episode of *The Bachelorette*, stuck with the difficult decision of who to hand out their final rose to. It doesn't work like that because, again, many of the human emotions (not to mention the institutions) we have here simply don't exist in Heaven. There's no competition; there is just pure love and togetherness.

Spirit tends to have a good sense of humor about it all too. Especially if they were known to be a jokester here on Earth. I've had women who've lost a spouse come to one of my live events after finding love again or getting remarried. If they're there with their new partner, Spirit will sometimes acknowledge that new person by saying something along the lines of, "Well, how awkward is this, bringing the new hubby to meet the old one?" And so I'll clarify, "Is this your husband sitting next to you?" and the person will nod their head while laughing through tears, along with the rest of the audience. I love these kinds of moments, since laughter raises the energy throughout the entire room. This type of message is usually followed up with something along the lines of, "I'm so happy you've found love again. I want you to know that I still love you so much and that you getting remarried could never diminish the love the two of us shared together. It doesn't change the fact that we'll get to be together again in Heaven one day."

YOU MADE THE RIGHT CHOICES

People who lose a loved one following an extended illness often wonder—and even beat themselves up over—whether or not they made the right choices. Spirit is very aware of this particular form of suffering. So many times, Spirit has come through to tell their family that they made all of the right choices and shouldn't torture themselves with questions, could'ves or would'ves. Don't dissect every decision you made and think about how it might have altered the outcome. Based on our soul contracts, the outcome is almost always going to be the same, regardless of how the situation plays itself out.

Spirit also likes to thank those left behind for how hard they tried and for all of the loving things they did. Even the most stubborn of loved ones (here on Earth) will also admit when "You were right after all." I hear different versions of this a lot: "Monica, please acknowledge the fact that I was stubborn as shit and that my wife was right when she told me to go to the doctor to get my nagging cough checked out. She knew something was wrong, but I didn't listen."

Still, many people continue to ask themselves if they did enough. Could they have done more? Or should they have done less? Maybe they should have encouraged their loved one to skip the chemo treatments altogether and just spent their final days together at the beach. The questions we ask ourselves can be endless.

Listen to Spirit when they tell you that everything was exactly as it was meant to be. Remember, Spirit has way more information than you do. They have already been through their life review and can see the big picture. They understand that, without a doubt, every single decision made was the correct one at that moment and that they were all made out of love. Whatever choices you made, they were right. I promise, you can let that go.

Also, regardless of whether or not your loved was coherent leading up to their passing, they are very much aware of everyone who had gathered by their side or cared for them. Whether they had Alzheimer's, were sedated, or even unconscious, they still know about all of the things you did for and said to them. You can let go of any concerns you may have about not saying the things you wish you would have said when your loved one could still hear you. They know what was said. They've heard your thoughts and prayers. They know if you were by their side until the very end, holding their hand. They know the precise moment in which you told them you loved them one final time or apologized for something that had been weighing on you, or when you whispered in their ear, giving them permission to go. For those of you who couldn't make it to your loved one in time or who never got the chance to say goodbye, they still know every single thing you have felt, said, or wanted them to know. And they know all of this whether or not you said it out loud.

Aside from the bigger decisions you made and actions you took on behalf of your loved one, Spirit also consistently acknowledges all of the small things their family and friends did throughout the course of their illness. All of the times you sat at their bedside, brought them meals, talked about the good times, your memories with them, and how much they meant to you—all of that is important. It was important to them in this lifetime, and it continues to be important to them in Heaven.

There's no need for any more should'ves or regrets over the decisions you made or things you did or didn't get to say. Spirit wants you to release any emotional burdens you're carrying around.

You should also know that making the right choices goes beyond their illness. Say you never discussed how your loved one wanted to be laid to rest, whether they wanted to be buried or cremated. You might wonder if you made the right choice or question whether or not it's okay that you spread their ashes, or split them up amongst siblings. Remember, the physical body is nothing more than a vessel to carry us through Earth School. The moment we return to Heaven, we are no longer attached to our bodies. For Spirit, it is not the exact manner of their final resting place that matters—whether they're buried or cremated, for example—but the love and attention you've put in making the decision. They know and can feel that. No matter what choices you make, they are happy.

The same goes even in circumstances in which you need to change the plan your loved one specifically requested prior to their passing. Maybe you realized after the fact that the cost of a casket, gravesite, or tombstone was far beyond your budget, so you had to have them cremated instead. Or you might find that having the huge funeral your loved one wanted you to plan is actually too overwhelming for your family to bear, so you decide to have an intimate memorial service at a relative's home instead. I promise you, Spirit isn't going to be upset with you for these changes now that they're on the Other Side. In fact, they crack jokes about their resting place all the time. They'll say, "While I'm so thankful she cares, tell my mom she can stop making the trip up north every year just to visit my gravesite. The truth is, I'm only there when my family and friends are. My Spirit hops in their car anytime they go to visit the cemetery. The last place you'll find me is six feet underground."

Can I Call Dibs on Grandma's Jewelry?

I have seen death bring many families closer together than ever before. I've also seen death pull families apart, whether it's because of resentment, jealousy, greed, or any other number of human emotions. Just like Spirit knows everything else, they also know when this happens. Not surprisingly, they don't like it.

I've definitely had some sassy mothers come through to deliver messages along the lines of, "Tell my daughter to cut the crap with fighting with her sisters over my jewelry," or a dad say, "If you guys can't divide up the money, then give it all to charity because I don't want to see my passing break the family apart."

If you find yourself in this situation, take a deep breath and think about what you and your family are really fighting over. Be kind, be fair, and remember what's important. Here's a clue: it's not the stuff. It's never the stuff that's important. The vast majority of people know this deep down, but especially during times of grief, it's easy to become stubborn.

Sometimes these reminders from Spirit are exactly what a family needs to hear to snap out of it, remember what's important, and move closer to healing—together.

LOOK AT WHAT YOU HAVE LEARNED

There are so many lessons to be learned from losing a loved one to illness. While you can't have all the answers right now, I encourage you to reflect back on that time. Think about some of the challenges, and notice how much you've grown and how far you've come. My guess is that you now have a very different perspective on living life in the present moment. You probably don't take your health for granted. I bet you appreciate the importance of taking advantage of the time you have now and not sweating the small stuff. Maybe you had a falling-out with a loved one prior to their illness and now realize that it's best to communicate openly and honestly with the people in your life; otherwise, you may lose out on extra time you could've spent with them.

Also, try to remember how your loved one responded to their situation throughout the illness. There are often so many lessons about compassion, love, grace, and patience to take away from these situations.

One day, I was sitting next to an elderly man while waiting for a prescription to be filled at the pharmacy. Out of the blue, he started telling me about his wife of forty-seven years who had died a few years prior after battling a long, drawn-out illness. As he was sharing this with me, I kept hearing the name Betty clear as day in my thought's voice. I was too nervous to tell this gentleman what I did for a living, considering the fact that a lot of older folks have never heard of mediumship, let alone experienced it firsthand.

So instead, I simply asked, "What's your wife's name?"

He looked right up at me and smiled. "Betty," he replied. "And, boy, was she beautiful."

I knew right then and there that I had to get over my fear and give this man a spontaneous message from his beloved wife. She came through with many healing messages, but the one that stood out, and that I could never forget, was this: "Please tell my husband how much I appreciate the way he sat with me around the clock while I was sick, and how thankful I am that he made sure I still had my cup of tea and crossword puzzle each morning."

The man's eyes immediately welled up with tears, and a huge smile spread across his face. Apparently, this was their daily morning routine for their entire marriage.

He said, "Tell my sweetheart that for as much as I appreciate her gratitude, *I'm* the one who is forever thankful. This woman taught me more about patience and love than anyone I've ever met. She also taught me everything I know about strength and perseverance. And she'd be damned if she didn't finish that crossword puzzle every morning! She somehow managed to get them all right even straight out of surgery while the anesthesia was wearing off. She's a fighter, I tell ya."

By this point, we were both laughing amidst the tears.

I've channeled many mothers and fathers who underwent terminal cancer. Their biggest concern throughout their illness was how their children would pick up the pieces and continue on. All of the time, I see from Spirit how people maintained an amazingly positive outlook and perspective during uncertain and difficult times, even at the point when they realized death was near. I also see how many of them fought with every fiber of their being to stay with their family and kids.

If you witnessed this, remember what your loved one would have wanted. Remember how they were able to look at the world, even under the most trying circumstances. Remember how much strength they had. Remember the compassion and patience that you saw, both in your loved one and in yourself.

And even if you didn't witness that, know that's what Spirit wants for you now.

8

Death by Suicide and Overdose

Man, I screwed up. I didn't mean for this to happen. I'm so sorry.

I made some really shitty choices in a desperate attempt to escape from my reality. To escape from despair and struggle. To escape from pain. But I now realize that the mistakes I made have only aggravated the pain. Not for me—I promise you, I'm okay—but for you and everybody else in my life.

If I could go back, I would have made different decisions. At the time, I couldn't see things clearly. I didn't have the clarity that I do now.

Don't get me wrong—I tried. I really did want to get better and to be better for the people that I love. I didn't want to leave you. Yet, in that moment, I wasn't in the right frame of mind. *All I saw was an opportunity to relieve myself from the chaos of life.*

The thing is, there are no freebies, even on the Other Side. The crap I didn't want to deal with (or that I didn't know how to deal with) in the physical world must still be dealt with in the afterlife.

It's an ongoing process of healing those unresolved issues. But, I promise you, I've been working on myself here. I'm learning from my actions. My soul continues to grow and evolve from all of this. I'm making up for mistakes I've made, now that I'm on the Other Side.

I wouldn't blame you if you're still angry with me. You have every right to be. You are more than justified in feeling whatever it is that you're feeling. But I want you to know that forgiveness is usually the first step in finding the strength to really start living your life again. That means not only forgiving me, but forgiving yourself too.

You did everything you could. Don't even think for a second that I blame you. This is no one's fault but my own. I take full responsibility for my actions and for any pain I've caused you.

Please stop reliving those final days and last moments. Instead, relive the good times. The moments in which I was the very best version of myself. That's the part of me that lives on in the afterlife. I'm not in some bad place. There's no such thing as hell.

This is paradise, one that is filled with peace and everlasting love.

LAYERS OF GRIEF

Grief and loss are often accompanied by feelings of guilt, responsibility, and a series of what-ifs. This is exponentially truer for people who lose loved ones as a result of suicide or overdose. This tidal wave of emotion is even more complicated by the fact that there is still a lot of stigma around these types of death.

I've met friends and family members of those who have died from one of these two causes who feel like they have to hide how their loved one passed. They often feel as if they have to suppress some of the intense emotions they are dealing with. All of this can leave those grieving to feel as if they have to go through the loss alone. Because of stigma and various religious and cultural beliefs, those left behind often find themselves without the support system other people who are grieving might have access to.

For those especially close to the deceased, such as parents and spouses, it sometimes even feels as though they are responsible or somehow played a role in their loved one's passing. Like if they would have loved the deceased just a little bit more or done something differently, they would still be alive. Or maybe if their loved one had loved *them* more, they would have stuck around. This leaves room for a lot of confusion and additional pain, on top of dealing with all of the emotions that already come with loss for all of us.

Grief is always layered, but there are several more layers than usual that have to be unraveled in the case of suicide and overdose. "Could I have done more to stop the addiction?"

"Could I have loved them more to prevent the suicide?" "Could I have said something different?" There can also be a false sense of responsibility from "ignoring the warning signs." All of this might be accompanied by anger, which is especially complicated when it involves someone who is no longer here.

Spirit knows about the guilt, shame, resentment, or anger their families and friends are feeling. They often express their sorrow and regret for putting them through this and tell their loved ones that they are not responsible for what happened. All too often, I see parents, siblings, and friends who poured their heart into trying to save their loved one. I have also seen these people come to a reading, crushed by guilt from never having known their loved one was suffering. The message from Spirit is always the same: "I'm so sorry for what I did, but it's not your fault. You couldn't have saved me." Spirit, with the wisdom and perspective that comes from being on the Other Side, recognizes your intentions and efforts, as well as your limitations.

Sometimes—and these can be some of the most difficult readings I do—family or friends reached a point where they were unable to continue to support or protect someone they dearly loved. Managing addiction, particularly, can be tremendously draining, both emotionally and financially. I have had clients overcome with grief when, after years of overwhelming effort and love, they had to let go. On the Other Side, Spirit can see how hard their loved ones tried, and they want nothing more than for them to release their guilt for doing what they had to do. It is my hope that some of the messages I've received from Spirit will help alleviate even a small amount of the shame, isolation, confusion, and pain you might be going through right now.

Luckily, I think that our society is getting better about having open discussions regarding mental illness, depression, suicide, and addiction. Hopefully, one day this will allow people who go through these experiences to feel less isolated and to have a better understanding of how mental illness and addiction really work. Maybe this will spare those left behind from the complicated maze of guilt and what-ifs.

One of the most powerful readings I've ever done happened at one of my live events last year. The soul who came through had been your typical twentysomething SoCal girl. She described herself as blonde, tan, athletic, and beautiful. She had a beachy, bubbly, go-with-the-flow, good-vibes type of feel to her. Her entire purpose on Earth was to do charity work and give back. She was beautiful inside and out. In short, she was the last person anyone would have ever in a million years expected to be struggling with depression or any type of mental illness. I have heard many other souls say that, from the outside looking in, no one would have ever guessed that anything was wrong. In fact, the average person would probably be very jealous of their life!

The message Spirit wanted to share with the audience that day was that we should all make the effort to ask people in our lives if they are okay. To open the door to these conversations, even if it's with a person who seems outwardly happy or like they couldn't possibly be struggling based on their life circumstances. Open up to the people around you. Ask what they are going through. Be willing to have vulnerable and meaningful conversations.

This Spirit also wanted to encourage people dealing with mental health issues to overcome shame and reach out for help. From the Other Side, she can now clearly see that many people would have dropped everything to be there for her had they known. They wouldn't have judged her or thought she didn't have the "right" to suffer when her life seemed to be so idyllic.

By the time Spirit finished delivering this message, there wasn't a dry eye in the room.

I have noticed that, at events, I often have a Spirit come through who suffered from mental illness that resulted in suicide or overdose. Often, these souls make it to the front of the line, even if they are communicating to a friend rather than a family member. (This is significant, because typically family members need to hear from their loved ones more than friends do.) I don't think this is an accident. I think that, as a society, we need to hear these messages. Yes, today we are able to have a more open dialogue about mental illness and addiction. But we've still got a long way to go. Spirit wants to help us with this conversation, to provide an understanding of both what those who cross over as a result of mental illness and addiction go through and, also, what their surviving loved ones are left to grapple with.

THE TRAUMA OF OVERDOSE AND SUICIDE

Before we get into the more spiritual side of these types of death, I feel like it's important to first address one of the specific issues I see with those who are left behind in this way. Losing someone can be traumatic in and of itself. It can be traumatic to see someone spend months or years battling an illness. It is traumatic to lose a loved one who passed well "before their time." But, by nature, overdose and suicide can feel uglier and come with more shame than other types of death. They are inherently traumatizing.

Even when people are able to discuss their loved one's experience and cause of death in an open and honest way, it's often still difficult to discuss some of the more nitty-gritty and perhaps even gruesome details of it. I've seen many instances in which the person I'm channeling for was the one who found their loved one's body upon their death. I only get a glimpse of the pain this causes for the people left behind when I'm channeling, and it is incredibly intense. Those who have actually been through this experience have to live with that painful memory for years or even their entire lifetime. That changes a person, and I can't imagine what a difficult experience it is.

Your loved ones in Spirit want you to know that they are no longer in pain with the hope that you, too, can move forward into a place of peace and understanding.

One thing that can help with this is remembering not just how your loved one died or the circumstances leading up to their death, but also the good times. Many souls who crossed over as the result of suicide or addiction come through to remind their family and friends that there were two sides to them; the side they showed on any given day was like flipping a coin. Some days were good, and other days were bad.

But when they were good, they were great! Spirit wants you to be able to remember the good days and to try to focus on all of the positive times you spent together. Remember them for the amazing ability they had to connect with others, for their compassion, for the gift they had for using their quirky sense of humor to bring a smile to someone's face. Remember them for the beautiful, intricate, and complex human beings they were. Like everyone else, these souls are not just a single experience. As one soul so beautifully put it when I gave her mother a reading, "Tell my mom I was so much greater than the problems I had." That message goes for all of us, but it is especially poignant in cases of suicide and overdose.

Those who have died from suicide often want their family to know that they were not in their right mind or were unable to think straight in the moment when they made that final decision. They explain that they were sick and that it was like any other illness a person is unable to recover from. To them, it truly felt like there was no other solution or way out. While there may have been other options to a clear head and inner peace, these souls were unable to recognize that at the time of their death. They want their loved ones to know that they never wanted to hurt them either; they just couldn't hold on anymore or didn't even have the presence of mind to think through the collateral damage of their actions. There is nothing you could have done differently, and you are in no way, shape, or form to blame. Release yourself from that burden.

THE DIFFERENCE BETWEEN SUICIDE AND OVERDOSE

There are a lot of overlapping elements between suicide and overdose, but there are also some key differences. On top of that, every situation has its own unique factors.

It can start to get a little complicated here. As we have discussed, nothing in life is set in stone. Despite our soul contracts, we all come to Earth with free will. Spirit has shown me that suicide is not a concrete aspect of anyone's soul contract. It is a choice made of free will.

We are never meant or destined to die by suicide. Instead, coming into a lifetime, some of us might have the *potential* for suicide in our soul contract. The experience of dealing with depression or mental illness could be part of someone's soul contract in a way that might ultimately lead to suicide. More often than not, Spirit tells me that the difficult experiences they went through in the physical world were meant to eventually bring them to a place of healing, learning, and acceptance. However, some people are unable to reach that place here on Earth regardless of how hard they try. In the event that someone does die by suicide, that choice and act is a decision made of their own volition. This is why the soul contracts of everyone peripherally involved in a suicide can shift; it's not an event that was dictated, so it can also alter the course of other people's lifetime trajectories.

While suicide is never specifically dictated in a soul contract, overdose does not necessarily fall under this same category. Addiction is usually written into soul contracts. Sometimes overdose may be part of a soul contract, but that works on a more case-by-case basis. This is because, unlike suicide, overdoses are often not intentional. Those who passed because of an overdose will take responsibility for their death, but generally they also say that it was an accident that they didn't intend for or ever mean to happen. Because of this, death by overdose works in a way closer to accidents, illnesses, and even old age: they pass when it's their time.

This, of course, begs the question of why anyone chooses to have these experiences in their soul contract. Personally, I view the souls of those who struggled with mental illness or addiction as great teachers. Spirit has shown me that these challenges, as difficult, traumatic, or heartbreaking as they may be, have brought them and the people around them a greater, more evolved understanding of themselves and the world (whether in this life or the next). They are sometimes the ones who have lived many lifetimes, because it takes a strong soul to contend with these experiences. They tend to get the growth and wisdom of ten lifetimes rolled into one in the process of living with mental illness or addiction. When a soul comes through who has died from one of these circumstances, they often talk explicitly and in detail about the experience of mental illness and addiction because there is so much that most people don't understand—and need to. Without having gone through mental illness or addiction firsthand, it's impossible to understand the hold it can have over a person and the toll it can take. It does not make for an easygoing life of rainbows and butterflies.

While death by suicide and overdose are both incredibly tragic and traumatic, there is a lot to be learned from them on the soul and big-picture levels. Despite the fact that suicide is a free will choice, it doesn't mean that the soul who takes their life and those who are impacted by it don't learn and evolve as a result. They certainly do; it's just that those specific actions were probably not a part of their contract.

SAFE AND SOUND IN HEAVEN

There are certain religious and cultural beliefs surrounding suicide and overdose that don't apply to other types of death. One of the big ones is the belief—or fear—that people who die in this way don't go to Heaven. Instead, they are sent to some sort of purgatory, or even hell. I am here to tell you that, just like everyone else, every single soul I have ever channeled who has died in this manner has expressed that they are safe and at peace in Heaven. They are now in a good place. In fact, they are in the best place.

Not only that, but Spirit has told me time and time again that there is no such thing as hell. Once we cross out of this realm and into the next, there is only one option: eternal love and complete peace. More than anything, your loved ones want you to know and trust in this. I would say this is the most frequent thing I hear from the souls of those who died by overdose and suicide. It is very important to them that you know this. While they may not have the same experience as everyone else here on Earth, they do in Heaven.

People who die by overdose or suicide are greeted by and reunited with their loved ones and surrounded by angels. They feel an immediate and overwhelming sense of peace and love. Everything about stepping into soul form is just as beautiful and peaceful as it is for everyone else who crosses over. They must then confront and work through the choices they made, but they can do so free of the pain and trauma that would have clouded them in the physical world.

LIFE REVIEW AFTER SUICIDE

The one aspect of crossing over that is a little bit different for those who die by suicide or for any soul who has made a terrible choice, regardless of whether or not they died at that point or many, many, years later (murderers, drunk drivers, and the like can all fall under this category) is their life review. It is here that they begin to understand and feel the consequences of their actions.

Like everyone else, they watch back over their life and get to see the bigger picture. They see their life not just through their own eyes but also through the eyes of everyone else who loved them or played a role in this lifetime. It is here that they understand the entire impact and consequences of those final decisions they made while on Earth. In that way, their life review is an extension of their human experience. They are continuing to learn and grow through the things they went through in the physical world. While this is true for all of us, it is more pronounced for people who die in these ways.

They might have regrets; I know this because I often hear Spirit express regrets when they come through in these circumstances. Part of my Spirit Dictionary is the phrase "I screwed up." For me, this almost always indicates an overdose or suicide.

Spirit will acknowledge that they realize what they did was a mistake, and during their life review, they do feel a great sense of responsibility, regret, and shame for the pain, anguish, and suffering they caused their family and friends who are left behind. They understand not only the initial traumatic impact but also that it will continue to affect others for the remainder of their lifetime on Earth. They realize that the choice to end their life was not a get out of jail free card or some kind of magic solution to all of their struggles.

From this vantage point, Spirit can see all of the things they are missing out on or the parts of their soul contract that they would have otherwise been able to accomplish. There is a sense of regret about the lessons they won't get to learn. This isn't just about them, though. On the Other Side, Spirit understands that they also did not fulfill their agreement to the members of their soul family in terms of the lessons they were meant to help them learn and the role they were meant to play in their earthly lives. They did not honor their commitment, and Spirit also feels some regret surrounding that. In short, during their life review, these souls understand the ripple effect their life and death had, just like all of our lives and deaths do.

I understand that these feelings of guilt, shame, and regret might seem to contradict some of the other things Spirit has shared about life on the Other Side. Nearly all of the time, Spirit talks about how all of these heavier human emotions do not have a place in Heaven. However, it's also true that suicide especially is an exception to this—and that is because of the distinguishing factor of free will. It's also important to clarify that these emotions apply only to the life review process and serve as a means for the soul to gain more perspective and to learn from their free will choices for lifetimes moving forward. Outside of the life review, these souls are just as peaceful and brimming with love as every other soul on the Other Side.

Despite the heavier experience of dealing with these emotions during their life review, these souls continue to grow and evolve as they get a clearer view of their experience in their most recent lifetime and how they might have done things differently. We are always growing, whether it's a result of our soul contract or free will.

Regardless of what the soul may be experiencing during this review, I promise you it's all internal. There is absolutely no shame, judgment, anger, or anything else of that variety toward the soul from their spirit guides, angels, soul family, God, or even their higher self. All of these entities fully understand what that soul went through in their lifetime and surround that soul with nothing but compassion and love. The soul will soon understand this and move to that place of nonjudgment as well. The feelings experienced throughout their life review are a purely individual experience that is merely an extension of their human experience. The same goes for everyone, even those who have had extenuating circumstances such as harming or murdering others in the course of their lifetime.

All of this is also part of the reason why it's so important to your loved ones on the Other Side that you are able to heal—that you don't beat yourself up and continue on to find joy. They understand that they have caused you sadness, grief, and perhaps even anger that you need to work through. They want you to go through that natural process for your own well-being. But, ultimately, your happiness and healing help their healing journey as well. Of course, this has to happen on your own timeline, but understand that no one is in more support of your renewed happiness than your loved one. With every layer of grief you are able to peel back, they will also become stronger, happier, closer to you, and more filled with light.

Does the Higher Self Judge?

It's important to distinguish between the experience of feeling emotions like regret, guilt, and shame as a soul in Heaven versus feeling them here on Earth in human form. Here, we have the tendency to beat ourselves up. We can hold on to those things we feel we have done wrong and cling to any sense of regret we might have about harm or pain we have caused others long past the point where those feelings are productive, necessary, or even relevant.

While souls who have crossed over do feel some of these emotions during their life review, they don't have the same impact they have on humans. The way Spirit understands emotion and impact is distinct—like the difference between self-criticism and self-reflection. On the Other Side, the soul is reunited with its higher self. That part of them that knows and understands everything about *all* of the lifetimes that soul has lived and can see a much, much bigger picture than we can imagine.

The higher self is aware of what happened in this past lifetime, but it also remembers all of the amazing, wonderful, incredible things that same soul has done and accomplished throughout all of time. It remembers all of the lessons the soul has learned and all of the acts of kindness and compassion that soul has done.

I often have souls who have died from suicide, overdose, or any other sort of mistake that they take responsibility for reminding their loved ones—particularly mothers—that the soul is not defined by the choice they made. They are so much more than their mistakes, problems, and struggles, and none of this takes away from the joy, happiness, and love in this past lifetime or any other.

IT'S NOT BECAUSE OF WHAT YOU DIDN'T DO

Everything we've talked about up to now brings us back to the same point: your loved one's death had nothing to do with you. There is nothing you could or should have done differently. Still, I know this feeling is incredibly difficult to overcome when you're going through it. I want to share with you a recent reading to help drive this point home.

Not too long ago, I did an event in Seattle. The morning after the event, I was still sensing Spirit even though I was trying to keep my light switch turned off. As I was going down the elevator to get breakfast, I overwhelmingly felt a woman's son trying to come through. He gave me the sense that she was in the very same building as I was. I heard, "Don't let my mom leave!" As soon as I walked into the area of the hotel where the breakfast buffet was being served, I noticed a woman talking on the phone at a table across the room. I immediately knew it was her son who was communicating, and that I needed to deliver a message. I felt nervous about approaching her, but walked up and asked the friend she was sitting with if I could pull her aside. "Of course!" she responded. Turns out, they knew exactly who I was and had actually been at my event the evening before. At first, it pained me that this woman hadn't gotten a reading the previous night, because I could feel how badly she needed it. But I later came to realize that Spirit meant for things to happen as they did.

As soon as we sat down together, I learned from Spirit that this woman's son had died of an overdose just six weeks prior. While I normally recommend that people wait longer to have a reading following the death of a loved one, I realized that this woman's son felt he needed to come through and had understood that the event was not the place to do it. This woman wasn't ready to go through all of these fresh, raw emotions in front of hundreds of people. She needed intimacy. However, she also needed to hear from him.

For the next thirty minutes, the son addressed all of the questions his mom was grappling with. The rest of what happened, I'll let you read in her own words. She sent in her story to share in this book, and I'm so glad she did.

> I walked toward Monica, and she guided me to a quiet spot in the lounge area of the lobby. We sat facing each other, our knees almost touching, and she looked me directly in the eye and said, "I hope you don't think that your son didn't

come through last night because he is in a bad place or that he doesn't want to give you validation and healing. I have no doubt that he is safe and at peace in Heaven, but that it was just not meant to happen in front of all those people."

Then, Monica took both my hands in hers and tried to speak as she held back tears. In a shaky voice she said, "This is going to sound crazy but just now, as I was coming down the elevator, I clearly heard an urgent voice say to me, 'Don't let my mom leave!' I could sense a young male trying to come through for his mother, and as I stepped out of the elevator, I knew I had to find you."

She paused and then said, "Is it okay with you if I share what he is telling me?" For a moment I felt like I was outside of my body looking in. Could this really be happening? I quickly nodded my head in stunned silence, not taking my eyes off Monica. She spoke calmly and said, "He's pointing to my fiancé, I'm getting the image of him clearly. Usually when I see this, it means there's a name connection. My fiancé's name is Tyler, was your son's name Tyler?" I shook my head no, and then she said, "Was his name Ty?" And with a huge smile I said, "Yes, yes that's what we called him. His full name is Tyrell." Then Monica said, "Okay, he's with us. I have him here now." I let out a deep exhale; I'm pretty sure I had been holding my breath the whole time up to that point. Monica continued, again looking me directly in the eyes. "He wants you to know that he's sorry." I burst into tears. I immediately knew this was my son, and I knew that "sorry" would be the first thing he would say. I know my son, and I know he would have deep regrets about his situation.

Through Monica, Ty told me that he was sorry for all the pain and suffering that he had caused his dad and I during his struggle with addiction, and that we needed to understand that there was nothing that we could have done differently. There was nothing we could have done to change the outcome. He said that I was the best mom and that I did everything right—it just wasn't meant to be. He said it was his time to go and that, for as painful as it is, he wanted me to not give up on living my life. He told me that I needed to go on without his presence in the physical sense.

This was especially meaningful because, a few months before, when Ty agreed to go to the recovery center, he said to me, "Mom, there is a good chance that I might die, and if I do, I need you to go on with your life. The thought of my death ruining your life is unbearable to me. I need you to promise me that you will be okay with it." Needless to say, it was impossible for me to make that promise, but now that he has passed away, I am doing my best to stay strong and continue on with my life for the sake of my husband and our twenty-one-year-old daughter. The fact that he mentioned this through Monica was so surreal. It proved how important this was to him, not only in life but also in death. He also said that he was at peace now and in a good place, so there was no need for me to worry. Ty and I were very close throughout his struggle with addiction, and he seemed to worry about me almost as much as I worried about him.

There was a lot of shame and regret on his part. Ty regretted that he had gone down this path and caused so much heartbreak to those who loved him. With tears streaming down my face and snot bubbles coming out of my nose, I told him (and Monica) that he had nothing to be sorry for and that we loved him no matter what had happened, and always would. He told me that he loved me and his dad and his sister, and also mentioned his love for his grandparents, who he was very close to during his struggle, and who supported him unconditionally. He then went on to say that he was with family of ours who had passed before him (and who Monica brought through by name).

Ty also said that he thought it would have been hard for me to stand up in front of all those people if he came through at the event. He was right; I would have bawled my eyes out. So, needless to say, I am thrilled that he found a way to connect with Monica and asked her not to let me leave the hotel. The way it all happened seems so unbelievable, but Monica explained that it was all meant to be. I thanked her over and over again for bringing Ty through for me and she said, "I appreciate that, but it's really Ty that you should be thanking. He planned this whole thing and made this meeting happen."

What a gift and a blessing! It's hard to put into words how amazing it felt to connect with my son in the Spirit World and to learn that he is okay and at peace. All I ever wanted for Ty was peace and happiness, and he assured me that he is in the best place he could be and wants me to focus on living my own life. Losing a child is the most painful experience a parent could ever face, and I don't think I will ever get over it. However, to honor my son's wishes, I will do my best to live in the moment and not take anything or anyone for granted.

After Ty passed away, my daughter got a tattoo on her inner left bicep because Ty was left-handed. It reads: Livin' the Dream. This is what Ty used to tell my daughter during their phone calls in answer to how he was doing at the recovery center. It is what he hoped for in the future when he was clean and sober. My husband also got a tattoo of a ram's head silhouette on his shoulder in reference to Ty's birth sign. And, yes, I got a tattoo as well. It is on my inner left forearm and it has his name with angel wings on either side of it because he will always be my angel.

This reading was definitely not the first time I've heard Spirit tell their family that they did not fail him or her; that it wasn't their fault, and that all they want for them is happiness. Just as this son did, so many other souls want their family and friends to know that there were certain struggles and experiences they had to go through. Most of all, Spirit wants those who are left behind to know that they recognize how much you love them, how much you did for them, and how much you sacrificed and set aside in an effort to lead them down any path possible to get them clean.

Remember that their soul agreed to the addiction or the mental illness and all of the experiences and challenges that come with it. Even in the case of suicide, where one's death may have been the result of free will, their struggles were always something they signed up for in their soul contract. The good, the bad, the ugly, the ups and downs, all of that was always meant to be. There was never anything that Ty's mom or anyone else could do to control these circumstances and all of the collateral impact. Of course, that is not to say their efforts are wasted or unwanted—in fact, they have a tremendous impact that we are unlikely to ever fully realize in this lifetime. The sincere effort we all make to be present, helpful, and supportive enlivens our soul and brings us growth, peace, and healing in this life and the ones that will come after. Because of this, not only do the souls of our loved ones agree to walk this path here on Earth, but, for as unbelievable as it might feel, so did you. No matter how weak you may feel in this moment, you are strong enough to handle all of this. Deep down, you know that about yourself.

This is all a part of your loved one's legacy, and it's also part of yours. Even if their death resulted from a decision of free will, the circumstances that led to it were not. They were meant to teach and evolve both the soul going through it and the others it impacted. That is why it's so important for Spirit to communicate the message to others: "Don't make the same mistakes I did." There *is* a net positive impact here. You just don't have the full perspective to see it yet.

In fact, this teaching often becomes part of the role of that soul on the Other Side. To share their story and teach people who are struggling that there *is* a bigger picture, there *are* options, and there *are* other ways out. Spirit wants those who are dealing with addiction, mental illness, or suicidal thoughts to know that there is hope and they don't have to go through it alone. For as much as mediumship and communication with Spirit is about bringing healing and comfort, another huge aspect of the work is to educate people through the experiences those before us have gone through and to save them from making the same choices and mistakes. Souls like this are teaching and educating even from the Other Side.

9

Losing a Child

For this chapter, I think it's really important that I take a moment to address a few things before we really dive in. In fact, it's not just me who wanted to do this—Spirit woke me up in the middle of the night with specific instructions and requests for me to restructure this chapter. Imagine my panic hearing these messages less than twenty-four hours prior to my manuscript deadline. But when Spirit speaks, I've gotta listen! As I've told you, Spirit can be a little pushy sometimes.

So, here are some things to keep in mind before reading this chapter:

If you're a bereaved parent, there's a strong chance you may have picked up this book for the first time, glanced over the table of contents, and then flipped through to skip ahead to this chapter. I completely understand why you would do this, considering this chapter was written with the sole intention of bringing the utmost comfort and healing to people like you, who have faced the worst kind of loss. That being said, Spirit wants to stress the importance of you reading the preceding chapters before this one. Otherwise, you'll be missing out on important pieces that will help you better understand this chapter. This goes for anyone reading this book who might feel compelled to skip ahead, but especially grieving parents.

If you'd like to skip the chapters where I share my background and how I came into my gifts—totally fine. But at the very least, I highly recommend you read the Introduction and Chapters Four through Eight before starting this one. Otherwise, you'll likely feel as if this one is incomplete, or you might be left struggling with a lot of questions and maybe even feel a bit frustrated. This is due to the fact that there are certain key concepts and messages that I've shared throughout the chapters leading to this one that I know Spirit really wants you to hear so that you can get the most healing and as many answers as possible.

This chapter contains content that might trigger difficult emotions you're still grappling with, especially if your loss was recent. There may be certain stories or examples that remind you of the way your loved one died or bring feelings to the surface that you've been shutting out for a while. My intention when working with any parent who has lost a child is to provide comfort, healing, and reassurance that their son or daughter on the Other Side is okay and at peace. Yet, as a medium, part of my duty to the Spirit World is to serve as a teacher (the same goes for many of your children on the

Other Side). Together, with Spirit, I'm meant to share certain messages and ideas. I try to do this as gently, yet honestly, as possible, but I realize that for someone who has faced the most horrific type of loss, the idea that your child died for the learning and soul growth of either themselves or for that of their family left behind can seem absolutely absurd and even downright disrespectful. I don't blame you if you feel that way. I can't even fathom the pain you must be going through, and, to be fully transparent, some of these concepts might only add salt to your wounds right now. But, over time, I hope this information will start to bring you clarity and comfort.

Please know that nothing in this chapter is meant to soothe your pain or put a Band-Aid over your aching heart. If there's one thing I've learned working with bereaved parents over the years, it's that grief is forever. You will never get over or move on from the loss of your child. The grief of losing a son or daughter you brought into this world will never end. It may soften over time, but you feel that pain in each breath you take until the day you die and are reunited with them. I realize better than most that everything I share in this chapter won't make the pain go away. There's nothing that I or anyone else could say that will make you hurt any less. I'm sure there are no words or answers that will ever address your mind or heart to your complete satisfaction.

Yet, Spirit has told me I'm meant to share what I do hear and learn from them. Many of these concepts are difficult to wrap your head around and are far bigger than our human comprehension. As you read this, I only ask that you do so with an open mind and an open heart. Take whatever resonates with you, and leave behind the rest. I only want this information to heal, not to hurt you in any way.

If you're reading this and you haven't lost a child, this chapter is still for you.

My hope is this information helps you support others in their grief, whether now or at some point down the road. I hope that you, too, can be a messenger for Spirit. Not in the mediumship sense of channeling Spirit, but in being there as a companion for someone who's lost a child. Perhaps you'll have an opportunity to start a conversation about death and grief, and provide some clarity or comfort to someone else through some of what you'll learn over the course of these pages.

When you lose a child, you join a club that no one wants to belong to.

An ugly, messy, downright unbearable kind of pain warrants entry into this club. No one truly understands this type of pain and loss unless they've been through the same unwelcome chaos. When I give readings to bereaved parents, the empath in me gets the slightest peek into what it feels like. While the circumstances that have led parents to me over the years varies across all types of death, their pain is always the same. Feeling even one percent of that pain is so intense that it impacts me for days after the fact. I can't even fathom what it feels like to go through this type of loss firsthand. I have yet to parent a child of my own, so I don't even know what that kind of love feels like. I've been told you never know what true love is until you have your own precious bundle of joy. That kind of love is not in my frame of reference (at least not yet), so I can't even begin to really capture or put into words what I wish I could. But I will do my best and can only hope I do right by each of you.

With that out of the way, I can now share the channeled message from Spirit for this chapter:

It doesn't matter how much time has passed. As the world keeps turning, yours still feels like it's come to a complete standstill.

I know you dream of the life I could have had, if only I hadn't been so cruelly taken from you. You often wonder what I would be like today. Who would I have become? Would I be bubbly and outgoing, or shy and reserved? Would my passion be playing sports, or would I want to spend my days making music?

I feel your pain anytime you think of all the milestones you won't get to celebrate with me in the physical world—teaching me how to drive, watching me graduate, helping me get ready on my wedding day, or being by my side when I have children of my own. Every milestone, every holiday, every birthday, and every angelversary. I know how hard these days—and every day—can be for you.

But I promise, I haven't left your side. I'm not missing out! My time on Earth may have been cut short, but my soul lives on forever.

I want you to know that it's okay to talk about me. In fact, I love it when you do! And I want you to remember the person that I was (and still am) rather than the person I might've become.

I want you to know that you will survive this, even if doesn't feel that way right now. You'll never stop missing me, but you will learn how to go on. You'll be able to move forward, and one day maybe even find the strength to form a smile without even the slightest trace of sadness resting beneath it. For through your tears and frustration, you will come out the other end as an even stronger and more adaptable human being.

Find ways to incorporate compassion and love into everything you do. I promise it will help you ease the sorrow.

Trust that I haven't left you; I've merely taken on another form. I see you, and I hear you. I find ways to send you signs that let you know you're not alone. The songs on the radio, hug dreams, heart-shaped clouds and leaves, butterflies, dragonflies, ladybugs, rainbows...there are so many signs I use to get your attention. You must simply open up your heart to receiving them.

More than anything, I hope you give yourself permission to live again, to laugh, to love, to forgive, and to enthusiastically celebrate each and every day of this crazy thing we call life.

I'll see you on the Other Side. Until then, look out for my hellos from Heaven. I promise you, I'm right here.

THE TOUGHEST LESSON

There are few stronger souls among us than those who walk the path of a parent who loses a child. Even though I talk to these parents frequently and have an understanding of the bigger picture thanks to Spirit, it's still so difficult for me to wrap my head around what they go through. Losing a child is one of the toughest lessons to take on in Earth School. It is so deeply painful.

Although it may be almost impossible to fathom, these parents chose this path as part of their soul contract. Sometimes, but not always, they chose it for the evolution and growth of their own soul. I don't know this for a fact, but I often wonder if the souls who chose this path are in their last semester here in Earth School and have decided to sign up for advanced quantum physics to roll all the lessons of ten lifetimes into one. I wonder if they go into this life knowing, "Okay, this is going to be a really difficult semester in Earth School, but then I'll finally get to graduate."

There is often a purpose for your child too. I can't tell you how many times Spirit has come through to tell me they learned more in the physical world in five years' worth of time than they would have in ninety years. They see life entirely through the outlook of a child, which provides them a unique, joyous, and beautiful perspective of the world they would not have otherwise.

Another thing to know is that the death of a child almost always rolls out to impact many more lives beyond that of the parents and children. It's almost like these souls are "taking one for the team." In this instance, that team usually consists of the soul family. However, sometimes it's bigger than that. Sometimes families go through this because their community, society, or the world at large needs to learn from their experience. Imagine the strength in that. Some of the parents who deal with this level of pain aren't even doing it for the sake of their own growth; they are doing it purely for the ultimate evolution of others. It's staggering to think about.

Despite the amount of pain you might be in right now, know that you can get through this, even though it may not feel like that at the moment. None of this is to take away from the pain you may be feeling. Losing a child is the most difficult experience any one of us could ever go through in this physical world. But also know that there is a greater purpose, and you can not only survive, but even thrive—no matter how unimaginable that might feel right now. In fact, that is exactly what your child wants for you.

Grieving is a bit like opening a present that has been wrapped a hundred times. We have to pull back layer after layer after layer until, eventually, we get to open the gift. With loss, we are peeling back the layers of grief until we reach the gift of peace or closure. Especially when it comes to losing a child. You will never forget, but you can start to heal. This might take five years, it might take ten, and it might take even longer than that. But I hope that, at some point, you will be able to see that there is a greater purpose. This didn't happen because you did anything wrong and somehow "deserve" this pain and grief. In fact, it is nothing but admirable that your soul agreed to take this on and is able to bear the burden of this loss in this lifetime for the growth and evolution of your child, yourself, and others around you.

In this chapter, we will look at losing a child through the lens of death by illness or accident, miscarriage, termination, and stillborn birth. Whatever the specifics of your situation, the messages from Spirit are largely the same: their soul lives on forever, they continue to watch over you, and no matter how abbreviated their time on Earth might have been, their soul still learned and grew in their time here. And now that continues in Heaven.

How Can I Help?

When someone we love is grieving any type of loss, but *especially* the loss of a child, many of us struggle with how to help or what to say. An important thing to keep in mind when you're trying to support someone through this kind of loss is that grief takes many forms. Shake yourself loose from all the shoulds and well-meaning expectations about how you believe the bereaved parents are supposed to act. What most people need is a judgment-free place where they get to decide what they need. Just the simple fact that you are reading this box, that you want to help, is a good first step. Let them know they are not alone.

Here are some recommendations:

- Offer your help. Run errands, clean up the kitchen, cook some food, do whatever little things you can to help alleviate some of the weight of daily life responsibilities. It can be difficult enough for a parent who has lost a child to get out of bed, especially in the early days. Give them one less thing to worry about.

- Be a steady presence. Their whole world has been turned upside down. Be someone they can rely on, a cornerstone upon whom they can take a breath. This can be as simple as texting every morning, going to church with them, or simply sitting quietly with them when they don't want to be alone.

- Remember their loss. Say their child's name, or share a memory of them. Donate to a charity in the child's memory, or send flowers on their birthday or the anniversary of their passing. Make sure the parents know their child will always be remembered.

- Listen. There's not much advice that can help someone in a time of grief. Instead, let them work through their emotions in their own time. Validate their feelings, and acknowledge how difficult it must be.

THERE ARE NO WHAT IFS?

So many parents who have lost children get trapped in a game of "what if?" What if I handled my child's treatment differently? What if I had looked twice before crossing that intersection? What if I hadn't had an abortion? What if I had done something differently during my pregnancy?

When it comes to matters of death—even with children—there are no what ifs. There is nothing you could have done differently to result in an alternate outcome. As a parent, this is very difficult to accept. Part of being a mom or a dad is feeling a sense of responsibility to care for your child and to keep them safe and healthy. You serve the role of protector. Because of this, I've noticed that even in cases where parents lose children from cancer or another terminal disease, they often still feel a strong sense of guilt and responsibility. They feel like if they'd only done something differently, their child would still be here. This feeling is exacerbated to the nth degree when a child dies in an accident or through some sort of fatal mistake, regardless of whether or not the parent was even present at that moment.

Every parent I have known, in my own life and through my work, does whatever they can to provide a good life for their child. They try to balance letting them grow with keeping them safe, a stressful endeavor even when things go right. But unfortunately, sometimes accidents happen, as much as parents try to avoid them. Every so often, I bring through a child that passed suddenly from a freak accident. Along with experiencing the grief of losing their child, these parents are often suffering through the guilt of what they perceive as failing to protect their child.

One of the most difficult readings I have ever done was for a mother who lost her child when her husband accidentally hit him as he was backing a car out of the driveway. During that reading, I got the smallest hint of the kind of pain this woman and her husband were in, and I knew how desperately they needed healing and forgiveness from their child.

When their son came through, he very clearly told me, "There's nothing to forgive!" He told me that he knew that it was an accident and that he had known on Earth, and still knew in Heaven, how much his parents loved him. Their son said that though he loved his time with his parents, it was just his time to go.

I know it can be difficult to understand how it could ever be time for a young child to pass, especially under these kinds of circumstances, but he confidently told his parents that he had lived the life he was meant to live. He reminded them that he was still and always would be with them and told them how badly he wished they could heal and move forward.

Spirit's message is consistent: forgive yourself. Don't hold on to the burden of what could, should, or would have been. You did not let your child down. You are not responsible for this. Your child has none of the feelings or judgments that you might be holding on to. Your child understands the big picture and the purpose. You can release yourself from all of the heaviness and pain that the sense of responsibility brings with it.

YOUR CHILD IN HEAVEN

People often ask me if their lost babies or children continue to grow and mature on the Other Side. Parents who lose a child through miscarriage, stillbirth, or termination tend to be particularly curious about this. They want to know if that baby's soul is aware of what's happening and if their awareness has advanced.

When souls who passed as babies come through, I usually see an image of a baby wrapped in a pink or blue blanket, depending upon their gender. I usually see children at the age they were when they passed. Just like anyone else, children on the Other Side have distinct personalities, mannerisms, and physical traits that love to shine when they come through in a reading. For example, if your child said their Ws or Rs funny in this life, I might hear that when they communicate from Heaven. This could be one of their ways of validating that it's really them. Despite the childlike appearance and mannerisms that are communicated to me during a reading, the souls of these children continue to grow and evolve on the Other Side. They can communicate at a very deep level, just like any other soul can. They are very aware of what's happening in your life, what you've gone through, and what they've gone through. They understand things that you cannot yet understand. Their cognition and awareness are no different than they would be if they had lived to be eighty.

The same applies for children who may have had disabilities such as autism or emotional or intellectual delays. When they initially cross over, I get a sense for who they were here, but then they will acknowledge they no longer contend with the same constrictions in Heaven that they did here on Earth.

Despite all the growth and wisdom these children attain on the Other Side, what makes these spirits so special is that they continue to hold on to their childlike essence. They are filled with wonder and appreciation; they are shy or funny; they bounce off of the walls; and they have the ability to make an entire room burst out laughing. It's beautiful and powerful.

Time on the Other Side

Time in Heaven isn't like it is here on Earth. There, it is endless and boundless. Time doesn't involve any restrictions.

It just doesn't exist there like it does for us here in Earth School.

Even if sixty years passes between the time when your loved one dies and goes to Heaven and when you die, it will feel as if no time has passed at all once you meet again. For them, no time has passed. Also, they've been with you all along. They've witnessed you growing and changing. They've been by your side the entire way through your lifetime here on Earth. Yes, you are being reunited in a different way on the Other Side, but the fact remains that they have never left you.

MISCARRIAGE, STILLBORN BIRTHS, AND ABORTION

All of the information in this chapter applies equally to cases of miscarriage, abortion, and stillborn babies. I don't want to get political, but I do feel like it is important to mention that Spirit communicates that the soul of a child exists beyond the confines of what we consider "life"—the soul is not suddenly created when a woman becomes pregnant. It has always and will always exist, but is then attached to a physical presence from the moment of conception. It is not nothingness; it is life. This means that regardless of how quickly you lost your baby, they will still go through a life review and continue to watch over you in the same way any of your other loved ones would.

Earlier I talked about how the souls of our babies hang out with our soul family on the Other Side until they are born here on Earth. If you're wondering how it can be simultaneously true that life starts at the moment of conception and your unborn children can be on the Other Side prior to birth, I'll take you back to the analogy of our physical bodies serving as the car we drive along this journey of life. We don't really get in that car until we are born. Until then, our souls can come and go between Earth and the Other Side. Prior to birth, souls are living more of a Spirit experience than a human experience.

As a parent, know that whether it is through miscarriage, stillborn birth, or abortion, the loss of your child is just as real as it would be to any parent under any other circumstances. Through my readings, it is clear to me that these parents experience just as much grief as do parents who lose their child later on in life. Grief does not discriminate. You are still losing a soul that you brought into this world.

The soul of your child still has a new experience from which it can learn and evolve. Babies don't have to be born into and live in the physical world for that to happen. They also still have the ability to impact and teach others. Remember, as is always the case, they agreed to this scenario in their soul contract. So did you.

The growth, understanding, and support from these souls are just as present and strong for those who have terminated pregnancies. For people with this experience, some may feel their own, personal grief along with an entirely separate level of guilt to contend with in the midst of their loss. I've had so many of these babies come through in Spirit form to let their parents know that they don't have to carry the burden of guilt, responsibility, or regret. Whether an abortion was a part of the soul contract or not, these souls have an immense understanding of the circumstances and rationale behind the choice, and embrace the need of the parent to make the best possible choice for themselves and their family. Both you and your child's soul will grow and learn from the experience.

As is always the case with death, you won't know what the entire purpose of this loss was until you reach the Other Side. But I have often heard messages about lessons of patience, timing, and being in the right stage of life from Spirit. Maybe someday in this lifetime, years later, you will be able to look back and see how the situation helped you grow, offered you a new perspective, and perhaps made you appreciate the child or children you do have with you here in Earth School that much more.

I found this to be true for a woman I read for about a year ago. I was in a store at the time, browsing the shelves, when I heard Spirit asking to come through for a woman who was close by. I asked her if she would be open to a reading, and when she said yes, we found a quiet corner. Immediately, her grandmother came through. They had been very close when she was young, but the grandmother had passed when this woman was a young teenager. Then I saw my symbol for a terminated pregnancy. Her child—a daughter, as I found out—was excited to talk to her. The woman seemed a little nervous, and I soon found out why.

Her daughter told me that her mother had been very young when she got pregnant, just a teenager. Scared out of her mind, the woman ultimately decided she was unable to care for a child at that point in her life. While she felt she had made the best choice she could, as time went on she would sometimes wonder *what if?* Her daughter was practically shouting, "That's why you have my brother and sister!" Her daughter could see the path that her mother took after she terminated her pregnancy. She finished school, found a career she loved, and, years later, had two children. Her daughter told her that she was proud of the life she had made for herself and her children. There was no anger or resentment, only total understanding.

The woman's grandmother stepped in then. She told me, "She thinks I'm mad at her! I'm not!" Apparently, her grandmother had been very religious during her time on Earth, and the woman had always feared that her grandmother would have been disappointed in the choice she made. Her grandmother assured her there was no judgment, and that the two of them were together on the Other Side, watching over her.

Is Karma a Thing?

This is a tricky topic for me, because I do believe that like attracts like; for example, negative energy attracts negative energy and positive energy attracts positive energy. What we put into the world we manifest to come back to us. Some people might call it karma, and if this is how you define it, then I'm on board.

I don't believe in karma in the sense that, for example, a parent who lost a child somehow earned that because of past actions. All of this was determined before you were born, and not because you somehow failed in a past lifetime. It just has to do with the Earth School curriculum that you've chosen to sign up for and the path you have decided to take to get you to those lessons and that growth.

The important thing to understand is that none of the experiences you've decided to go through in this life stem from a place of judgment or punishment, whether it be from God, your spirit guides, or yourself. As souls, we strive to have and know all types of experiences, from all angles. These are the lessons we can only achieve through having an earthly existence. Therefore, in one lifetime you might have lost a mother at an early age. And in another lifetime, you could be the mother who's lost a child. While sometimes we have another go at certain experiences if we couldn't check off that lesson from our Earth School to-do list the first time around, the challenges we face are mostly about our souls having the opportunity to fully know all aspects of a particular experience. This is what helps us to truly learn and reach the soul growth we've set out to achieve.

THEIR SOULS LIVE ON

When I'm talking to parents who have lost babies, especially through a miscarriage or termination, I'm often told that a part of the soul of the child they lost lives on in their children who came after. I've also talked to many parents who lost older children in tragic circumstances then went on to have more children. So often I hear, "When I look at my baby, they remind me so much of the child I lost." This could be because a part of your child's soul has come back to you, and you can pick up on that essence. Many parents naturally understand this without me having to tell them. Not every soul comes back to Earth in the form of another child, but it certainly does happen.

For instance, I once brought through a five-year-old girl who had passed away from cancer. She came through strong and bright, saying, "Tell them they're not imagining it! She has a piece of me!" It turned out that she was referring to her little sister, who was born a year after she passed away. Her parents, wide-eyed and shaken, confirmed that, every day, their younger daughter reminded them of the daughter they'd lost. The way she laughed, how she liked to dance, the look in her eyes. They felt like they could see their older daughter in her very soul but were questioning whether it was even possible.

It's hard to understand exactly what this means or how it works, but from what I've been told, I believe that sometimes the next lifetime of a child's higher self (or the next slice of the clementine) will be sent down to the same parents and bring that essential, familiar energy with them.

MOVING FORWARD AFTER LOSS

I've talked to so many parents who find it almost impossible to move on after the death of a child. A lot of them leave their child's bedroom untouched. The drawers are still filled with their clothes, the teddy bears are still lined up against the walls, and the books are left in the exact same position on the shelves. Some parents need this—at least for a while. They feel close to their child when they're in their room, sitting on their bed, holding their favorite toy. And if that's what feels good, that's okay!

But, on the flip side, understand that your child wants nothing more than for you to give yourself permission to keep moving forward in life. They want you to do the things that make you happy, whether that's following a passion, moving out of the house where the child lived, having another baby, or anything else that puts color back into your world. They want your life to continue, and most of all, they want you to feel joy.

In one reading, a young boy who had passed away from a car accident came through to his parents. He told me that his parents had kept his room exactly the same in the two years since he had passed, but that he knew they were considering moving out of the house. They were struggling to leave the place that held so many memories of their son, afraid they might slip away with distance.

"It doesn't matter where you are," he told them. "I'm always with you!" He brought through the fact that they kept the blanket he had slept with every night. He was happy and laughing, and joked, "You need to wash that blanket! It's getting pretty gross."

His parents walked away knowing that they had their son's blessing not only to move out of their house but also to move forward with their lives. This is a message that has come through with every child that I've connected to.

How Do I Survive the Holidays?

The pain that follows the loss of a child exists every day and, for many parents, every second of every hour of every day. Yet, I've found that many parents' pain is amplified during the holiday season. It usually brings a flood of memories that are impossible to avoid. A parent will go to hang up stockings and find the one with their lost child's name on it. Halloween rolls around, and the bucket of costumes is impossible to sort through without remembering their child's excitement to dress up in each one. But many parents, particularly those with other children, try to power through the holidays with a smile plastered on their face. It can be grueling and heartbreaking to try and enjoy something when there is a hole where a child once stood.

Be patient with yourself. Too often, I hear parents express deep feelings of guilt around the holidays. It might stem from "failing" to make a fun holiday for their other children or feeling guilty because they dared to feel joy without their child there. If this resonates with you, I want you to cut yourself a break. There are no rules when it comes to grief, and you should give yourself permission to work through it in whatever way works for you.

Around holidays, birthdays, and the anniversary of your child's passing, set aside some time to check in with yourself. It is important to nurture yourself and allow self-healing. This could mean taking a break to walk in nature, meditate, or do anything else that helps you feel grounded. Don't let that little voice in the back of your head—you know, the one that whispers, "You don't have time for this. You should be taking care of your family. You're being selfish."—get in the way. By taking care of yourself, you are helping bring out your best self. This includes allowing yourself to feel whatever comes your way. If you wake up on your lost child's birthday and find that you want to cry and rage against the world for a while, then do that.

You can also try setting up a ritual in your child's memory. Maybe you can listen to their favorite Christmas song before you open gifts, leave a place for them at the Thanksgiving table, or share a favorite memory on their birthday every year. Your child is always with you, and in that moment, you can honor their presence and remember that they are still very much a part of your family. Avoiding or hiding from your grief can be exhausting, and making space for both your love for them and your sadness at their passing can be therapeutic.

Lastly, remember that your child wants more than anything for you to be happy. If you find yourself talking, laughing, reveling in the holidays, you have no reason to feel guilty or ashamed. Your child is right there, laughing with you! Know you are capable and deserving of living a joyful life and, in fact, that is what your child wants for you.

BRINGERS OF JOY

Your children want you to know that it is okay to grieve on your own timeline. It is okay to feel what you need to feel. But they also want you to know that you don't have to suffer. In fact, they want nothing more than for you to feel joy, to feel hope and happiness, and to feel all of this without guilt.

In fact, your children are at their happiest, strongest, and closest to you in those moments when you are filled with joy.

They are practically jumping off the walls with happiness!

While most of our spirit guides are not people we have known in this lifetime, the one big exception is babies and young children. These kids often take on the specific role of joy guides for their parents to help them heal and experience the beauty of life once again. How beautiful is that? Your child's purpose is now to bring more joy into your life. If you're having a rough day, it's your little joy guide who will swoop in to somehow lead you to a circumstance that will bring a smile to your face. The ability to do this is their greatest joy.

If you have the inkling to follow a dream or a passion, do it! Your child is probably behind that nudge. If you are pregnant again and scared or worried about moving on or feel as if you are somehow unworthy, you don't have to. No one is happier about this than your child, and they know that your new child will never replace their memory. No one feels that you are a more worthy parent than your child.

So many times, relationships fall apart when parents lose a child. There is too much lingering blame and sadness. Your child doesn't want you to blame each other and reminds you that, even in a case where their death appeared to be an accident, it wasn't. Children want their parents to be able to turn to one another for support as they pick up the pieces and move forward.

The desire and ability of children on the Other Side to bring joy through is no surprise. They do the same thing here on Earth! I get chills when I think of all the stories I've heard both in life and through Spirit of children going through terrible illnesses like cancer, all the while with a smile on their face and the desire to make everyone around them happy. Kids are masters at finding the positive and joy in everything. In this way, they are our greatest teachers. They teach us to have patience and to find the joy in even our greatest struggles. They teach us not to sweat the small stuff. They teach us about perseverance and resilience. There is so much to learn from children, both in this world and the next.

I think it's probably for exactly this reason that, of all the spirits I communicate with, children come through the strongest and are the easiest to connect with. They know how badly their parents need to hear they are safe and happy. They understand how desperately their parents need to understand that their child didn't suffer. Their biggest hope is for their parents to go on to live happy lives, as incomprehensible as that seems to the parents who are left behind.

Because of this strong energy and ability to communicate, if you think you're receiving signs from your child, I can almost guarantee you that you are! If you sense their energy in the room or have a visitation dream, your child is absolutely right there with you. That rainbow, dragonfly, special song, or penny from Heaven is almost surely for you. Your children want you to know that they are very much still with you and are always watching over you. Your children know that you need these signs, and they are strong and powerful in their ability to make sure you receive them.

Should I Do Something to Honor My Loved One's Memory?

After losing someone close to them, many people want to find a way to honor and memorialize them. Sometimes this means having something that serves as a reminder of who that person was (and still is), sometimes it can be a physical place to visit, and sometimes it can be doing something good in their name.

I want to make sure you know that your loved ones are entirely aware of and proud of your efforts. Even if you haven't followed through on the memorial yet or simply thought about something you'd like to do. Maybe you were planning on getting a tattoo but found you were too scared of needles. It's okay! It truly is the thought that counts.

Your loved ones have no expectations, and they will not be disappointed regardless of what you decide. Make whatever choices help you in your journey toward healing and recovery. Your loved ones appreciate the things you do in their memory, but by no means should you feel you have to do anything grand. Merely talking about them is the perfect way to honor them and have their legacy live on.

MY SPIRIT HELPERS

I have a small group of souls that I have channeled in the past years who I call my "Spirit helpers." These souls will come around as needed to help me channel. My Spirit helpers tend to come through when I am speaking with someone who has experienced a similar loss or who can in some other way connect to one of these helpers. Of my Spirit helpers, several of them are children, all of whom came through at different events over the last few years and each of which passed as a result of cancer when they were about four-and-a-half years old. As I've said, most of the time I don't remember spirits after I channel them, but the souls on this team of helpers are a few of the handful that have stayed with me.

I don't think it's an accident that so many of my Spirit helpers come in the form of children. Some spirits communicate better than others, and I've found that children tend to have such a strong energy and presence, they are among the strongest communicators and are able to connect so easily. My guess is that this is because kids, in general, operate at a higher vibration.

I never fail to be impressed at the beautiful ability of my Spirit helpers to swoop in and assist, even if just for a moment. It is profound and powerful to witness and connect with and speaks to the power of children—both on Earth and on the Other Side.

Typically, my Spirit helpers know when their presence will help me connect, and it's usually because they have some connection to the reading. So now when I do an event and someone has lost a child to a similar form of cancer, I'll see the little boy Logan's face in my mind's eye, feel his energy, and know he's trying to help another child come through. The little girls who are also part of my Spirit helpers work in the same way.

As Logan's mother explains in the following passage, the role of a Spirit helper and the joy they bring is something that has brought peace to the families they've left behind. As you'll see, he is definitely one of the strongest souls I've had the pleasure of connecting to, and I'm honored to now have Logan as part of my little Spirit helper team.

I watched Monica's television series long before anything bad ever happened to me. I had no need for a medium back then; I just found the idea fascinating. Well, six months after my son Logan unexpectedly passed away, I heard that Monica was having an event, and I wasn't about to miss out on an opportunity to possibly have Logan come through. Every single day leading up to the event, my daughters and I talked to Logan, asking him to come through to Monica. I specifically told him every single personal detail I wanted him to bring up and repeatedly told him, "Please go to Monica. She can hear you, she can talk to us for you."

Finally, the day arrived. It was October 2016. I thought the odds that we would get a reading were slim, but I continued to talk to Logan in my head throughout the event, just as I had done every single day since he passed. As the time flew by and the event was drawing to an end, I began to feel desperate and started begging Logan to come through, please God!

Monica said she had time for one more reading. She held her hand up to about four feet off of the floor, and said, "I have a little boy, about this tall, four years old, cancer connection." My husband and I raised our hands; Monica zeroed in on us, and told us to come up on stage. She went on to describe our son exactly, from his spiked hair to his stylish clothes and gray TOMS shoes to his "shrunken little man" appearance. That was my Logan!

She went on to say that Logan visited her in a dream the night before the event and excitedly told her, "You're going to meet my mom tomorrow!" They then proceeded to play piggyback rides and Legos. Logan showed Monica a blue blanket, and she went on to say that Logan is with his brother, that I had lost a baby and that he was a boy.

No one knew that I felt that the baby I lost during pregnancy a year before Logan passed was a boy; it was something I knew in my heart but had never shared with anyone. But Logan confirmed that it was, indeed, his brother, and that both of my boys are in Heaven waiting for me. Monica went on to describe the color of our living room sofa bed Logan passed on, the box where I keep his ashes and where I keep it, including describing my nightstand where it sits. Monica gave us specific details pertaining to our son, his brief illness, details of what I had done in his memory after he passed, and named every single thing I have done to honor him since.

She told us things that literally no one but us and our son knows. Monica even knew that my son sends me hearts, which wasn't something I shared with anyone at the time. She named the item I placed in my son's hands at his funeral, something no one saw since I placed the object there after the ceremony, and she knew I later bought an identical version of this object to keep for myself. Logan literally conveyed every single detail I had spent months asking for to Monica, and she relayed it to me! I feel so blessed to have had this incredible experience, which I won't forget for as long as I live. I am so grateful that my broken heart felt a little less broken, even if only for a moment.

In October 2018, I saw that Monica was having another event, this time in our home state of New Jersey. Being that my mom lives in New Jersey and we visit as often as we are able, I decided to go to see what would happen. Maybe, just maybe, Logan would pop in again. Leading up to that event, again, every day I asked Logan to please come through for me, even if it was just to say something short and sweet. As my husband and I sat at that event, I talked to whatever spirits were listening and to Logan, asking them to please let Logan come through for me. About halfway through the evening, Monica said, "I have a little boy coming through, about four years old, spiked hair." She went on to say, "Wait, he feels so familiar to me, like we are buddy-buddy."

Monica went on to tell me that Logan is one of the spirits that has come through to her very often as one of her "Spirit helpers" at events and that he assists other young souls in coming through to connect with their parents, which explains his familiarity.

At one point, Logan said, "Mom, you connect with me so much already. You don't need a medium to connect! You know this, though." Then Logan stomped his foot to be silly and said, "I'm important here. I have jobs to do!" This was his personality to a T; you couldn't get more Logan!

All my experiences have led me to where I am, all I believe, and know today, giving me immense peace and a faith bigger than I imagined. I have full trust that Logan will continue to help and guide us on our Earth journey, until we are with him once again.

The hardest thing to accept about grief, particularly when it comes to the loss of a child, is that it is a lifelong process. When you wake up every day and go to sleep every night weighed down by grief, it is only human to wonder when the pain will end. I've also had parents tell me that they're afraid to stop feeling grief, in case the memory of their child starts to fade away. From what I've seen, the pain never disappears, but it does change. The sharp edges start to soften. The weight of it lessens over time. What once occupied every cell in your body will instead live only in your heart. Eventually, you will learn how to carry it with you in a way that doesn't feel suffocating.

You can find a way forward, but unfortunately no one can tell you what that way is. It looks different for everyone, and only you can decide what steps are right for you. But I can say that at the very core of healing is a commitment to take care of yourself. You've lost your child, but you've also lost the person you were before. Take the time to figure out who you are now and who you want to be going forward. Remember that you will keep going, and your life will be joyful again.

10

Animals Have Souls Too

Throughout our time together, many major milestones occurred, including new homes, new family members, new jobs, and so much more. Over time, you grew older and wiser. People came into your life and people walked out of your life.

But the one thing that never wavered throughout all of this? Me.

I was your constant cuddle buddy, pal, and best friend. I was by your side through it all, and wouldn't have had it any other way. Nothing made me happier than to get to be that constant source of companionship and unconditional love for you, even when the rest of your world was inevitably changing.

While I may have been only one part of your world, you were my entire world and then some. (Well, actually, I must say that toys and treats fall under the same umbrella—because you know how much I love those!)

Thank you for the beautiful life you gave me. You provided me with a home, a sense of safety, and lots of yummy meals. My days were filled with hugs and belly rubs, which gave me more joy than you'll ever know. Thank you for all the memories of fun, love, and mischief.

In the physical world, I couldn't speak through words and may not have always understood exactly what you were trying to get at. (And sometimes the stubborn side of me simply chose to ignore you. Sorry about that!) But at the end of the day, all it took was hearing the affection in your voice or being held in your arms to know that I was loved.

I missed you every single second we had to be apart. But, looking back on my life, I now have an even greater understanding of why you couldn't be there constantly or entertain me twenty-four hours a day, seven days a week. I know how blessed I was to have had a place in your heart and in your home, something that so many animals don't get to experience on Earth. But, don't worry; those guys are here too, and they are now enjoying all of the things they might not have had the chance to during their most recent lifetime in the physical world.

Believe it or not, animals do have souls. The rainbow bridge you all speak of? It's real! Well, not in the literal sense. But it's true in terms of everything that it represents. Furry friends go to Heaven too!

Please don't feel bad for any of the decisions you had to make or things you wish you would have done differently. You did the best you could. And nothing was left unsaid. I hear your thoughts and know how you feel. Upon arriving in the afterlife, I got to experience the same life review that human souls go through. With that being said, I should probably take this opportunity to apologize for all of those times I had an accident, got too loud, made a mess, was too rowdy, scratched up the house, tore up toilet paper, ruined your things, or ate your food. On the flip side, though, you're welcome for teaching you loads of patience. But, seriously, part of my purpose was to teach you many different lessons throughout my lifetime.

Don't you worry. No matter the circumstances, my passing was peaceful and seamless. I'm whole again and free from any complications I may have faced before I died. I can now run as fast as I'd like to and leap so high it's as though I'm flying through the clouds. Heaven is whatever I want it to be. Sometimes that means chasing my buddies through fields of flowers; other times I lazily snooze under the warmth of the shining sun.

You'll be seeing me again one day. We'll get to play and have fun together, just like we did in the physical world. Not only that, but my Spirit is with you, even now. I visit you all the time and do what I can to let you know I'm still there. When you're spending time with other pets, and they start acting funny even though you can't see any reason why? I can almost guarantee you, that's me! I send signs too. Keep your eyes wide open so that you don't miss them. These signs could come in the form of things like songs on the radio. On the other hand, you may find yourself hearing the pitter-patter of my steps around the house or occasionally feel the sensation of my coat brushing up against your leg. It's not wishful thinking or you making stuff up! It's me. And these are only some of the many ways I let you know when I am near.

People used to laugh and joke about how I was like your child. It's true, though. I was more than just a pet. We were family, and always will be.

Just as I was loyal to you in life, I continue to be in Spirit. So when you need me, I come running. That's a promise.

Forever and always.

THE PET CONNECTION

If you have a pet, I'm sure it comes as no surprise to you that animals have souls just like human beings do. Next to children, some of the strongest communicators in the Spirit World are pets who want to connect with their owners. In fact, pets are *so* communicative that I have to be careful about them at events or I'm pretty sure that I would end up channeling dogs and cats for two hours straight. Before I go onstage, I ask Spirit to be aware of the fact that there are a couple of hundred people in the room, so we really should do our best to focus on human loved ones.

To be honest, though, most people are just as excited to connect with their pets as they are to any other member of their family who has passed. For many of us, our pets *are* our family and are just as important as anyone else.

Especially when I used to do private readings back in the day and even now when I do spontaneous readings or one-on-one sessions for giveaway winners, pets love to come through and make their presence known. They want to validate for their owners that they are around just as much as every other member of the family on the Other Side. Through these readings, I'm constantly struck by how beautiful and profound our connection with our pets is. Our pets offer us one of the greatest examples of unconditional and transcendent love that we can experience in this lifetime. I see the depth of this love not only from the spirits of animals but also from their owners' reactions to them. I have seen people cry more when their dog comes through than when a grandparent does plenty of times. It's always a reminder to me that sometimes we do not take people's grief seriously enough when they lose a beloved pet.

HOW ANIMALS COMMUNICATE

I never once doubted that all animals return to the afterlife as souls, just as we do. However, it took me a while into my work as a medium before I realized that I could communicate with and bring forth messages from the souls of pets, just the same as I do with the souls of humans. Since I never had pets as a kid (although Tyler and I now have two dogs we love more than life itself), it wasn't really a part of my frame of reference or Spirit Dictionary.

I don't specifically remember the first time an animal came through in one of my readings because channeling pets was sort of a process for me that I became adjusted to over time.

When it first started happening, pets came through to me as a part of another Spirit's message. For example, I would be talking to someone's father on the Other Side and in my mind's eye, he would show me the image of a dog. I began to connect the dots and realized that the animals who popped up in these readings had crossed over too, and the dad was passing along the message that the dog was safe and at peace. Each time this happened, the person who I was sitting with confirmed that was the case. Although the cameo appearances of these pets surprised me at first, it always made perfect sense to their owners.

After a while, those pets I was being shown through their human counterparts started to communicate in their own right. At first, I tried to keep my focus on the human, but then I realized that the pet had other ideas. These pets were showing me things from their point of view. Before long, pets started coming through to me without their human "escorts."

It is now crystal clear to me that animals on the Other Side communicate just like the souls of humans do. Especially at events, I'll sometimes sense a WTF vibe coming from the audience when I first start to bring through messages from someone's pet. They're like, "Wait, what? Is this lady really talking to a cat the same way she just spoke to that woman's aunt?" I know that it probably looks a little crazy (especially if you've never had a close bond with an animal), but the reality is that there is no such thing as language barriers when it comes to Spirit, and that goes for pets too.

Pets talk to me exactly the same way anyone else in Spirit form would, through signs, symbols, and my own frame of reference. In fact, nothing about an animal's energy feels different to me than a human's energy. The only thing I notice, which may or may not be the same for other mediums, is that I sometimes have a more difficult time distinguishing between male and female energy with animals, along with their various physical characteristics, than I do with humans. Again, this might be because I didn't grow up with pets and I'm by no means an expert on the hundreds of different breeds that exist in this world. If I had more experience (or maybe worked as a veterinarian on the side), then my Spirit Dictionary would expand, and that might make it easier to pick up on these types of details.

But when it is a part of my frame of reference and they're able to communicate the information, animals describe their earthly physical appearance just like a human soul would. They do their best to provide details about themselves in ways that I can easily translate. It's a lot like how a human Spirit might come through and explain that she was a heavier-set woman in her seventies with gray, curly hair and larger ears.

Following is a perfect example of how pets will often come through to connect with their human loved ones:

I thought I would treat myself to the experience of one of Monica's live events. I went into the evening with hopes, but no expectations. My aunt and I were both huge fans of Monica's show, so I asked if she wanted to come along.

As we settled into the room and chatted with the people around us, a woman seated in front of us mentioned that she had recently lost her dog—I could relate; I had lost my dog two and a half years prior and still, at times, felt the grief as if it were yesterday.

The readings that evening were intense. I remember thinking it was completely okay if I didn't get a reading because the experience of seeing others connect with their loved ones was well worth it. As soon as I finished having that thought, my heart started to pound and Monica walked across the stage toward the side of the room where my aunt and I were sitting.

Monica looked straight at me and asked if I had a dog on the Other Side. I nodded as I fought back a flood of tears.

"A white chihuahua?" she asked.

I nodded again and she said, "Your grandmother has your dog, and he's happy!"

I felt a huge weight lift from my heart. My grandma had passed away three weeks before I had to put my dog to sleep. It was the most difficult decision of my life, and it had weighed so heavily on my heart in the time since. Hearing Monica say that he was happy and with my grandma gave me a sense of relief I never thought I would feel.

Monica also mentioned the trouble he'd had walking and asked about his two front legs. My dog was a rescue, and before I adopted him, he had two broken front legs. They were crooked, scarred, and even had metal plates and screws in them, but he never let that slow him down. Monica said that he no longer has any physical problems, and that he is fully healed now that he's crossed over. At the end of the reading, Monica mused, "See, all dogs go to Heaven!"

I'm so thankful for that night. I got more from it than I could have ever hoped for. The grief of losing my sweet puppy and my grandmother so close together was a huge hurdle to overcome. I still miss them, and I still cry, but I now know that they're together and happy. I was also reminded that no one is ever really gone, and that the love we share always remains.

Just as I do with human souls, sometimes I even *hear* certain words and phrases from animals. Pets often share their name, birthday, and other types of factual evidence that makes it very clear to their owner who is coming through. They allow me to feel the type of relationship they had with their owner and how the two of them interacted.

Just like human souls come through with their personalities fully intact, so do animals. I find that what usually provides the most validation for people is the capacity for animals to capture the essence of who they were on Earth. A cat might explain himself as practically doglike, always cuddling and wanting attention. Or a dog might show me that she had a tendency to get jealous, always keeping an eye on where your attention was directed at the dog park.

WHY ANIMALS COMMUNICATE

Animals come through from the Other Side for all of the same reasons human souls do. They want you to know they are still right here with you. They want to validate any decisions you had to make on their behalf. They want to let you know that you did all of the right things, that they are grateful, and that they love you. That you can let go of any heaviness you might be holding.

Many people carry around a lot of guilt because they feel as if they didn't notice that an ailing pet was sick soon enough. They bear a sense of responsibility for their animal's death. Ultimately, human beings have a greater ability to express physical symptoms than animals do. Animals tend to mask their pain and ailments. Just like humans, pets come through to let you know that it was their time to go. They have soul contracts too! Often, they want to thank their owner for not letting them suffer. If you had to make the decision to put them down, your pets understand that it was a choice made out of love and that you only wanted what was best for them. They want to let us know they are okay and everything is as it should be. Our animals know how much we loved them and that we did right by them. As with humans, there is no need for guilt or what ifs when it comes to your pets. If you couldn't afford an expensive surgery that you were told was necessary for them to live for another year or two, don't beat yourself up. They understand and have a complete view of the circumstances surrounding their death. Just like the souls of humans, they are by no means disappointed and they don't hold a grudge against you.

Animals who suffered a quick or painful death also want you to know that, just like humans, they didn't feel it. They were already in transition, feeling more peace and experiencing more beauty and love than we could ever imagine here on Earth.

Animals go through a life review just like humans do too. They see every little thing their human has ever done for them. So often, they come through wanting to express gratitude for how much their person was there, especially at the end. If a dog or cat had to be put down, they will often show me how their owner held them in their arms, saying goodbye. The pet will communicate that they were aware of all that love down to the final moment, and that they are so grateful.

Just like humans, animals also share information about what is happening in their human's present-day life. They do this as a way of letting you know that they are still right there with you, aware of every little thing that is happening in your life. There are any number of other specific messages, too, just like there are when human souls communicate.

Even though I know firsthand how well and how enthusiastically animals communicate from Heaven, it still never fails to thrill and move me every time a pet appears—this just happened for my own family a few months ago. My stepmom lost her dog, Gaston, who she and my dad were very close to.

Less than forty-eight hours after he passed away, I was sitting in circle. (Circle is what it's usually called when a medium joins together with a group of other mediums and lightworkers, and they collectively quiet their minds and expand their energy, thus reaching a deep and shared level of connection with the Other Side.) Oftentimes during circle, whoever is sensing something will share it with the rest of the group. Prior to this particular medium meetup, I didn't tell anyone about Gaston's death, though I wondered if there was a chance he might pop in. I wasn't surprised when three different people clearly brought him through. All of them described seeing a vision of a dog that was fluffy, white, and looked similar to a wolf. As I'm sure you've already guessed, this is *exactly* what my stepmom's dog looked like.

They went on to explain Gaston's personality and conveyed the message that he was okay, at peace, and very much a wise soul who has now taken on the role of being an animal spirit guide for some of my family members. Yes, animals can evolve to the point of becoming a spirit guide as well!

To be completely honest, I wasn't particularly close to Gaston. He was always very slow to warm to strangers, and it required quite a bit of time and effort to get him to like you, which I unfortunately never had the opportunity to do. But other members of my family—the ones who'd eventually coaxed him into not only tolerating them but loving them so much he'd follow them around the house and cry when they were out of sight—needed to hear these messages.

Still, even I teared up when Gaston popped in the circle that day. It was wild and reassuring, even for me. Especially because he came through so soon after he had crossed over. My guess is that Gaston probably knew he might not have another chance to do so for quite some time since, admittedly, I don't get the chance to attend these kinds of spiritual circles as often as I probably should. And, remember, I can't connect to Spirit for my own family the way I can for strangers.

All of this brings me to one of my favorite readings of all time, which happened more than five years ago. I was talking to a woman over Skype. She didn't tell me who she hoped to communicate with, which, as always, is how I prefer it to be.

I turned on my light switch and invited Spirit to come in, one at a time. Most people almost immediately have at least a few different souls lined up to communicate with them. That didn't happen this time. I didn't say anything to the woman, I just continued waiting for Spirit, inviting them to come through. Finally, I had to tell the woman, "I'm really sorry, but I'm not sensing any human loved ones stepping forward. The only thing I'm getting is an orange cat."

The woman started bawling. I mean, she completely lost it. "Oh, my God! This is how I know you're the real deal," she said. I felt my tension release. "Monica," she continued, "I've been to six different mediums. Every single one talked about my grandmother, who I was never close to. Not one of them brought through my cat, and that's who I've been waiting to hear from this whole time."

I'm guessing that this woman's cat probably *did* come through to at least some of the other mediums, but they got stuck on the fact that most people come into a reading wanting to connect to their human loved ones so they either ignored the cat, or they may have let their own bias or doubt start to creep up and second-guessed whether or not she really did have a cat on the Other Side. It's hard not to do. I too sometimes question the information coming through (or not coming through, as it were), but I have to force myself to remember that readings aren't about me. The important thing is that I tell the person I'm reading for the truth. In this case, I accepted the fact that I might look like a crappy medium to this woman when I told her that nobody was there other than a cat. Of course, it turned out to be exactly what she needed.

The longer I do this work, the more I realize there's a reason for everything and that Spirit won't ever let me down.

I swear this cat went on to describe himself and communicate more strongly and clearly than most humans do. He showed me his fat chub rolls, expressed his personality, and came through in such a way that completely nailed his earthly essence. He even told me that his nickname was Mr. W.

Mr. W walked me through his entire life, from the moment this woman had adopted him as early as she possibly could when he was just a kitten, all the way to the very end when she held him in her arms as he transitioned to Heaven more than eighteen years later. Mr. W showed me the type of cancer that had spread through his little cat body and talked about specific instances when his human had brought him to the doctor for treatment. All of it was crystal clear. He validated that the woman had done the right thing by cremating him and showed me the wooden box etched with his initials and hearts that now held his remains. He even showed me that the woman kept this box in the third drawer on the right-hand side of her computer desk.

At this point, the woman was totally amazed. "Before I came into this reading, I told Mr. W that if this reading was for real, he would have to describe the box his ashes were in and where I keep it!" she exclaimed. "Monica, I've never told anyone about this. There's no way you would know."

It gets even better, if you can believe it. Mr. W then started talking about all the signs he was constantly sending his owner. He described specific moments in which the woman had felt his energy and confirmed that it had been him, right there with her. The one that stands out to me the most is a vision he showed me through my clairvoyance, of this woman looking up to see both a paw and heart-shaped spot of clear glass on her foggy kitchen window. "That happened a week after he passed," she cried. "I had just been looking at his little food bowl and was feeling extra sad. I looked up at the window and there appeared to be a paw print next to a heart. I knew in that moment that it had to be a sign sent from Mr. W."

The woman left our call that day without a shadow of a doubt that she had connected with her cat. She wasn't married and she didn't have kids. In her eyes, Mr. W *was* her baby. I mean, it makes sense. He had been this woman's life for more than eighteen years. Even if cats do have nine lives, that's still a long time. You know by now that Spirit comes through the strongest not for who wants it the most, but for who needs it the most. This woman *needed* to hear from her cat in the same way any mom needs to hear from her son.

THE PURPOSE OF ANIMALS

Broken record here: I don't have all of the answers. But I do have a feeling that more than animals come to Earth School to learn, they come to *teach*. We humans are meant to learn from our pets.

As cheesy as it might sound, I believe that animals teach us about unconditional love. Whether it's a dog, a cat, a horse, or any other type of pet, humans are often in the type of relationship with them where the human (or family) is the pet's sole source of love and care. Pets don't have an entire village looking out for them like our children do. A pet's owner is everything to them, which adds a very special energy to that relationship. And just like you are everything to your pet here in the physical world, you are also everything to them in the Spirit World. More than anything, pets love to come through for you and to connect. They crave the opportunity to bring you comfort, just like they did here on Earth. And, also, just like you have always done for them.

I doubt that any of this comes as much of a surprise to any pet owner because we can see all of this down here in Earth School. Sure, we give to our pets, but our animals give just as much back to us on an emotional level. Our pets can love us in a way that even our own family members cannot. I know plenty of people whose relationship with their family members is not all rainbows and butterflies. It is their pets who they turn to for unconditional love and support. Many people who adopt a furry friend will tell you that it's not they who saved the pet, but the pet who saved them. So often, pets give their owners the very thing that their heart has been longing for: a source of hope, a compassionate companion, or a best friend. Our pets often come into our lives just when we need them the most.

Kelsi, the girl whose story I shared in Chapter Six about losing her mother in a house fire, also received validation about her dog's purpose, in that same reading. While her mother was coming through, she showed me clairvoyantly the image of a fluffy, brownish-looking dog. Over the years, as part of my Spirit Dictionary I have developed a different symbol Spirit uses when referencing a living dog as opposed to one that's on the Other Side. The mother showed this symbol for a living dog to me and made me feel like it was in connection with her daughter Kelsi. Kelsi validated this information, saying that yes, she had a twelve-year-old dog named Bailey.

I got the message that Bailey was brought into her life to save her, in a sense. That Bailey and Kelsi shared a soul bond that was undeniable and unique. Spirit communicated that Kelsi's angels and loved ones had helped send Bailey her way; he was quite literally Heaven-sent. Kelsi was supposed to have this dog as a form of support throughout the tough times; part of his purpose was to provide motivation for Kelsi to keep going, even during her darkest moments.

Kelsi expanded on the backstory of her relationship with Bailey when she had shared her story for me to use in this book:

Twelve years ago, I stopped by a friend's house and discovered that his dogs had just had puppies. "You want one?" he asked.

I was eighteen and still living at home, so taking a dog home with me wasn't an option, although there was an all-white one who I had my eye on. The dogs had been born just days ago, so my friend told me that I had seven weeks to change my mind. Six weeks later, I randomly visited my friend again and saw the puppies. They were all so much bigger and cuter and fluffier, and I couldn't resist. I picked up the all-white one and said, "This is the one." As I was getting ready to leave, I went back to say goodbye to the puppies. I can't tell you what came over me, but I think that the universe works in marvelous ways.

I put down the white puppy and picked up a fluffy multi-colored brownish dog. "Actually, I think I'm going to take this one," I told my friend.

"You don't want that one—he's the runt," my friend replied.

For some reason, his comment made me want this puppy even more. I proceeded to tell my friend it was fine, and he agreed to let me take him.

During my reading with Monica, she confirmed all the ways I already believed Bailey was special and sent to help me. I was a troubled teen, in and out of drugs, and hanging with a bad crowd. A few months before meeting Bailey, I had been in a drug-induced coma and spent several days on life support. It was a dark time.

Bailey helped me through so much. He gave me a sense of responsibility and purpose. To this day, my friends think my dog is weird. He's too attached to me, follows me everywhere, gets anxiety when I'm sad. Bailey feels my pain. This dog is special. We share a soul bond. I know that.

I didn't need Monica to tell me this, but the reassurance was amazing.

Even for those of us who do come from healthy, functional families, the love of our pets is still its own separate, special thing with a different energy about it.

Also, much like children, our pets teach us about the simple nature of joy, being in the moment, and not sweating the small stuff. I look at my dog Luna all the time and think, "Man, she doesn't have a care in the world." She's just happy as can be every single day, constantly giving love without thinking twice about it.

I'm constantly floored by how dogs in particular are so intuitive about their humans. They know when we're upset or grieving. They know if and when their "mom" is pregnant. They are so tuned into our energy that many dogs even know when their owner has passed away. Dogs are the epitome of being attuned. It's not a mistake that dogs often serve as emotional support and service animals as well as police dogs.

I've seen a lot of people who feel what seems to be almost a sense of guilt about how deeply the loss of their animals affects them. After all, it's not a person, and we have all either lost or know people who have lost human loved ones. It feels like we don't have the *right* to miss our pets that much. I'm here to promise you that every single feeling you have about the loss of your pet is valid and real. Our pets are incredibly special and important, not just in our lives but also in the more cosmic sense. Also know that just like the human souls you've known are now in Heaven looking over you and waiting for you, so are your pets.

ANIMALS' CONNECTION WITH THE OTHER SIDE

Much like I believe children tend to be more attuned with the Other Side, I believe animals are too. In fact, I think animals are even more attuned than children are because society has no chance of getting into their head with "facts." Unlike humans, this isn't a "phase" that animals grow out of.

I feel that animals are acutely aware of the energy around them to the point where they recognize things that go completely over our head. My guess is that they pick up on the difference between a human and Spirit presence through some sort of sensory cue along the lines of, "Something's not right here. I can tell what my mom had for lunch by sniffing her, but I can't do that with this other person in the room."

Spirit has validated this for me through many readings. Just recently, a mother came through and talked about her daughter's Golden Retriever, who was still alive. The mother told her daughter that whenever the Golden Retriever starts barking at "nothing" or is strangely focused on the wall, it is because the mother is in the room, and he knows it. Anytime you get a sense of a loved one's energy in the room and notice that your pet is acting weird, I can almost guarantee you that's confirmation. Pets are often keenly aware of Spirit's presence.

I've even had dogs do this with *me*. When I used to walk into people's homes for private readings, their dogs would often start running around and going crazy. I feel like it was probably a result of the fact that I had a lot of spirits walking in with me and the dogs were wondering why the room was suddenly flooded with (dead) people. I even watched some dogs' energy and personality change throughout the course of the readings. I always had a sense that they knew exactly what was going on.

I've seen my own dog do this too. Remember how I mentioned that I'll feel Spirit on either my right- or left-hand side, depending on whether they belonged to the maternal or paternal side of someone's family? When Luna was a puppy, she had pretty bad separation anxiety, so to stop her from barking and disturbing my college roommates at the time, I would often give readings with her in my lap. Whenever I channeled Spirit and began shifting my attention to one side or the other, I would notice my dog Luna's attention go to that same place, even before mine did. A few minutes into the reading, she would get really, really quiet and calm, which, trust me, is not how Luna (who we often lovingly refer to as Lunatic) normally behaves. Most times she'd even fall asleep during my readings; it was almost as if Spirit knew she would otherwise be a distraction, so they went ahead and helped lull her to bed for me.

Spirit knows our animals are sensitive to their energy, so they love to use them as a conduit to communicate their presence to us. While most of us don't see dead people perusing our kitchen cabinets, we do certainly notice when our furry sidekicks are reacting to something that is invisible to our human eyes. It's a cue that those feelings we have that there is a familiar presence in the room aren't just in our head—that something more is going on, even if we can't see it for ourselves.

IV

You Don't Need a Medium

11

Understanding Signs from the Other Side

talk to a lot of people who are all about signs. They get so excited to tell me all about the signs they receive and, often, even have an innate understanding of specifically who those signs are from. But then there are other people who are like, "What the heck? I don't get any signs!" Sometimes people who don't receive signs—or, as is usually more accurately the case, who don't *recognize* signs—feel like their loved ones aren't around them. This only adds to the struggle they're already dealing with after loss.

I always share with these people what Spirit has told me time and time again through readings: it's not that your loved ones aren't sending you signs; it's that you're likely either not looking for them or you're not acknowledging the signs for what they are. This is so common that I even have a specific symbol in my Spirit Dictionary for when people are not seeing the signs they're being given. Spirit wants us to know that they *are* there and that they *are* in fact actively trying to send us hellos from Heaven.

Signs are not a one-way process with all of the effort on the side of Spirit. It's a give-and-take process. It takes a lot of effort and energy for Spirit to send signs. At the same time, it requires the right frame of mind on your part to receive them.

Let's take a look at some of the ways you can assist this process of connecting with your loved ones on the Other Side—and, also, at how you might open your eyes to see signs that are already right in front of you, just waiting to be noticed.

WORKING TOGETHER

Over the years, I have noticed that a significant amount of the people who tell me they are asking for signs but not receiving them are still pretty heavily in the grieving process. I think this is because the cloud of grief around them is still so thick. It's like they want the signs so badly that they can't even see them. Sometimes this turns into a vicious cycle and these same people start to wonder if their loved one is "stuck" between this world and the Spirit World or if they're not okay. I promise you, they are not stuck and they are doing great. Better than you can even imagine.

There can be other concerns too. Some people are worried that if they open the door to Spirit at all, they'll start seeing dead people—and they *don't* want that. (I get it. Because like I mentioned at the beginning of this book, I'm the first one to admit that the thought of waking up to a dead person standing at the foot of my bed scares the bejesus outta me.) Many people want to connect with their departed loved ones but only in more subtle, not frightening types of ways. When I talk to those who feel this way, I let them know that they always have control over how they feel and sense their loved ones. They have the right to remain in their comfort zone. Rest assured, Spirit only wants to make you feel happy and comforted—not freaked out! Although it's not required since Spirit hears your thoughts and already knows how you feel, it can still help to lay down the ground rules. Let your loved ones on the Other Side know specifically what your boundaries are in terms of communication. I promise you, they will abide by that. If Spirit knows something is going to frighten you, they will never make their presence known in that way.

Receiving signs requires a balance between keeping an open mind and not getting so caught up in wanting to receive them that it turns into an obsession. A lot of people get to the point where they look so hard for signs that they can't even see what's right in front of their face. It's sort of like when you spend hours desperately searching for something you lost, only to find it in exactly the place it's supposed to be (hopefully that doesn't just happen to me!). When people feel like they're not receiving signs, it's almost never the case that those signs aren't actually there. Sometimes it's similar to how when a person who's been unlucky in love finally stops looking, and only then do they suddenly meet the man or woman of their dreams—and it happens in a place they've frequented all along. Maybe the signs haven't come yet, but that's only temporary. You *will* receive them when the time is right and when you are ready.

When I'm channeling Spirit, and either the person receiving the reading tells me they aren't getting signs or I get my symbol representing that they're not, Spirit will often follow up with specific examples or situations in which they *were* sending a sign. The person I'm reading for almost always responds with some version of, "Oh, my God. You're right, that *did* happen!" They'll often be slapping their head like, "Why didn't I notice that?!" or "How could I have not realized that was a sign?" These hellos from Heaven are almost always right in front of our face. Literally.

Another thing that happens frequently is that people *do* notice the signs that are sent their way, but they still remain skeptical. They write them off as a mere coincidence or wishful thinking. They get stuck in their head, questioning whether or not they are just making up things that aren't really there. Again, Spirit almost always confirms that, yup, the things we think are signs *are* actually signs. You can stop all of the doubting and overthinking, I promise.

I believe that everybody has the ability to receive signs from the Spirit World. All you have to do is be open to it. If you feel like you are open-minded but still aren't connecting with your loved ones—well, try asking! Get specific about what you want to see so that it will be easier to spot the signs when they arrive. This doesn't have to be complicated. Before you go to bed, just say, "Hey, Dad. I would love it if you could work on trying to send me your favorite song over the radio."

Or, "Hi, Mom! Can you please send me a license plate with your initials on it?"

Then, be patient. The sign might not come in the next hour or day, but if you put that intention out there, Spirit will hear it. Your loved ones want to communicate, so they will be more than willing to work on your terms to get their message to you, assuming you're ready to receive it.

Let me expand on this for a moment. I've had a lot of parents who've lost a child say something like, "I don't get it, Monica. I *am* ready to receive a sign or message from my daughter! I want nothing more than some reassurance that she's okay and still with me. But I promise you I'm not obsessing over it; I'm doing all the right things and simply trying to stay open. So why is it still not happening for me? Why aren't I getting any signs?"

Trust me, I feel for these parents (and anyone experiencing a similar thing). Of course they want those hellos from Heaven—we all do. But, again, remember that your loved ones know what's best for you, even when your version of what's best for you might look completely different from theirs. If you're doing all the right things and the signs still aren't happening, then it truly may just not be the right time yet. While you may think or feel that you're ready to receive an in-your-face kind of sign, your loved ones know if and for how long to hold back from sending it in order for you to go through the natural grieving process *first*.

It's similar to what I spoke about earlier; sometimes Spirit won't come through in a reading if it's too soon or if you're not emotionally ready to hear from them yet. The same goes for receiving signs and dreams. If some people were to experience that jaw-dropping sign too early on in their grieving process, they may feel as though it was their only form of relief from that point forward. And *that* is precisely how a person can become obsessed with searching for signs and how signs can turn into an unhealthy coping mechanism. Some of you might only need a few days or a week before Spirit knows that you're ready to receive their hellos, while, for others, it could be three months, a year, or even longer before you're in the right headspace to connect that way.

Also remember that Spirit needs some guidance too. They have to learn how to communicate with you in the best way possible, and there's a bit of a learning curve in the time after a soul transitions despite the fact that we've all been in Spirit form long before this lifetime. It's like any skill that needs to be brushed up on.

I'll share a story I love that exemplifies the power of asking for specific signs. A woman told me about a trip she took to Salem, Massachusetts, several years ago to see where her deceased mother had grown up. While she was on the trip, she asked her mom to send a sign letting her know that she was aware of this hometown visit. This woman got very specific with her request and asked her mom to send her a sign that would in some way relate to Bingo, because it was one of the mother's favorite pastimes and she made a point of playing every week.

When the woman arrived in Salem later that day, she felt drawn to go into a specific store. She walked in, looked up, and there it was hanging on the wall—a framed photograph of a building that had a large sign in front of it with BINGO written in capital letters. But that's not even the best part! Below that the sign read: "Every Friday at 6:15 p.m." That just so happened to be the exact day and time her mom played Bingo every single week.

Spirit's got a great sense of humor, and sometimes they like to up the ante to *really* let you know that they are sending you a message. As I'm sure you can imagine, these types of signs leave a lot less room for doubt.

As for that framed Bingo picture? The woman purchased it and it now hangs in her living room as a daily reminder that her mother is always with her.

BUT HOW DO I *REALLY* KNOW IF IT'S A SIGN?

I get asked about how to tell if something is a sign or not a lot, and I get it. It's not like you can just call 1-800-HEAVEN to get ahold of your loved ones or angels to confirm the sign, so, as the human beings we are, there's always room to wonder and question when it comes to signs.

Spirit loves to say, "If you feel in your heart that it's a sign from me, trust and know that it is." Spirit wants us to trust our own ability to connect, our own intuition and gut feelings. If you have a feeling that a loved one is reaching out to you, trust that.

During readings, when people ask me about the signs they've seen, I always tell them that if they even remotely suspect something is a sign, chances are that it is. Even if these people are asking for answers from Spirit and me, the truth is that they already *have* the answer for themselves. No one else can know and feel what you do, including me. You have the ability to pick up on and identify signs. You even have the ability to intuit who signs are from and perhaps even understand why you are receiving that sign. It's just a matter of trusting.

I will never stop saying this: you don't need a medium to connect with Spirit. *Spirit* doesn't want you to only connect through mediums. They want that channel between you open on an ongoing basis; they want a day-to-day relationship with you. I get the appeal of receiving some of the more tangible, concrete, and specific messages a medium conveys, but the fact of the matter is that Spirit is always right there, doing their best to connect with you every single day. Signs are one of the most effective ways to keep this connection vibrant. All you have to do is open your eyes, open your mind, and open your heart.

WHO'S TALKING TO ME?

When people have multiple loved ones who have crossed over, they are sometimes unsure about specifically who a sign is from even when they recognize the sign itself. In these cases, just ask for clarification. Begin with the loved one you suspect the sign is from and say something like, "If this sign is from you, I want to only see this sign when I'm specifically thinking of you." Or, you can offer guidance in the form of something along the lines of, "Dad, I would love you to communicate with me by sending me pennies." As you should know by now, Spirit is happy to work in your framework, so this is an easy way to clarify things for yourself.

Spirit also sometimes works collectively. Not every sign is from a specific soul on the Other Side. Signs can also come from your entire Spirit squad, including your loved ones, angels, and guides.

TIMING OF THE CONNECTION

Spirit wants to communicate as much as possible, but it's easier for some souls than for others. That doesn't mean that you will never hear from some loved ones, it just means that you might not hear from them every day. While Spirit can be in more than one place at once, it does take a lot of energy for them to lower their vibration to connect with the physical world, and sometimes they're devoting all of their energy to the important work they're busy with on the Other Side.

A very common theme I have noticed is that Spirit tends to communicate more during certain times. You are more likely to hear from your loved ones in those moments when you need it the most or when they are at the forefront of your mind. As you'll see in this chapter, instances like this are rampant, especially on the days that are difficult or meaningful, such as anniversaries, holidays, milestone moments, or anything else that might serve as either a happy or sad reminder. Spirit knows what these days and moments mean to you, so they work that much harder to send you whatever signs they can. Again, even if you can't see them, your loved ones are still right there with you, attuned to your life, your thoughts, your feelings, and your well-being.

COMMON SIGNS

Signs can come in various forms. If you feel in your heart that something you saw or experienced was a sign from your loved one, then it almost certainly was. Having said that, there are some common ways that Spirit tends to communicate through signs. Some of the ones I hear about most include: butterflies, dragonflies, birds, pennies, songs on the radio, and repeating numbers. However, this is by no means an all-inclusive list. There are dozens, if not hundreds, of ways in which Spirit can send signs to the living. Signs also commonly appear by way of anything that is personally meaningful to you. For example, I once spoke with a woman whose dad sends her signs in the form of nails. I had never heard that one before, but it makes perfect sense because her dad was a carpenter. I don't know for sure, but I expect that the reason such a thing as "common" signs even exists is because we are programmed to be on the lookout for them, which makes it easier for Spirit to get our attention.

I'm going to break down some of the signs people receive so that you are able to see and understand the many different ways Spirit can connect with us. Maybe you've only ever looked for your mom's favorite bird but never listened for her favorite song on the radio. Or maybe you're convinced the lights keep flickering for no reason, without consciously realizing it tends to happen when you think of your loved one. It's important to pay attention, or you might miss the signs you've been wanting so badly to receive!

PHYSICAL SIGNS

This category includes all sorts of things, like animals, coins, flowers, and heart-shaped leaves, clouds, and other objects. You name it, and I've probably heard it from one Spirit or another!

Winged creatures in particular tend to show up a lot: birds, dragonflies, ladybugs, butterflies, and so on. And it's not always just the "cute" ones either. I've met some people who receive bumblebees and even flies as signs from their loved ones. I'll never forget an older lady who I gave a reading to years ago. Her husband came through right away, wanting to acknowledge flies. I was so confused because at the time I had never seen this before. The woman explained that before he passed away, her husband had thought all this Spirit stuff was a bunch of hooey and always cracked sarcastic jokes like, "Alright, hon, if this shit's for real, none of that butterfly crap will be coming from me. You bet my ass will come back to you as an annoying little fly that never stops buzzing around you." At his funeral and on every significant day since (including birthdays, anniversaries, and holidays), a single fly appears and follows this woman around for hours on end. It's gotten to the point where the family jokes that if any of the grandkids use a flyswatter to squish it, they're going to piss off Grandpa.

Along with various insects, another common sign is feathers that seemingly drift out of nowhere or that you find where you would least expect them.

A lot of people also see forms of change, such as pennies from Heaven or dimes that just randomly appear. Maybe you open your car door and find a penny on your driver's seat. "How did that get there?" you might wonder. Yup, that's from Spirit.

Of course, we see pretty much every object I've mentioned here all of the time in the course of day-to-day life. The difference is that when these objects are put in your path specifically as signs, something will feel or seem...different. Or they will appear at a time when you *really* need something to hold onto. For instance, a ladybug will land on your hand on a day you're particularly missing your brother, or your wife's favorite flowers will suddenly bloom on the anniversary of her passing despite the fact that it's not the right season for this to be happening. Your attention will be somehow called to that sign. And while signs can come at any time (Spirit also often sends signs on a random day just to say hello), they tend to be even more frequent at times where it couldn't be more fitting—or necessary—to receive one.

You might also see an object, picture, graphic, or figurine featuring a particular creature in a strange place or at an uncanny time. For instance, my best friend Krista gets dragonflies from her mom, who passed away the summer following our freshman year of high school. Most often they're living dragonflies, buzzing around Krista for extended periods of time. Not too long ago, Ryan (Krista's soon-to-be husband) took her to Washington, DC's National Museum of Women in the Arts. The very first thing Krista saw upon walking inside was a beautiful tapestry entitled *Rainmaker*, by the artist Hung Liu, which featured two large dragonflies. Krista took a moment to silently say hello to her mom, knowing that it was a sign she was there. To Krista's surprise, on their way out of the museum, Ryan proposed! There's no doubt that Krista's mom was present when Ryan popped the question. I can only imagine how overjoyed and excited she was for her daughter as she watched it all go down.

It's important to note that signs won't always come exactly how you've envisioned them. You might get stuck on wanting them to be a certain way, but Spirit sometimes has plans of its own in store for you.

A twentysomething guy named Jake was dragged to one of my events by his girlfriend Brittany earlier this year. I later found out that ever since that night, he had experienced a complete change of heart about the afterlife and began opening up to the idea of signs from Spirit.

While the couple was enjoying a beach day on vacation, Jake told Brittany that he would only believe his sister was with them if he found a penny on the beach that day. The two of them left the beach feeling discouraged because he had found no such penny. As they were walking back to their hotel, Jake and Brittany stopped in for margaritas at one of the local beach bars they hadn't yet had a chance to visit. They took their seats and, to Jake's surprise, attached to the metal utensil holder was a single magnet—a magnet of a penny lying on a beach! It was the exact sign he had asked his sister for, only delivered in a slightly different way than he had imagined. Jake's sister clearly guided him to find that penny on the beach from her (and at a beach bar no less, which is appropriate since Jake's sister was known for being the life of the party and she, too, had a love for margaritas). Oh, and believe it or not, it gets even better. The waitress who came up to take their order? She shared the same name as Jake's sister! So. Freaking. Amazing.

Is My Mom a Ladybug Now?!

Every now and then, when people receive signs from their loved ones in, say, the form of a butterfly or ladybug, they become concerned that their loved one is now that little insect. If you happen to have accidentally squished a ladybug—don't worry. It's not your mom. She hasn't suddenly reincarnated into a ladybug and is now flapping all over the place. The ladybug is just the middleman in these scenarios. Spirit's simply sending the ladybug to you as a hello.

REPEATING AND SIGNIFICANT NUMBERS AND SEQUENCES

Numbers and number sequences can come from anyone on your Spirit squad, but they often overlap with signs from angels. These frequently come in the form of repeating numbers—like my personal favorite 444—or they could be a number that was meaningful to or reminds you of your loved one. For example, you might see numbers associated with their birthday or the date on which they passed, or if playing sports was a passion of theirs, you might notice their jersey number everywhere.

These numbers can appear on clocks, receipts, confirmation codes, and pretty much anywhere else you can think of. But for me personally, I see them most often on license plates.

A few years back, a woman named Diane sent me the sweetest thank-you card a few months after having a reading with me that she and her husband won through a charity auction. In it, she shared a jaw-dropping sign she had received from her son not long after the reading. She said:

When our son died, it felt like a part of us did too. His messages were exactly what we needed to hear. For the first time in a long time, we felt hopeful about the future.

After our reading, we decided to move to another state to have a fresh start with our family. Not long after the move, I had to get a new license plate for my car. This wasn't a personalized plate; we didn't pick it out or anything like that. The numbers on the license plate just so happened to be my son's birthday! I knew this was a sign from him that moving was the right decision and that he'll be continuing to watch over us, no matter where we live.

And it's not just number sequences that appear as signs on license plates. Many people see names or initials too. A girl named Libby shared this story about a license plate she saw on the anniversary of her grandpa's passing:

I come from a very big Irish Catholic family. When my grandpa passed away, it was a big loss for all of us. He was the most loving, warm, incredible man. His name is Joseph, and one of his nicknames was Big Joe. This past October 5, on the anniversary of his passing, I was driving to work a different way than I usually do. As I was driving, I decided to call my mom to say hello. While I was talking to her, I stopped at a red light and looked at the car in front of me. The license plate said BIGJOE3. In that moment, I knew it was my grandpa saying hello on the day he knew we needed it the most.

LETTERS FROM HEAVEN

Some of my favorite signs from the Other Side are handwritten notes or letters from loved ones who have passed on that have never been unearthed before or have been long forgotten about. These letters often contain poignant messages such as "I'm here" or "I love you."

It's no coincidence, especially when you find specific messages like this at exactly the right moment. A girl once shared with me that on Father's Day, she, her older brother, and sister were all out in their dad's garage working on their cars. Their dad was a jack-of-all-trades and had taught his children a lot about cars. As they were in the garage that day, this girl happened to stumble across a box that was taped shut. Inside, she found birthday cards and other little trinkets her dad had saved.

When the kids were little, their dad worked out of town a lot and used to send them cards. He had kept one that he sent to his son. The card read: "You're the man of the house since I'm gone. Take good care of Mom and the girls. Love, Dad." It brought them to tears because they knew they were meant to find it on the day they were missing him most. Their dad's written words couldn't have been more fitting, even all of those years later.

Another woman named Stacey shared a similar experience:

As I was packing the same suitcase I had used a million times since I was seven years old to go to my sister's out-of-state wedding, I had a strange urge to clean out the front pockets that I hadn't looked in since I was a little girl. I pulled everything out and smoothed out all of the crinkled-up receipts and papers to see what they were. One piece of paper had a note from my grandmother that read: "Dear Stacey, Have a great time. I love you. xxx ooo —Grandma." Directly above my grandma's words were two kisses in her red lipstick.

I instantly got chills and started crying. My grandma had passed away a few years before, and the family was hurting because she wasn't going to physically be there for such a special occasion. I knew this was a sign from her, telling us that she wasn't going to miss it. She gave us kisses from Heaven.

Spirit will often validate their handwritten notes or long-lost letters when they come through in a reading. One time I gave a reading to a woman from her deceased husband. He kept showing me a handwritten love letter. She was adamant that nope, that wasn't something she would have from him. I couldn't stop seeing the letter, though, and told her to keep it in the back of her mind since it would likely make sense after the fact.

I heard from her a few days later. It turns out that less than twenty-four hours after the reading, the woman came across a love letter that her husband had sent her back in college and that she had since completely forgotten about. He ended the letter by saying, "Please take this as a sign of my love for you." That's exactly how she took it.

FAMILIAR SCENTS

Signs aren't just limited to things you can see. They are also frequently delivered as sensory experiences, such as smells. It might be a sign when you catch a whiff of a specific scent or fragrance you associate with someone who has passed, such as a flower, perfume, cigar smoke, or a type of food that reminds you of them. Or, say they were a mechanic; you might randomly smell oil or gasoline.

As I mentioned previously, I sometimes catch these smells during readings too. One time I was onstage and started to smell something rotting, like garbage. I couldn't figure it out until the woman I was reading for told me her dad was a garbage man. The entire room burst out laughing. (I should probably also add here that sometimes I smell really wonderful things too!)

You might pick up this smell when there is no logical explanation for it whatsoever. But even if you are smelling a reminiscent scent for earthly reasons such as walking through a mall and picking up a whiff of your deceased husband's cologne, it can still be a sign. Spirit has the ability to orchestrate who walks by you at any given moment or might subtly guide you into a store you wouldn't have gone into otherwise. If something like this happens as your loved one is on your mind or you are going through something, chances are it is not a coincidence at all. Just the other day, a friend of mine sent me this text:

Monica! I have to tell you what happened last night! Remember how my cousin, who was also one of my best friends, passed away last year? Well, her absolute favorite scent in the world was a Japanese cherry blossom candle. Anytime I would go over to her house, she would have it lit and the whole place smelled like cherry blossoms. I've never once had that kind of candle at my apartment and I don't own anything that smells like it. Yesterday was the anniversary of my cousin's passing, so I was thinking of her all day and really missing her. Then, just around 9:15 p.m., which is the time she passed, I walked into my room and it smelled exactly like her candle! There was zero explanation for it. I have goosebumps even now, just thinking about it. It was so amazing. I definitely feel like it was my cousin's way of letting me know she's still with me.

To which I responded, of course it was!

SOUNDS AND SONGS

Spirit uses sound in a few different ways. A common manifestation of this is hearing a meaningful song on the radio at just the right moment or a sound that gets your attention. I understand that, for some people, sudden noises like closing doors or footsteps might be scary. Spirit does these things mainly when they were a jokester or playful like that here on Earth, but if it freaks you out, just let your loved ones know, and they will find a different way to get your attention. There are also plenty of ways in which your prank enthusiast loved ones can still make you laugh without turning it into a full-blown scene out of a *Paranormal Activity* movie.

I once gave a reading to two sisters, whose brother was coming through. I got an overwhelming message to talk about the smoke detectors. "That was me!" I heard him laugh, as if Spirit thought it was the funniest thing ever. The girls knew instantly what their brother was referencing. On the day in which the younger sister, Lynn, had brought home her first baby from the hospital, the smoke alarm randomly went off at her house—despite the fact that no one was cooking. There was no explanation for it. Come to find out, the smoke detector had also gone off at both her sister's condo and at their parents' home that same day. Clearly, Lynn's brother was wishing her congratulations and letting the family know that he wasn't missing out on their lives.

Another woman once shared how her five-year-old son who had passed away was obsessed with loud holiday decorations like singing pumpkins and dancing elves.

After listening to a particularly obnoxious singing snowman for weeks on end, this woman had enough and removed the batteries. A while later, she lost her son unexpectedly. Leading up to the first Christmas without him, she set out all the decor her son had always loved, including the snowman with no batteries. Christmas morning arrived, and the family was trying their hardest to enjoy the holiday despite the sadness. As her daughter opened up presents and the woman thought about how happy her son would've been, the singing snowman suddenly lit up and started singing! No one had touched it, and it still had no batteries. It only lasted for a brief moment, but everyone in the room witnessed it and knew it was their sweet boy letting them know he was still celebrating the holidays with them in Spirit. I, for one, would've been totally spooked by something like this but for others, like this family, it's exactly what they need.

Very rarely, people will hear Spirit whisper their name. When this happens, it often occurs when someone is in a meditative state or late into the night when the veil between here and the Other Side is the thinnest, and when we are in a greater state of receptivity. This has happened to me before, and I have also heard about it happening to others who are not mediums.

One other sound I hear of people experiencing somewhat regularly is a buzzing or ringing in their ears. This generally tends to happen to those who are in the midst of a spiritual awakening and becoming more receptive to the Other Side. It's almost as if they are being fine-tuned to the sensitivity of these higher energies and vibrations. (Of course, this same thing can happen with people who are developing ear problems, so also be sure to visit a doctor if you experience this on a persistent basis!)

When the Veil Thins

A lot of people notice that they routinely wake up at a very specific time of night shortly after a loved one dies—down to the exact moment. This time generally falls somewhere in the window of 3:00 to 5:00 a.m. It's during those hours that the veil between the physical plane and Other Side is at its thinnest. Between these hours, it's easiest for us to feel the presence of Spirit. It doesn't mean that this is the only time our loved ones are around us—not at all. But it does mean that it's when many of us can feel them the most easily.

I don't have an explanation for why this is the case, but I suspect it's because our inhibitions are lowered when we are sleeping. Our normal thought processes are relaxed, so we are more open to the energy around us.

ELECTRICITY AND DIGITAL DEVICES

Electricity and other digital devices are another one of the common ways for Spirit to communicate because they, too, are energy. Earthly forms of energy can be fun for Spirit to manipulate. How exactly they're able to do this is one of those areas I won't fully understand myself until I'm dead. But these types of signs can come in many different ways. Some common ones are: flickering lights, radios, clocks, or children's toys that randomly turn on and off; phones ringing or never-before-seen voicemails from when the person was still living suddenly popping up; and lightbulbs that seem to blow out for no reason at all, no matter how often they are replaced. These things don't just happen in your home. You might have the experience of having a streetlight flicker or blow out just as you're parking or walking under it.

One woman recently told me that while she was waiting for one of my live Messages from Above events to begin, she accidentally butt-texted herself. When she looked at her phone screen, she saw her loved one's name and the phrase "I love you," right there in the middle of a jumble of random letters. While she didn't get a personal reading that night, Spirit clearly came through for her!

Another time, a gentleman shared a story with me about how he and his kids were visiting his wife's gravesite on her birthday, taking turns talking to her and leaving flowers. Suddenly, the lights surrounding her headstone turned on. The family thought this was strange since normally the lights don't come on until the sun goes down, and none of the other headstones' lights were turning on. They thought maybe it was due to a sensor that detects motion, so they walked up to several other gravesites throughout the cemetery—still nothing. When the man and his kids walked back to his wife's headstone, he said, "Honey, you here?" The lights immediately flickered. From that moment, that man had no doubt that his wife was making her presence known and sending love to him and her children.

PHYSICAL SENSATIONS

Do you ever get the chills, goosebumps, or a flush of heat throughout your body, either out of the blue or when you have a loved one on your mind? This happens to me all of the time. Other people feel a distinct and sudden temperature drop in the room, whether it's a cool breeze or a hot spot. Again, hello from Spirit! Either that, or maybe it's time to get your HVAC checked.

You might also feel the sensation of a hand resting on you or a leg or arm brushing up against your own. This seems to happen primarily when people are either drifting to sleep or in a deep meditation. I've talked to people who have woken up in the middle of the night only to find a physical impression in their mattress, as if someone has just been lying down next to them—not surprisingly, this seems to happen mostly in the case of departed romantic partners. Shortly after my stepmom lost her previous husband to cancer, she vividly remembers waking up one night to the feeling of her husband's presence, and she even *felt* him softly kiss her on the lips. She says that moment is what gave her the strength to continue because she knew it meant that he was okay and still by her side in Spirit.

A girl around my age, Sydney, told me about a similar instance she had experienced.

> My best friend and maid of honor passed away in a tragic accident just a month before my wedding. We couldn't afford to lose thousands of dollars to reschedule the date so, hard as it was, the wedding went on as planned. As my bridesmaids and I were all getting ready that morning, I felt someone come up behind me and put their hand on my shoulder. When I looked back, I swear I saw that hand moving away. At first I thought it was the makeup artist or maybe one of the bridesmaids, but they were all across the room. I started crying then, because I just knew in my heart it had to have been my best friend. I'll never forget that moment. I thanked her for being there for me, just as she always had been while she was still alive. I could always count on her.

We sometimes feel a loved one's presence without a physical sense of touch. For example, someone might *know* their departed sister is in the room without actually seeing her. It's just a feeling—not that different than the feeling most of us have with the living too. I'm sure you've been somewhere with headphones blasting music and your back turned, only to know exactly when someone else physically walked into the room. You may not have seen or heard them enter the room, but you knew they were there. We are so attuned that sometimes we can even tell *who* is in the room just by sensing their familiar energy.

Physical sensations also frequently occur close to or during a soul's transition. I've spoken to many, many people who experience a sensation they describe as a powerful energy flowing through them either at the moment of a loved one's passing or in the short time leading up to it. The phrases "flowing through me" or "washing over" seem to be very common when people describe these moment-of-passing sensations and feelings. Many of the people who experience this also seem to have some understanding of what's happening in that moment, even in cases where their loved one's death was unexpected.

While this next one is more to do with sight than sensation, it still seems most appropriate to mention here. Every now and then, people tell me that they see a flash of light or glimpse of their loved ones out of the corner of their eye. As crazy as you might feel in that moment, I promise you, that it's in fact almost always your loved one, provided that you have given them permission to communicate with you in this way.

OTHER PEOPLE

Spirit will communicate through other people or circumstances too. We generally like to file these sorts of events under the category of coincidence or synchronicity. And, sure, that's what it might look like from the outside. But I've heard countless stories that tell me Spirit has a hand in these "coincidences."

People have told me that on days where they were thinking about their loved one in Spirit more than usual—maybe a birthday or anniversary—they suddenly run into an old friend who knew their loved one here on Earth. Maybe they got to talk or reminisce about their loved one or were simply comforted by a friendly face. Sometimes it seems like Spirit is moving us around like chess pieces, although I promise you they're not doing so in a creepy or controlling way—think of it as more of a gentle nudge in the right direction. For example, I sometimes give readings at my events where someone receives a message to pass on. Occasionally, these messages are for people they haven't seen or spoken to for years. I can't tell you how many times those people have come back to tell me that they just happened to bump into the very person they were supposed to speak to in the days following the reading. I believe Spirit has a way of sending people onto our path, and these run-ins often happen when people most need a sign or a message.

Before I wrangled my gift under control, I used to experience things like this all the time. One instance in particular stands out to me. I was at the Penn State library, desperately trying to finish a paper that was due the next day, but I just could not concentrate for the life of me. I kept having this weird urge to walk downtown by myself, and I couldn't fight it. It's also worth mentioning that, at this point in time, I was thirty pounds heavier and a lot less active than I am these days. The last thing I would ever *decide* to do at that point in time was to go on a long-ass walk.

I did, though. Finally, I got downtown and decided to go into a bar I'd never been to before. Did I mention this all happened around eleven o'clock in the morning? Again, this is not something I would normally decide to do, especially by myself. The waitstaff were still setting up for the day, but they let me in, so I decided to sit down alone at the bar and order some food. You can probably guess what happened next.

It turned out that the bartender serving me had lost her mom just six weeks before. Looking back, Spirit had me get up from the library, walk downtown, and plunk myself down in a random bar before it officially opened. Listen, Spirit can't *force* us to do anything, because we have free will. But they sure do know how to work their magic when they have something to say, and they have the ability to guide us into certain scenarios!

Many of us have also had the experience of seeing someone while we're out and about who reminds us of a deceased loved one. While this isn't an apparition, it's still a hello from Heaven. Remember, Spirit has the ability to guide you into certain circumstances so that you're in the right place at the right time.

A lady named Sheila shared her experience of this:

My sister and I were supposed to go to an old family friend's funeral that she had read about in the local paper. Neither of has had seen that friend in a while, but we had many fond memories from when we were younger, and we wanted to pay our respects. My sister came over to my house that morning and, as we were getting ready, she grabbed the newspaper to get the address for the funeral home. She then realized that she had mixed up the dates, and we had missed the funeral. Instead, we decided to go to brunch. When we got to the restaurant, the hostess who greeted us looked exactly like the woman whose funeral we had missed. Talk about crazy timing! We took it as her way of saying, "Well, hey! It's the thought that counts. I still love you both."

What About Ghosts or "Negative" Spirits?

I'm the furthest thing from a paranormal investigator or ghostbuster. I don't connect with any kind of negative or earthbound energy—I won't even watch movies or TV shows that have to do with hauntings or anything like that. Since I don't communicate with these energies, I can't offer a full explanation for what causes some spirits to get "stuck" between the two realms in the process of transitioning. To be honest, I'm not even entirely sure what my personal beliefs are about all of this. All I know is that, while it doesn't happen very often, sometimes a spirit will exist at a much lower vibration, to the point where they seem to be in an almost "in-between" state, like they never fully crossed over to the Other Side.

From my understanding (again, I choose not to focus on the paranormal side of things, so I really don't know much about it), I think this can happen when the spirits don't yet understand something or still need to process information. These situations are generally tied to people who made some majorly twisted or heinous decisions of their own free will while here on Earth and are terrified of what may lie ahead for them as a result of their actions. To be clear, the vast, vast majority of people transition peacefully. These are outlier cases.

Having said that, I do regularly protect myself from any negative energy, which I see as a preventative measure.

I do this by placing very firm boundaries and making it clear that I only connect to the peaceful, positive, loving, and wholesome spirits in Heaven. I also ask for God's and the angels' protection before every single connection or reading that I give.

I've learned that when it comes to connecting to Spirit, like attracts like, and fear attracts fear. The same goes for the energy we all feel in our everyday lives. I maintain a positive mindset in every instance that I channel and, in doing so, it helps block out any unwelcome energy.

I highly encourage people to stay away from lower vibrational entertainment and things like Ouija boards (and, by the way, it will never cease to blow my mind that things like this are created by a toy company and marketed as a game). While there are occasional instances when people have used tools like a Ouija board to connect to peaceful energy, more often than not, it opens the door to icky energy. You might as well hold up a sign that reads: "Our home is currently accepting applications for ghosty-ghost tenants."

If you're experiencing or sensing a negative presence in your home, call upon your angels to assist in clearing out that energy. Some people use sage or smudge sprays, which can also work, but I feel that setting the intention and taking a moment to communicate out loud that these energies are not welcome in your space and to please leave, should do the trick.

While I'm no longer tied to any religion, I do still believe that holy water is very powerful as well, so you can also try displaying a bottle in your room if these other methods don't seem to be helping.

HELLO FROM HEAVEN

I am so moved by stories about people's experiences receiving signs from Spirit and I think they are so important to share as affirmation for others that I started an entire Instagram account dedicated to sharing and spreading these encounters. I sometimes share some of my own signs received from Spirit on there too. People often joke with me that it's funny how I still get so excited about these signs, even though I communicate with the Other Side for a living. I always remind them that, yeah, that's true, but I also can't connect with *my* loved ones the way I can with other people's. So, these signs are just as important, meaningful, and thrilling to me as they are to everyone else.

I'm going to share a few more stories of signs from Spirit that have been shared with me over the years. And if you'd like to follow along for even more Heaven-sent signs, you can find us at @signsfromspirit on Instagram (and while you're at it, follow @monicathemedium, as well).

THE BADASS BIKER CHICK

Chelsea's mom was a badass biker chick who loved her Harley-Davidson and spent a lot of time hanging out with her biker gang. Shortly after her mom passed, Chelsea was on a field trip with her son. As they were leaving, her son decided that he wanted to buy a little trinket to remind him of the day. He walked up to the counter of the facility's gift shop and saw that they had a basket that contained angel carvings with words such as peace, love, and joy inscribed on the back.

Chelsea told her son they needed to get back on the bus and urged him to pick one out quickly. He grabbed an angel and Chelsea paid for it, then shuffled her son back on the bus. It wasn't until they got home that Chelsea looked at what he had picked out. She flipped the angel over and, on the back, in big capital letters, was the word "Biker." Not exactly the most common message to find on angel carvings like these.

Chelsea knew right away that it was her mother letting her know that she was still right there with Chelsea and her son.

SMILE!

One day Candice and her boyfriend Elando went to buy a dozen donuts from Krispy Kreme, then stopped at another restaurant to grab dinner. As they ate, Candice reminisced about her cousin Sean, who had died many years before. Elando said to her, "I wonder if Sean ever tries to show his presence to me, but I just don't realize it since I never met him."

When their bill came, Elando opened up the little booklet and gently tossed Candice a smiley face pin that their server had included along with their check. Candice could hardly believe it when she saw it. That was exactly the sign that Sean has always sent her family and, now, was sending Elando. The two of them sat there in shocked silence. They had asked the question, and almost immediately, Spirit responded.

Later that night, Candice told Sean's sister what had happened. "Oh, my God," she replied. "The last time I saw Sean, I brought him Krispy Kreme donuts. I didn't get to see him because he was sleeping, so I wrote him a note to tell him that I was sorry I had missed him, but here's some donuts for him."

As this story demonstrates, the more you share the signs you receive with other people, the bigger, more extensive, and more specific you find out those signs actually are.

A SIGN ON A SIGN

Erica had gone to visit her grandma Lola at the cemetery. She said, "Grandma, please give me a sign that you are still here with me."

Later that afternoon, she decided to grab lunch. As she was turning in the parking lot, she started bawling her eyes out when she saw the sign from her grandmother. It was her name, Lola, written on an empty sign holder. And if you knew her grandmother's personality, you could hear her saying, "You asked for a sign, so I gave you a sign!" She literally gave her granddaughter a sign, on a sign.

FLIPPED JACK

Eve lost her dog Jack early one Saturday morning. That afternoon, she painted a picture using an abstract method that leaves a lot of room for random chance. When she finished her abstract painting, Eve took a picture of it and shared it online. Once the picture uploaded, Eve saw that it had been posted upside down.

As Eve looked at the flipped picture, she realized that all of that random chance had actually resulted in a painting of Jack. She held another picture of Jack up next to the flipped painting and, sure enough! There was Jack, clear as day.

Eve is sure that was Jack's way of telling her that he was okay and had found his way to the light. Just like we all do.

TRUST YOUR GUT

By now, you can probably see a common theme to all of these signs: trust your gut. If you feel like something is meaningful or is from a specific person, trust that it really is. Don't logic your way out of it. Don't come up with a million other explanations (which, ironically, are often a lot less logical) for what happened.

Trust your instincts, trust your intuition, trust your feelings, and trust your senses. Trust yourself. We came into this world with an inner knowing. You have probably heard the saying that goes, "We are not human beings having a spiritual experience. We are spiritual beings having a human experience." It couldn't be more true. On an innate level, we are all born with this ability to connect with the Other Side. We all come from the same place and are made from the same energy Spirit is; the only difference is that we are currently in physical form.

Also, understand that Spirit is not God. They can do a lot to let us know they're right there, but a message from Spirit can't always appear in the form of a blinking neon sign. So, you have to do your part too. And sometimes a bird really is just a bird. But, other times, it's so much more. If you're just willing to listen and trust your gut, you will know better than anyone else when there is a hidden meaning designed specifically for you to receive.

More Than Just a Dream

Spirit often sends their family and friends signs and symbols like the ones we discussed in the previous chapter. The upturned penny, the feather floating past our window—these are, as I obviously like to call them, hellos from Heaven. But there is another way Spirit can communicate with us, though it takes more dedication and energy—both on their part and ours—to accomplish. Spirit visitation dreams, which I will explain below, are an experience that brings us closer to the Other Side than almost anything else.

VISITATION DREAMS

Sometimes Spirit will visit through dreams. But these Spirit visitation dreams are far different from your average dream.

Remember when I spoke about deathbed visions in Chapter Seven? While many of those people literally see, hear, or feel their departed loved ones gather in the room as they near their death, others experience this connection through a visitation dream. Yet, visitation dreams are definitely not limited to just those who are dying, so please don't jump to the conclusion that if you have recently had one of these dreams it means your time is running out. People of all ages and from all walks of life have experienced these amazing dreams at various points in their lifetime.

Most people feel emotional when they wake up from a visitation dream. They'll usually be overwhelmed with happiness, or they might even start crying (tears of joy). The difference between a Spirit visitation dream and a regular dream is in how they look and more importantly, in how they *feel*. They are overwhelmingly clear and vivid, and they seem real in a way that normal dreams do not. That's because visitation dreams *are* real. It's your loved one coming to visit you in that exact moment. Whereas the details of a regular dream usually start to slip away as you wake up (or even before you wake up), that's not the case with visitation dreams. They stick with you and are much easier to remember. I still encourage you to write them down, though, so that you can look back and read through them in the future when you need a little reassurance that your loved ones are okay. Having said that, visitation dreams are usually so vivid that most people don't forget them anyway, even if they don't take a single note. They tend to remain a very conscious memory.

I like to call visitation dreams "hug dreams" because often Spirit will come through and give you a hug in the dream. Like everything else, the hug feels real and so beautiful. Again, that's because it *is* real and beautiful. Other times, Spirit will talk with you, whether it's to apologize, relay a message of comfort, or convey any other type of information that is meaningful to you. In other instances, no words are spoken at all. You and your loved one might instead take part in certain activities that you loved to do together, or they may simply sit beside you with a smile on their face or reach out to hold your hand. Like any other visit you would have with a loved one here on Earth, the possibilities are endless, depending on your relationship with that person.

What About Nightmares?

On the flip side of visitation dreams are nightmares or frightening dreams about loved ones who have passed. People worry that these types of dreams are also visitation dreams—but that it means something bad about where there loved one might be now or could represent the fact that they're not okay.

Spirit clarifies that these are *not* visitation dreams. Sure, you might have regular dreams about those who have passed, and those dreams might even be nightmares. But these types of dreams are the result of your own personal experiences, fears, or emotions, not Spirit. These dreams are still worth paying attention to though, because there could very well be a lesson imbedded in them or they might point to a lesson you still need to learn or feelings you need to work through and release. But they are not a visitation dream and they are not connected to Spirit.

A few months ago, one of my students shared with me how she and her husband had to put their dog down. Shortly after, her husband started having recurring nightmares that start off with him playing with their dog, but then suddenly their dog starts bleeding out and dying in his arms. I explained to her (and the same goes with any negative dreams or nightmares you might have about human loved ones) that this was not a Spirit visitation dream, but rather, her husband's subconscious mind trying to tell him something through these dreams. He was holding onto feelings of guilt around their dog's passing, and the visual of the dog bleeding out represented the feelings that he could've done more or gotten their dog help sooner. He needed to forgive himself for any decisions he did or did not make and take the time in the waking world to process and work through these emotions that needed healing. For most people, the nightmares stop once they've truly let themselves feel the heavy emotions because only then are they able to start releasing them.

When Spirit is present, you will only feel love. In fact, this is one of the key ways to identify a visitation dream: when you feel a sense of comfort, healing, happiness, and even joy. It is the very best kind of emotional reunion.

HUGS FROM HEAVEN

Tons of people have shared their visitation dreams with me, and no matter how many times I've heard or read these stories, they still bring the biggest smile to my face. Following are just a few of the experiences I've heard about over the years.

Shortly after my brother died while on active duty, he came to me in a dream. In the dream, we spent what felt like ages together, hanging out and doing all the things we always loved to do. Before I woke up from the dream, the last thing I saw was him walking on a beautiful beach toward the sunset in his full army gear. When I asked him, "Where are you going?" he looked back and said, "Don't worry, munchkin. I will see you again. I love you."

And then he kept walking toward the setting sun. I will never stop missing him, but I have a complete sense of knowing that he is okay and at peace.

—Maddie

A few weeks after my dad passed, I had the most vivid dream. I was walking through a park, and the grass, trees, and leaves were the most rich shades of green and brown I've ever seen. I was walking along a paved path with a man who was wearing a white robe and listening to me talk. I looked in front of us, and there was my dad sitting on a park bench. I ran up to him, saying, "Oh my God, oh my God, oh my God, Dad!" He looked up at me smiling, and said, "Hi, babe," just like he always did when we talked on the phone. I'll never forget it and he's been gone for about twelve years.

—Patty

This next dream I'm sharing demonstrates another trend I've noticed across visitation dreams. It's when a loved one not only comes into a person's dream but also communicates information about something that has yet to happen as a way to validate that they're watching over their loved ones and know what's in motion. Sometimes this foretelling involves the dreamer, and other times it might be about future occurrences in the life of another mutual loved one.

My mom died about five years before my daughter was born. When I was ready to tell my dad that I was pregnant with my first child, I sent him a text saying: "Hey, Dad. I have some news to share. Can I call you later?" He responded, "You're pregnant, right?"

I freaked out, thinking that my husband had spoiled the surprise since he was the only other person who knew. But it turned out my dad had gotten a special visit from my mom in a dream. He told me, "Your mother came to me in a dream a couple of weeks ago and told me you were pregnant with a baby girl. It felt so real, I had no choice but to believe it was her, and so I've been waiting for you to tell me."

I was early in my pregnancy, so I didn't even know the baby's gender yet. But when my dad told me that, I immediately felt my mom's loving presence and warmth. When it came time for an ultrasound to find out the gender, I already knew it would be a girl. Sure enough, I now have the sweetest little girl who shares my mother's beautiful blue eyes (and her middle name too).

—Amber

The reason these types of visits happen in dreams is because our dreams can act as the middle ground between our world and the Spirit World. It is the place where our attention, focus, and awareness are completely withdrawn from the constant hum of our logical left brain. When we have these experiences in our dreams, we don't start to doubt them, explain them away, or become fearful. We're not filling in blanks that don't need to be filled in or that *can't* be filled in with the logical mind. We don't ask, "Why?" or "How?" We just accept the experience for what it is.

It's very hard for me to explain how I do what I do, but in some ways it works similarly to visitation dreams. I also meet Spirit somewhere in the middle by raising my vibration; meanwhile, Spirit lowers theirs.

While this may seem hard to wrap your head around—because after all, Spirit has the ability to be in more than one place at a time and to do what they please—it still takes a lot of energy and effort on their part to come through in dreams. It's worth it to Spirit because they want to get your attention, to let you know that they are around and that they're saying hello and sending love from the Other Side. However, it's not something that tends to happen on a regular basis. Visitation dreams are usually a special, rare gift. The more you can do to recognize these dreams for what they are, the happier and closer to you Spirit will be. For them, just like for you, it is worth every last little bit of energy necessary to make this incredible connection happen. Just like some people feel their loved one's energy flow through them as they transition to the Other Side, I've heard many instances of Spirit appearing in a dream even before the person has found out their loved one has crossed over.

One woman's experience provides the perfect example of this:

> The reading was winding down and Monica mentioned my grandma coming to me in my dreams, which hadn't really happened since she passed, so I was a little confused. Then Monica asked, "Did your grandma drive a taxi? A yellow taxi?" As soon as she said that, I knew she was referring to my grandmother Alice, who had passed away twenty-two years prior. I shared with Monica that my grandma Alice always took taxis to her doctor's appointments, and that the night my grandma Alice passed away, she came to me in a dream. In that dream she told me that she had to go. A yellow taxi pulled up to the curb outside her house, my grandma got in, and the taxi drove off into a bright light. When I woke up, I heard my dad on the phone with the hospital. My grandma had passed away during the night.

I love that Spirit came through to validate what this woman always knew deep down—that it really was her grandma Alice who came to her in that dream. It was her grandmother's way of saying goodbye since they didn't have that chance to do so in person. Not only that, but it was a beautiful opportunity for Alice to let her family know that she was going to be okay and at peace.

Another girl, Becca, told me about a similar experience she had when her grandfather passed:

The night my grandfather passed away, he came to me in a dream. In my dream, everyone was telling me that my grandfather had gone to Heaven. I refused to believe them. But then my grandfather appeared to me as his younger self. I had never seen him like that before, but I instantly recognized him. He sat with me in the dream and told me that it was his time to go. I asked if I could go with him, and he smiled and said, "I'm sorry, no, not now. But one day many, many, many years from now, you'll get to join me here." He then stood up and hugged me. It was the most real feeling I've ever experienced in a dream.

I woke up the next morning and my mom broke the news that my grandfather had passed away a few hours before. When I walked into the memorial service, they had a table set up with different photos taken throughout my grandfather's life. That's when I saw a picture of him that looked exactly like the younger version of him I'd seen in my dream a few nights before. Same clothes, same haircut, same everything. I felt chills all over my body. Knowing it was really my grandfather in that dream was the best feeling in the world.

OPENING YOURSELF UP TO A VISITATION DREAM

To make it easier for Spirit to get through, I think it helps to request a visitation dream. Ask your loved ones to come to you in this way and open yourself up to the experience. Do everything you can on your end—environmentally, physically, emotionally, and mentally—to get yourself into a state where you can drop into a deep sleep. You want to be as unaware of the physical, earthly world around you as you can possibly be. Of course, there are no guarantees, but doing this definitely makes a visitation dream more likely to occur.

This experience is open to all of us; it's just a matter of stacking the deck as best we can to put all of the necessary elements in place. I've found, though, that if it's not in your best interest to connect with Spirit in this way for whatever reason, there's a chance a visitation dream might not happen, no matter how much you may think you want one. Remember that our loved ones have a perspective from the Other Side that we do not. They probably know you better than you know yourself. You might think a visitation dream is exactly what you need when the reality is, you might be better off receiving a sign from Spirit through a different medium (no pun intended).

Also, if Spirit isn't getting through to you in *your* dreams for whatever reason, they might come into another family member's dream because they know it's a gift that will keep giving as that person goes on to share the story of their dream with everyone else in the family. This even happened in my own family.

When my grandmother passed away, my family went through the grieving process all families experience. Despite what I do for a living, we still couldn't help but feel those nagging questions everyone does: *Was she okay? Were our grandparents reunited?*

Just a few days after my grandmother died, my sister Jessica had her first visitation dream. In the dream, our whole family was together, sitting around, laughing, and talking as we always did. Our grandmother was there, looking younger than she had when she died, like she did when we were kids. She appeared happy and calm. Suddenly my grandma got up and walked out of the room. Jessica followed her out and found her at the foot of the stairs. Jessica says my grandmother reached out and gave her a hug, smiled at her, and reassured her that everything was okay. Then she turned around and walked up the stairs.

Jessica woke up from that dream feeling overjoyed and at peace. As soon as she could, Jessica told the rest of my family what she'd seen. She gave us all a gift that day.

Of course it's only natural that, for as much as it is a gift to hear about a visitation for a loved one, most of us still want to have the experience for ourselves if possible. Keeping in mind that you do not have complete control over this situation, it's still helpful to know about the ways in which we can enhance our own connection to Spirit and open our souls and minds to their messages while simultaneously improving our own spiritual well-being.

A great way to enhance your connection with Spirit is through a regular meditation routine. I know, some of you might be thinking, "Ugh." You don't *have* to meditate to connect with Spirit. It's by no means a prerequisite. Whether you meditate or not, Spirit is still going to send you signs or visit you in your dreams. You are still capable of making a connection in those ways but, with meditation, the easier it will become.

Meditation will help you become more open to sensing, feeling, and experiencing communication with the afterlife. This is especially true for those of you in the process of developing, strengthening, or coming into your own mediumship gifts. Over the years, I've had students enrolled in my mediumship course who, without question, have a natural ability to connect with Spirit. They do all of the exercises, assignments, and practices that are laid out for them in the course to help them strengthen their connection with the Other Side. Yet, if they don't take the meditation aspect seriously or start slacking in that area, they almost always struggle to reach the point that would make the difference between them being a *good* medium and a *great* one.

Even for those with little to no mediumship abilities, Spirit still sometimes uses that state of meditation to communicate. Meditation helps clear away mind clutter and puts us in a better place to receive so that we can more easily feel, notice, and even see (if you want) the more subtle energies around us. During a meditation, you might feel a hand on your shoulder or chills running up and down your spine. It's possible you'll even receive a message or have a conversation with one or more of your spirit guides.

I'll never forget one of the most profound experiences I've ever had with Spirit, which happened during a deep meditation. This occurred back when I was still struggling with accepting my gifts and trying to figure out whether or not mediumship was something I should be doing.

My main spirit guide, Lily (who I had met in a previous meditation), came to me during this meditation and brought me to a library. In this library, she pulled a huge book off of one of the shelves. On the spine of this book, I saw the title, *Monica's Spiritual Journey*. Lily opened up this gigantic book on a table before me and started flipping through the pages. Page after page, there were photos of people of all ages and ethnicities. It was like a never-ending collage of various strangers—every type of individual you could think of, along with groups of friends and families, and even animals! At this point I looked up at Lily, clearly confused by what she was showing me. "What is this?" I asked her.

With a loving look in her eyes and the sincerest smile, she told me, "Monica, these are the thousands upon thousands of people that you will help by doing this work."

At the time, I hadn't given even one official reading—only spontaneous messages from Spirit here and there. This was long before I started seeing clients or had a television show.

Lily continued to flip through the pages, saying things like, "Oh, and here's a gentleman you'll give a reading to after he unexpectedly loses his wife" and "Look! This is a little girl who will come through to you after passing in a tragic accident. And these are her parents, whose lives will forever be changed for the better when you deliver healing messages from their daughter."

Lily continued to show me all of these different people and families that I would reach and help through sharing my gift. Then she looked up at me and said, "Monica, *this* is your life purpose. *This* is what you're meant to be doing. So get ready."

I was in shock, but it was also the first time I felt completely confident about further developing my connection with the Other Side and sharing my gift with others. I might've still had my doubts, but I no longer felt crazy. This experience happened while I was in a meditative state, but it felt just as real and vivid as any interaction I've ever had in the waking world. I knew in my heart that it wasn't just wishful thinking or a daydream. It was my spirit guide communicating with me, and I was meant to hear those messages from her to help me prepare for my future. To this day, I still get chills thinking about this particular meditation and the visual of that library. It entirely changed the way in which I viewed my purpose and my gifts.

But don't be alarmed if it freaks you out to think of having such a clear interaction with a spirit guide in meditation. This experience is definitely not the norm when it comes to meditation. For most people, the power of meditation has more to do with the regular practice of settling, clearing, and coming into the present moment, which—bonus points!—also helps you move about life in a more mindful way. The more mindful we are of everything around us, the more attentive and receptive we are. The less distractions there are to muddle through.

Meditation also provides a great opportunity to set intentions and talk or pray to your loved ones through your thoughts. Although you probably won't hear them talk back, I promise you they're listening. Let them know that you're ready and willing to receive and that you truly have the desire to accept the signs, or see them in a dream. It's helpful when you're able to ensure Spirit that you'll be open to recognizing the signs and messages they set forth the effort to send. It really is that simple.

As I always mention to my podcast listeners or to my audience at the end of my events: you may have believed up until this point that you were not receiving messages (or perhaps you never even knew of all the ways in which Spirit tries to grab our attention), but now that you have a better understanding of it all, you will likely start to see the ways you have or will have that connection. I'm sure that, for many of you, the same applies to reading this book and all that you've (hopefully) learned from it. With this new awareness, open-mindedness, and frame of reference, I can almost guarantee you that you'll soon begin noticing what's likely been there all along.

Love Never Dies

Death is not the end.

If there's one thing I know, it's this. I know that death might seem like an end, and in some ways it is. But it's only the end of a single chapter of a very, very long book. Ultimately, this single idea underlies everything Spirit wants you to know: love never dies. Your loved ones are never gone, and you can rest assured that they are now in a better place.

No matter how much you are hurting, I hope you can find some comfort in the fact that every single person you have loved and lost is in a more beautiful, peaceful place than you can ever imagine. They are filled with the purest form of love, joy, and peace that exists. You can call it the Other Side, the afterlife, Heaven, or whatever feels right to you. What matters is understanding that their soul continues to live on far beyond this physical world. They know your love—they can feel it. And they love you just as much as they ever did here on Earth because love never dies. That bond is never broken.

You can let go of any regrets you might have about things you wish you would have said or done. Spirit has a complete understanding of all of it, just as if you've already said or done it. As far as they are concerned, you have. They know it all. They hear your prayers. They hear you talk to them. They know every feeling you have, or ever did have and were unable to express. Anything you might feel like you need to be forgiven for has already been forgiven. They are not holding on to any anger or pain, and they want the same for you.

People always ask me to tell their loved ones this or that. "Tell my mom I love her" or "Can you let my brother know that I'm sorry?" You don't need me or anyone else to do that. You can tell your loved ones every single thing you want them to know. And you don't even have to *say* it. Thinking it or feeling it is enough. They know it all.

Part of what hurts so much about death is that those of us who are left behind can feel so incredibly alone. I know it feels that way, but trust me: *You are not alone.* Your loved ones are right here by your side, even as you are reading these words. They are your biggest cheerleader. All of those milestone moments you wish your loved ones were here for? They are. Please trust that they're not missing out on a single thing. As far as they are concerned, there is no separation, no matter how much you might feel like there is. The reality is that you are forever connected with everyone you love. For eternity, in this life and beyond. One day, you will be reunited again. But they want you to know that you don't have to be in any rush. Spirit often says that jokingly, but they mean it.

You are here for a reason, just like they were here for a reason and now they have left for a reason. Be here in the present moment. Live your life now. Spirit knows better than anyone that none of us are guaranteed tomorrow. If you want to travel somewhere and you have the means, *do it*. Don't work at the expense of your life. Don't mourn at the expense of your life. Spend more time with your family. Do the things you love. Pursue your passions. Say "I love you" to the people who you love as often as you possibly can. Never once has Spirit told me they wish they worked harder. I have heard, many times, that they wish they spent more time with their loved ones or let the people they loved know how they felt.

Spirit wants you to know that happiness is possible again, even if it doesn't feel like it right now. They want it so badly for you and are cheering you along the road to healing every step of the way. So often we feel like a part of us dies when someone we love dies. Know this: they are not dead at all. In fact, they are more alive and whole than they ever were here on Earth. So, keep living, even if at first, you're only doing it for them. Hopefully, over time, you will get to a point where you are living fully and joyfully again for *you*. That is what Spirit wants for you more than anything. They want you to love, to laugh, to experience joy and, most of all, to not feel any sort of guilt about it.

It's okay to find love again. It's okay to have another child. It's okay to move out of the house you shared together. It's okay to change their room. None of this is replacing their memory or forgetting about them. No one is happier to see you moving forward than your loved ones. They want to see you live, forgive yourself, let go of the coulda, shoulda, wouldas, and find peace.

Each of us deserves happiness, but ultimately happiness is a choice. No one can make that choice for you, not even Spirit. Only you have the power within to choose to see your loss, your struggles, and your ups and downs through a lens of growth, learning, and even joy. Begin by looking at all of the silver linings in your life, even the ones that came as a result of your loss. I'm willing to bet they are there. They always are, even in the most difficult situations.

The phrase "time heals all wounds" is something we like to say in an attempt to alleviate pain. But here's the truth: there is always going to be a part of you that still hurts and misses your loved ones. There will always be a hole in your heart, even if that hole feels smaller and smaller as time goes on. As much as I wish that an incredible reading or sign from Spirit would erase your loss, it won't. That is part of being human. But, with time, you *can* move beyond your loss.

Time can and will make things easier. Even in those moments when it might seem like there is no light at the end of the tunnel, Spirit always says, "Tell them it's going to get better." I promise you, it will. Even if it doesn't feel like that today or even next week or next month. Trust in knowing that, over time, it will slowly start to get a bit easier. And know that, as you walk that path, Spirit will be right there by your side, comforting you and walking with you as you go through the grieving and healing process.

Know that all of this pain is not meaningless suffering, nor are any of the other struggles you've been through in life. Just like your loved ones have a bigger purpose, so do you. And this experience right now? It is part of that purpose. It's part of your evolution. Try to find the lesson in your struggles and the opportunity to grow and learn, even through this. Especially through this. There is a lot of truth in the old saying that everything happens for a reason.

Some people are afraid to even attempt to begin this process of moving on because they don't want to forget the tangible things about their loved ones. They don't want to forget how it felt when their loved one hugged them, or the way they laughed and smelled. Spirit wants you to know that, yes, your memories might start to fade over time. But that's okay! If and when that does happen, it's a sign that your heart is slowly healing. If you're really worried about forgetting, write down those details and memories so that you can rest assured that they will always be there, even as you move on. Ultimately the bond and connection you have is the most important thing. And *that* will never fade; it's unbreakable.

Also know that there are no right answers about how or when to do all of this. It's okay to grieve on your own timeline and to take each small step forward only when you feel ready for it. It's also okay to talk about your struggles and your process. Talk to Spirit. Talk to your friends. Talk to others who have been or are currently going through their own loss. Share your lessons and learn from others. Make new connections, even as you cherish and celebrate the old ones.

Over time, you can let go of what doesn't serve you or bring you happiness, and bring with you what does. Let go of the pain, sadness, and worries. Take with you the stories about the quirky things your loved one used to do. Cook the recipes they loved, tell their stories, you might even save them a place at the Thanksgiving dinner table. Keep their memory alive and share their legacy. But, also, know that you don't have to do any of these things. Spirit knows if you even *think* about doing any of these things, and they love it. That's enough. There is no pressure to any of this. Only encouragement to find the path that ultimately leads to your own happiness.

Take it from me when I tell you that you don't need a medium to connect with your loved one or to receive messages from them. You have the ability to receive hellos from Heaven on a regular basis. It's purely a matter of being open to receiving them. Trust in those moments when you feel your loved one's presence and know that when you call them, they are there.

Know that they are actively seeking out ways to let you know that they are still right here with you.

And since I feel it's only fitting for Spirit to have the last word, I'll leave you with this channeled message:

When you take a breath and all that seems to flow into your chest is the pain you've been holding on to, the guilt you can't seem to let go of, or the anger that's been building up, I want you to close your eyes and let yourself feel your feelings for what they truly are. Cry, yell, scream, laugh. Whatever you

need to do. By allowing yourself to fully feel—and even welcome—the emotions, you can start to work through them.
This process is your path to healing and will move you toward
wholeness and peace.

Your soul has known sorrow, but it has also known love.
One day you'll be able to transition any harsh thoughts and
feelings into something entirely different. You can start to
rebuild and replenish your energy. With time, you will dis-
cover your new normal and learn to live again. You have
the power to take on a new perspective, a new attitude, a
new beginning.

When the voice of regret is all you can hear, let the voice
of love speak louder. If you find yourself consumed with guilt,
remember that all has been forgiven. When the pain of missing me hits you with unexpected sharpness, hold fast to the
dear memories that we shared together. When the burden of
grief becomes too heavy for you to carry silently, talk about
me. Share my stories and remember the parts of me that live
on through you.

Honor me with your ability to find even the smallest sliver
of joy during times of sadness. Honor me with your happiness. Honor me by loving life and loving hard.

Remember that love transcends death.

You can't see me, but if you allow it, you can feel my presence. Listen for my whispers of courage when you need it
most. Smile when you see the signs that make you know that
I am near.

Even when your heart feels broken, it still has so much
to give. Have faith in the resilience of the human spirit.

Find reasons to replace your tears with laughter. You can rise above pain and grief with hope and strength. After all, you are not doing this alone. I am with you every step of the way.

Acknowledgments

This book has been, without a doubt, one of the most challenging (and yet most rewarding) projects I've ever undertaken. In fact, there were many times when I thought I wasn't going to be able to complete it. I think the hardest part about it was not so much the writing process itself, but the enormous pressure I felt to do right by the Spirit World and my readers. I think that's why when I attempted to write this book several times over the last five years, I became overwhelmed and had to put it on the back burner until now. (Also, I'm a full believer in divine timing, and in hindsight, I now realize I still had so much more to learn and experience before I was ready to share Spirit's insights in written form.)

It's no exaggeration when they say that it takes a damn village to publish a book. This couldn't be truer with this one. I want to thank everyone who played even a small role in making this book come to life. Not only have you helped *me* tremendously, but I hope you realize that your contribution will help people around the world. You're making a difference that goes far beyond helping an author—you're helping the Spirit

World, too, and are playing a part in spreading healing and hope to those who need it most.

I read in an article somewhere that authors should try to keep their acknowledgments to a page or two, but considering this might end up being my one and only book, I say screw it to that recommendation.

With that being said, I want to extend my deepest gratitude and thanks:

To Spirit, without whom this book would not exist. Thank you for your guidance, for sharing your wisdom, and for allowing me to share your healing messages. And thank you to God for giving me a gift that I cherish each day.

To my guardian angels and the rest of my spiritual support squad, for sending me signs throughout this project (and throughout my life) when I needed them most. You always swooped in at exactly the right moment and gave me the reassurance—and many times even a boost of energy—to finish this book.

To my fiancé and future husband, Tyler, for putting up with more tears and meltdowns throughout this process than I care to admit. You stood by me through it all, and you are hands down the reason I somehow kept my sanity—especially in those final weeks of revising the manuscript. Thank you for being so caring and patient and for being my greatest source of support. I love you more than I could ever express in words. I cannot wait to be your wife, and look forward to a lifetime of love and friendship with you. Also, thank you to Lori, Marissa, Trav, and the boys for welcoming me into your family and for always opening up your home (and your pool) for us. I love you guys, and the rest of the Scott family as well.

To my mom, Marlene, for bringing me into this world and for supporting me and my gift. I know you've had to work through a series of struggles with your own beliefs and faith in order to do that. I know it hasn't been easy for you, and I've put you through a lot of stress and worry over the years. I know that all of this has only ever stemmed from your love for me and your desire to protect me. At the end of the day, you've only ever wanted the best for me. Thank you for being an amazing mother to your four daughters. Thank you for being one of my biggest fans and for helping me in every way that you can. Thank you for never being afraid to tell me how it is and for always giving me your honest feedback in order to help me succeed. Thank you for all the time you spent helping me review the several rounds of revisions for this book cover. You have no idea how much I appreciated your attention to detail and your unwavering support throughout that process (and in all other areas of my life too). I love you.

To my dad, Michael, and my stepmom, Susan, for your never-ending love and support. Thank you for always leaving your door wide open for me and offering your home as a much-needed escape whenever I needed it. There were several times throughout this project (and throughout the last few years) where the stress got to be too much, and a huge form of relief came from getting to spend the occasional afternoon in the oasis of your beautiful backyard, surrounded by all your luscious plants and the comfort of family (not to mention Dad's awesome BBQ). Dad, I so appreciate how much you've grown spiritually and how much more open-minded you've become. Susan, I have you to thank for that. Thank you for your words of wisdom, New Age insights, and love for all things woo-woo. In addition to being a spiritual guru that I can so relate to, thank you for being the best "nurse mom" and for always texting or calling with comforting words and the very best healing remedies.

To my younger sister, Joanna, who may be a year and two weeks younger than me but often appears to be years ahead of me with her level of maturity, intelligence, and compassion for others. Joanna, I don't think I've ever felt more grateful and appreciative for you than I did throughout this project. You've helped me time and time again in my life and in my work, but with this book especially, you have done so much more than I could have ever asked for. You truly went above and beyond in ways I can't even put into words. Thank you for the countless late nights, early mornings, and long days reading page after page, helping me edit revision after revision, and for being the only person I trusted outside of my publishing team to read and edit this book before it went to print. I needed someone who knew me on such a personal level and who has also seen my gift firsthand to help me through the revision process. You were the perfect person for this. By the way, I'm sorry if I've ever given you shit for being a bookworm. Because, my gosh, has it paid off! You're the fastest reader I've ever met, and you blew my mind more times than I can count with your ability to help me put certain things into words that captured *exactly* what I was trying to get at. So many times, I asked you for help throughout this project, and you dropped everything to assist right away. And never once did you bitch about it.

I know I've joked when I've said this, but honestly, if you decide to switch career paths, I wouldn't blame you. You'd make a fabulous writer or editor, and I'm going to hold you to that idea we came up with over hard ciders for that novel we'll cowrite together (and yes, I promise your name will go on the cover, LOL). Now that it's in writing, we better make it happen—even if it's ten years from now. I thank you and I love you so much.

To my sisters, Jessica and Vanessa, for always being there for me when I needed feedback on something, reassurance, or advice from an older and wiser sister. Jessica, thank you for putting up with my endless FaceTime calls and requests for adorable videos of my beautiful nieces, Sienna and Evelyn. During some of the toughest days I encountered while writing this book, you were always there to offer words of encouragement and sisterly love (not to mention the fact that seeing Evie's little smile or hearing Sienna's cutest little British accent was often just what I needed to lift my spirits). Vanessa, thank you for taking care of me after my ORIF surgery and for being the best dog auntie to Luna and Chubba. Thank you for driving down for much-needed sister dinners, even though you can be such a grandma sometimes and insist on eating at five o'clock. Nonetheless, I'm so happy to have a sister in San Diego and so grateful to have you and Jake, not just as family, but as friends too. That applies to all three of my sisters, who truly are some of my best friends in this world.

To my entire publishing team. Without you, the perfectionist and procrastinator in me would've never been able to get this book finished and ready for print. First and foremost, a huge thank you to Nikki, for believing in this book and for being a major player in making it happen. Thank you for your tireless work and never-ending patience. You bent over backward to make this entire process as seamless for me as you possibly could. I don't think you'll ever truly know just how thankful I am for you and all of the hours, energy, and hard work you put into this project. Thank you for putting up with all of my calls and texts, endless edits and track changes, deadline extensions, rescheduled meetings, and emotional breakdowns. I've told you before, and I'll say it again: you would make a bomb-ass therapist or life coach if you ever get sick of the writing world. Thank you for going far beyond your job description throughout the last eight months and for realizing the importance of what was being shared. You helped me structure this book in the best way possible and put into words various emotions, concepts, and ideas that I would otherwise not have been able to share with my readers. Thank you for being so open-minded about a topic that so many people are still closed off to and for never making me feel judged even in the slightest bit. There's zero doubt in my mind that Nick is smiling down on you with such pride and adoration for his incredibly talented sister. You are amazing, and I'm eternally grateful.

Along with Nikki, thank you to everyone else on my publishing team. Thank you to Ellie, for being on top of the timelines and details. For responding to emails so promptly and for always being there to answer any of my questions with an enthusiasm and kindness that is hard to come by. Thank you to Erin, Cindy, and the rest of the design team, for the countless revisions to make this book's cover the best it could be and even better than what I always envisioned. Thank you to the copy editors, proofreaders, layout and marketing teams, and everyone else who played a role in making this book a reality.

Thank you to my *Monica the Medium* family. Without the television show, I probably would've never had the opportunity to write this book, let alone share my gift in all of the ways I've been so lucky to get to over the years. *Monica the Medium* provided me with a platform that I am forever grateful for. Thank you to EP Malachi McGlone along with Dave Caplan, Lauren Rosenberg, the other producers, and an incredible cast and crew of #champions (you know who you are), Brian Tannenbaum, and everyone else at Lionsgate, Freeform (formerly ABC Family), and Disney for allowing me to share my gift with more people than I could've ever thought possible and who helped create two seasons of *Monica the Medium*. Thank you to Penni and Amanda at Freeform, along with Anderson PR Group, for your efforts in marketing the show. Special thanks to Tricia Durrant for recognizing the potential for something special and for setting up several of those initial meetings with production companies and networks, and to my awesome agent at the time, Nir Caspi. Also, thank you to Matt Gaffney for making it possible for me to use the Freeform attribution on the cover of this book. I really appreciate you guys giving me permission to add that.

Thank you to Krista, for being more than a best friend—you truly are like a sister to me. I'm so grateful for our monthly Facetime dates and your constant DMs with dog vids, LOL. I freaking love you. Thank you to Alina, Mimi, and all of my other friends back home, who've known and loved me as just Monica, but who've also continued to love and support me as Monica the Medium. Thank you to my Rawmana Fitness family, especially Sia, for being a constant source of motivation and support since I moved to San Diego (not just in health and fitness, but in all areas of my life).

Thank you to my medium mama and good friend, Maureen, for always giving me the best advice and for being there whenever I need to talk to someone who completely relates. Thank you to my friend Beth for always thinking of me and providing me with angel guidance. Thank you to my photographer, Danielle, who captured the perfect photo for this cover, to Peggy for doing my makeup, and to Hailey for being the queen of awesome blowouts and curls. Thank you to Danielle, from Garnet Lash Studio, for giving me the best lashes a girl could ask for and for continually inspiring me as a fellow boss babe and good friend.

Thank you to those of you who've been a part of #teammedium over the years and who've helped me manage multiple projects, plan and host Messages from Above events, and so much more. Thank you to Francesca for being so thoughtful and for always going the extra mile. I'll never forget you coming over to surprise me with a bottle of rosé and other goodies to cheer me up when I first broke my ankle. Thank you to Rachel, for being so understanding and patient with me while I was simultaneously creating *The Empath Oracle* (a project that I hope you know I'm equally as excited about) throughout the entire time I was working on this book. I've learned the hard way that two giant creative projects like these are probably best suited for working on one at a time. Without you and your support, there's no way I would've been able to complete them both.

Thank you to all my other friends and extended family members, both the ones who are living and those who are watching from Heaven. I wish I could name every last one of you, but these acknowledgments would never end. If you're someone who feels they should've been mentioned, please know that it's not because I don't love or cherish you, but more likely because I forgot. I swear my brain is officially fried after months of very little sleep and too much caffeine.

Finally, thanks to everyone who has been following my journey over the years. Because of you, I'm able to do what I love for a living and get to help people around the world. Trust me when I say that I don't ever take that for granted. I look forward to continuing to share my gift with all of you through my live Messages from Above events, free reading giveaways, charity fundraisers, podcasts, courses and workshops, oracle decks, and who knows, maybe even future books. Many of you have been supporting me even long before *Monica the Medium* ever aired, and I'm so lucky for your constant encouragement and love. Thank you to those of you who sent in your amazing reading stories and signs from Spirit for consideration for this book—there were literally hundreds of them—and I so badly wish I had the space to include them all. But please know that I read every last one of them, and it made me so happy to learn how much your experiences with me have positively impacted your lives.

Lastly, if you've made it this far, thank you to my readers. Thank you for allowing me to share with you what I've learned from Spirit. I hope this book was everything you hoped it would be and more and that it brought you healing, hope, and reassurance that death is not the end.

About the Author

Monica Ten-Kate is an extraordinarily gifted spirit medium and star of the Freeform television series, *Monica the Medium*. At the age of fifteen, Monica realized that her empathic tendencies were accompanied by a sense of feelings, signs, and symbols, which she later discovered was Spirit communicating. Monica now travels to cities across the country for her live Messages from Above events. She also teaches online courses and workshops for those coming into their own gifts, is the creator of *The Empath Oracle* deck, and hosts a podcast, *Wine & Spirits with Monica the Medium*. Follow @monicathemedium on Instagram and learn more at monicathemedium.com.

Printed in Great Britain
by Amazon

55183022R00208